1,001 Prescription Secrets
for SENIORS®

How to Pay Less for Medicines,
Find Natural Alternatives,
and Avoid Rx Ripoffs for
Every Prescription

Publisher's Note

The editors of FC&A have taken careful measures to ensure the accuracy and usefulness of the information in this book. While every attempt was made to assure accuracy, some Web sites, addresses, telephone numbers, and other information may have changed since printing.

This book is intended for general information only. It does not constitute medical advice or practice. We cannot guarantee the safety or effectiveness of any treatment or advice mentioned. Readers are urged to consult with their health care professionals and get their approval before undertaking therapies suggested by information in this book, keeping in mind that errors in the text may occur as in all publications and that new findings may supercede older information.

"He gives strength to the weary, and to him who lacks might He increases power."

Isaiah 40:29

Contents

Allergies

Generics can save up to 80 percent

Allergies have become the sixth-leading cause of disease in the United States, affecting more than 50 million Americans and costing the health care system more than $18 billion a year.

You can be allergic to almost anything, with reactions ranging from a slightly stuffy nose to life-threatening anaphylactic shock. The most common allergy is allergic rhinitis or hay fever. Some scientists think better health and hygiene are partly responsible for rising allergies. It could be that children who are kept away from germs have less chance to build up an immunity to viruses.

Drugstore shelves are full of prescription and over-the-counter (OTC) remedies, so it's easy to spend a lot of money searching for allergy relief. Here are some things you can do to make yourself feel better without breaking the bank.

Reap big savings with OTC drugs

You don't need a prescription to fight off your allergies. Research shows that two of the old over-the-counter standbys, Benadryl and Sudafed, work just as well as prescription drugs that do the same job.

Take antihistamines to avoid symptoms. Antihistamines are the primary allergy drugs. They work to stop the itching, sneezing, runny nose, and watery eyes caused by the histamine chemicals your body makes when it tries to get rid of allergens.

The original antihistamines make you sleepy, but the newer, second-generation antihistamines do not. Experts caution against using the old medicines if you're at risk of dosing off, especially if you're older. But you can offset the sedative effect by taking them at home a few hours before bedtime and avoiding alcohol and tranquilizers.

Benadryl and Chlor-Trimeton are the original over-the-counter antihistamines, and you can now get second-generation Claritin without a prescription, too. One recent study claims Benadryl is better than Clarinex, one of the most-expensive prescriptions, and many doctors believe Chlor-Trimeton is just as effective as newer drugs.

Generic over-the-counter drugs usually cost about half as much as name brands, depending on the quantity you buy. Save money with diphenhydramine hydrochloride instead of Benadryl, chlorpheniramine maleate instead of Chlor-Trimeton, and loratadine instead of Claritin. If you have a prescription for Allegra, ask your pharmacist to substitute generic fexofenadine HCI instead.

The graph on the following page illustrates the dramatic differences in the average cost of a 30-day supply of three similar drugs — Clarinex, Claritin, and loratadine. By buying the generic drug, you can save 80 percent over the cost of the prescription drug, Clarinex.

Clean your air with ivy. New research shows English ivy can wipe out airborne allergens from things like mold spores and animal feces.

Stop stuffiness with decongestants. These allergy remedies relieve nasal congestion by shrinking the vessels in your nose. Pseudoephedrine, sold under the brand name Sudafed, is a common non-prescription

Save dollars at the drugstore

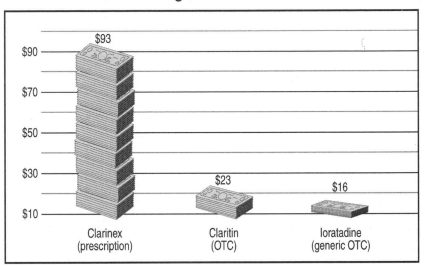

decongestant. You'll see it in many generic and brand-name cold and allergy medicines.

A study at the University of Chicago found that pseudoephedrine hydrochloride (Sudafed 24 Hour) worked just as well as the prescription drug montelukast sodium (Singulair), which costs four times as much. Patients took the pills in the morning and avoided the insomnia and nervousness pseudoephedrine can cause.

Nasal decongestant sprays work faster but don't last as long as pills. Don't use nasal decongestants more than three to five days at a time, though. Continued use causes rebound congestion that stops up your nose even more than it was. This can lead to a vicious cycle of overuse and eventual dependence.

Decongestants in general have risky side effects for people with many medical conditions, including high blood pressure and diabetes. Don't use them without a doctor's guidance. A simpler solution is the saltwater nasal wash, used for centuries and still recommended by some doctors. Check your drug store for a large rubber ear syringe or special nasal wash system to clean out your nose. For a cheap, do-it-yourself method, see instructions in *The bottom line on decongestants* in the *Colds* chapter.

Treat serious allergies for less

A generic version of Flonase, a much-used corticosteroid nasal spray, has recently been approved by the U.S. Food and Drug Administration. That means you can treat more serious allergies for a lot less money.

Steroids are becoming the most effective way to treat severe allergic rhinitis. They block allergic inflammation and are the same drugs used for more severe asthma cases. See the *Asthma* chapter for more details on this kind of medicine.

Like the newer second-generation antihistamines, steroids must be prescribed by a doctor and are generally quite expensive. A 16-mg inhaler of Flonase, for instance, costs from $75 to $90, depending on where you get it. But an inhaler of generic fluticasone propionate — the ingredient in Flonase — costs $20 to $25 less.

Exciting allergy cures on the horizon

You may soon be able to block pollen with a simple nose cream. A German company has come up with an ointment that traps pollen before it can cause trouble for your allergies. A study paid for by the manufacturer found the cream cut allergic symptoms by nearly 60 percent with no adverse effects.

A Swiss vaccine company is experimenting with a DNA-based dust-mite vaccine they say reduces hay fever symptoms. It is also working on vaccines against cat hair as well as grass and tree pollen. In Japan, an edible vaccine made from genetically modified rice also shows promise. It has been shown to cut allergy symptoms in mice.

That can translate into big savings when you consider you have to take these medications regularly, even when you don't have active symptoms. Doctors generally advise you start them a couple of weeks before pollens and other allergens appear.

Fight to get the right medicine

Your health insurance may no longer pay for the allergy medicine that works best for you. Since Claritin is now available without a prescription and as a generic, insurance companies are raising deductibles or refusing to pay at all for prescription antihistamines.

But the substitute drugs don't always work as well for some people. If that's the case for you, talk to your doctor about convincing the insurance company you need a particular medicine. He can submit a "prior authorization" form to your insurer saying the drug they'll pay for doesn't work for you. Then you can ask the company to cover the drug you like.

Another solution is to talk to your doctor about using nasal corticosteroids instead of antihistamines. Nasonex and Rhinocort, for example, don't have as many restrictions as Allegra and Zyrtec. For many people, the steroids also seem to be more effective.

Shut down sneezing with allergy shots

Allergen immunotherapy can be a successful solution to your sniffing and sneezing when all else fails. You need to see an allergy specialist, who will run tests to find out exactly what you are allergic to. Then the allergist will inject you with increasing amounts of those allergens over a period of several months.

The shots work like a vaccine and, after a while, you build up an immunity to the allergens. The American Academy of Allergy, Asthma

Some cats don't produce as many allergens, and a California company is using selective breeding to produce more of them. Look for the first "genetically divergent" kittens in the near future.

& Immunology (AAAAI) says this treatment is successful in up to 90 percent of patients with seasonal allergic rhinitis.

Allergy shots are a drastic measure because of the time, trouble, and expense they involve. But they could be worth it, depending on the extent of your allergy problem and whether you can control it with drugs. You'll eventually make up the cost from the money you save on allergy medicine.

To find a certified allergist/immunologist in your area, call the AAAAI at 800-822-2762 or go to *www.aaaai.org* on the Internet. You can also use the American College of Allergy, Asthma & Immunology at *www.acaai.org*.

Best way to breathe allergen-free air

Pollens, molds, and animal dander can float around inside your house as well as outside. If you sneeze even when you're indoors, an air cleaner may be what you need to keep allergens from bothering you. Here are some things to consider before you buy.

▶ Air filtration alone is not a solution for reducing indoor allergens. You also need to control sources of pollution, have adequate ventilation, and keep surfaces clean where allergens come to rest.

▶ The Clean Air Delivery Rate (CADR) for tobacco smoke should be at least two-thirds your room's area in square feet. For a 10′x12′ room (120 sq. ft.), you need a machine with a CADR of 80.

▶ Not all air purifiers actually filter particles out of the air. Some are intended to kill bacteria or eliminate odors and gases. See the chart on the following page for the different ways air cleaners work.

Air cleaner	How it works	Pros and cons
Mechanical filter	Air is forced through a mesh that traps particles of pollen, tobacco smoke, pet dander, and other irritants.	HEPA (high efficiency particulate air) filters catch pollutants .03 microns or larger. ULPA filters catch even smaller parts.
Electronic or ionization filter	Static electricity causes particles to stick to the filter.	Some units may create ozone above an acceptable level.
Ozone generator	Uses ozone to oxidize organic compounds that produce odors.	Has little effect on allergens. Creates ozone above acceptable levels.

Secret to cheap prevention

One of the least expensive things you can do to allergy-proof your home is to clean it often and well. Among the allergens you need to eliminate inside your house are dust mites, mold, animal dander, and cockroach droppings.

Target dust mites. Get rid of the allergy-causing residue from microscopic pests by dusting surfaces and washing bed linens in hot water at least once a week. Launder blankets and mattress pads four times a year.

Keep humidity low. Dust mites, mold, and mildew thrive in a damp environment, so keep humidity levels below 40 percent, and don't let moisture build up in the kitchen and bathroom. You can use mold-killing cleansers in sinks, showers, and tubs. A study partially funded by The Clorox Company found that diluted household bleach not only kills mold but also neutralizes mold allergens.

Vacuum frequently. Most experts recommend vacuuming once or twice a week. But some say it's not effective at removing dust mites, even with the use of expensive filter bags. Although vacuuming sweeps up some allergens, it also stirs up dust in the air. It's best to wear a mask when doing housework or have someone who isn't allergic do it. Better yet, replace carpets with hard surfaces, and confine pets to areas where you don't spend a lot of time.

Keep pests from coming back. You may need an exterminator to get rid of cockroaches, mice, and other pests. But that's only half the battle. The allergens come from their body residue and droppings, so you need to clean your house thoroughly after the exterminator is finished. Discourage the return of these pests by cutting out food and water sources. Don't leave dirty dishes in the sink, and clean up spills and crumbs immediately.

Save money with natural antihistamines

Histamines are naturally occurring chemicals that cause allergic reactions in your body. It shouldn't be surprising, then, to know that naturally occurring antihistamines might counteract those reactions. Try these naturals instead of expensive allergy medicines.

Vitamin C is perhaps nature's best-known solution for allergies. It seems to keep your white blood cells from releasing histamines and

Avoid herbs that add to your woes

Be careful about drinking herbal teas when you suffer from allergies. They may contain leaves or pollen you're sensitive to. For example, people take echinacea to help prevent colds, but it helps boost their immune system, not relieve symptoms. If your nose is stuffy and you think echinacea will help ease your congestion, you could be making a big mistake. It may actually worsen your symptoms or even trigger some you've never experienced before.

then neutralizes the ones that do appear. Research shows your histamine levels rise when you don't get enough C, so eat peppers, citrus fruits, and other foods rich in vitamin C regularly. It works best when you get it all the time, not just when your allergies flare up.

Quercetin is another food chemical that regulates histamine release, and you'll find plenty in apples and onions. Quercetin is even more effective when combined with bromelain, an anti-inflammatory agent found in pineapple. Bromelain boosts quercetin's absorption.

Herbal supplements may be the answer if you don't get enough of these nutrients from foods. Other herbal aids for allergies include freeze-dried stinging nettle and butterbur extract, which are only available as supplements. Talk to your doctor before you take extra pills, though. If you take other allergy drugs along with the naturals, you can get in trouble from too much antihistamine activity.

Sweet way to ease symptoms

Here's an oh-so-sweet way to ease allergy symptoms without using drugs — if it really works.

Some people swear by the powers of local honey to build up your immune system so you won't be bothered by the sniffing, sneezing, and itchy eyes of hay fever. It has to be made by bees that gather pollen in the area where you live, and it has to be unfiltered. The idea is that your body won't react to pollen in the honey because it comes into your body through your digestive system. After a while, your immune system also stops reacting to the pollen when you breathe it in.

For whatever reason, people say it works. But research to back it up is hard to find. If you love honey, it may be worth a try to find a local beekeeper and start eating the honey before allergy season begins. But be careful — it's also possible to be allergic to honey.

Doctors aren't sure if it's because of the pollen or for some other reason, but if you notice any unusual symptoms, stop taking it.

Beware of money-wasting therapies

Homeopathy has a lot in common with local honey as a cure for allergies. It's based on the idea that the same substance that causes a disease can also cure it, but there is no clear scientific evidence it actually works.

Homeopathic allergy medicine is just a highly diluted form of a specific allergen, so you can't be sure exactly what is in the bottle. Active ingredients are repeatedly diluted, so the medicine may contain only water or alcohol and won't cause any harm. But, in some cases, products are diluted only a little and may contain significant amounts of the active ingredient. This can lead to problems with side effects.

Acupuncture is another complementary-alternative medicine (CAM) used to treat allergies. Like homeopathy, scientists have trouble proving acupuncture and other CAMs are effective. They urge caution when using alternative remedies because of their high cost and potential risks, such as dangerous side effects.

Alternative remedies may work like a placebo in some cases, but most people are better off saving their money for proven allergy remedies.

Children from the former East Germany had more allergies when they were exposed to a Western lifestyle. Among the changes: more wall-to-wall carpet, damper homes, and more cats.

Alzheimer's disease

Get treatment without breaking the bank

Alzheimer's disease (AD) is a type of dementia that slowly destroys memory and mental abilities. It affects about 4.5 million people just in the United States, but that number is estimated to triple in the next 50 years. The heartbreak of AD is that while there is no cure, it is possible for a loved one to live for decades with the disease. The Alzheimer's Association estimates the average lifetime cost of caring for someone with AD at $174,000.

Researchers are working hard to discover a better treatment for Alzheimer's disease, but in the meantime, know your options. The good news is some drugs can help manage AD or slow down the process. The better news is certain lifestyle changes can lower your risk of getting the disease in the first place.

Read on to learn what medications work, which ones you should avoid, and what can help you manage this condition.

Steer clear of heart-hazardous treatments

Recent studies suggest the risks of using two popular Alzheimer's drugs, Aricept (donepezil) and Razadyne (galantamine), may outweigh their benefits. More of the study participants taking either of these drugs died — mostly from heart attacks and strokes — than

Beware the hazards of similar drug names

Some doctors and pharmacists got confused when the Alzheimer's drug galantamine was still called Reminyl. They would mix it up with Amaryl, a diabetes medication. The snafu caused several cases of hypoglycemia and at least two deaths. So to make things less confusing — and less dangerous — the pharmaceutical company changed Reminyl's name to Razadyne.

those taking a placebo. Some experts are concerned about this increase in heart disease risk, especially when the drugs produce only mild benefits. Talk to your doctor if you have questions.

Vaccine spells hope for the future

This time, scientists are hoping they've got it right. The first vaccine they tested a few years ago was supposed to work just like any other vaccine — by triggering an immune response in your body. It contained a small amount of the protein beta amyloid thought to cause sticky plaques in the brain. Once your immune system created antibodies to destroy this protein, you would be safe from Alzheimer's. But a dangerous side effect sent researchers back to the drawing board. Now they plan to bypass the immune response entirely and inject the antibodies directly into patients. Keep an eye out for news on this promising treatment.

Watch out for memory-stealing drugs

The medicine you're taking for high blood pressure, asthma, allergies, pain, nausea, irregular heartbeat, ulcers, or Parkinson's disease may be stealing your memory. Anticholinergic drugs are prescribed for conditions like these because they block a certain neurotransmitter — a chemical that regulates nerve impulses. While these drugs help control your heart, or your breathing, or your muscles, for example, they can also inhibit memory. So, if you feel your attention, recall, or reaction time is suffering, it may not be dementia at all.

Sidestep AD with common meds

While some drugs are accepted treatments for Alzheimer's symptoms, there are other options you might not have considered.

Lower your cholesterol and your Alzheimer's risk. The medicine you may already be taking could be the key to preventing Alzheimer's. Statins — drugs that keep your cholesterol levels down — could help you avoid this dreaded disease. Studies have shown that Alzheimer's patients who regularly took statins experienced a slower mental decline along with lower cholesterol.

Manage BP to slow dementia. Got high blood pressure? Don't wait to deal with it. Research shows that for every year you treat this damaging condition, your risk of dementia goes down three percent. If you're already taking a potassium-sparing diuretic there's more good news — you may be lowering your risk of Alzheimer's by up to 70 percent. This medicine helps your body hang on to potassium, a mineral that allows your brain to send signals between nerves. And no matter what, control your numbers — avoid large swings in blood pressure readings throughout the day. Japanese researchers think big changes can lead to more memory lapses.

Black currants and boysenberries may protect your brain from Alzheimer's disease with potent compounds called anthocyanins and polyphenolics. British black currants have the most benefit because they're darker.

Although not everyone agrees controlling blood pressure decreases your risk of dementia, it's such a smart move anyway that even a slight chance of Alzheimer's prevention is a nice bonus.

Take two aspirin and remember me in the morning. Most experts agree inflammation plays a role in the development of Alzheimer's. That's why, in theory, preventing AD with nonsteroidal anti-inflammatory drugs (NSAIDs) like aspirin, acetaminophen, or ibuprofen just makes sense. And even though not all clinical trials have proven this to be true, enough studies on long-term use are positive to keep the research community interested. Talk to your doctor about NSAIDs because there are potential side effects.

Eat right to protect your memories

What you eat can affect every aspect of your health, and it turns out eating a Mediterranean diet rich in fruits, vegetables, and fish can reduce your risk of Alzheimer's disease.

Columbia University researchers surveyed over 2,000 people aged 65 and over and found the ones who ate foods from the Mediterranean diet were 40 percent less likely to develop

Diabetes drugs may hold key to dementia cure

Because diabetes changes the way your brain uses sugar, some experts believe it could also cause Alzheimer's disease later in life. One group of researchers found that diabetic patients who received a drug that "resensitized" their bodies to insulin — or essentially improved their brain's sugar use — had a lower chance of developing Alzheimer's years down the road. Studies are currently underway to further test this theory.

Alzheimer's. Follow their lead with these helpful foods.

Try the catch of the day. Fish is the entrée of choice when it comes to healthy hearts and minds. It is low in harmful saturated fat and high in healthy unsaturated fats like omega-3 fatty acids. In one study of seniors, those that ate fish at least once a week were 60 percent less likely to develop Alzheimer's disease compared to those who rarely ate fish. Good sources of healthy omega-3 fatty acids include salmon, halibut, mackerel, and sardines, but you can also get it from walnuts, almonds, and soy.

Ping-pong isn't just a way to kill time. In one study, playing the game increased blood flow to the brain and decreased symptoms in dementia patients — regardless of how well they played.

Eat your fruits and vegetables. Energize your brain naturally without dangerous drugs. Jump-start it with the folate you get from foods like broccoli, spinach, asparagus, beans, papaya, and orange juice. Scientists studied 300 older men and found that eating folate-rich foods protected them from declines in memory and thinking skills.

Pour a glass of wine. It doesn't make sense to start drinking alcohol for your health, but wine in moderation can be good for you. Red wine, especially, has resveratrol — a chemical found in grapes that reduces the protein that causes damaging plaque in your brain. Red wine has more resveratrol than white wine, and Pinot Noir has the most of all.

Save that thought with helpful herbs

Drugs aren't the only way to improve your memory. Natural herbs and supplements can help, too.

Put the kettle on. It tastes good, it's inexpensive, and you know it's healthy. Now, it could save your memory, too. It's green tea, and it contains an antioxidant called epigallocatechin-3-gallate. Otherwise known as EGCG, this natural ingredient kept harmful, sticky plaques from forming on the brains of mice that had been engineered to develop AD. Drink three to four cups a day of decaffeinated green tea for the most benefit. Steep a teaspoon of leaves or a tea bag in one cup of boiling water for three minutes. Then strain and enjoy.

India may have the world's lowest rate of Alzheimer's because of curry. Curcumin, the spice's yellow pigment, keeps beta-amyloid plaques from forming and even breaks down existing plaques.

Get jazzed up with ginkgo. Some medical studies have shown that taking ginkgo biloba extract on a regular basis increases circulation and offers antioxidant protection from dangerous free radicals — a one-two punch against memory problems. It's not a sure thing, but scientists are still hopeful. If you want to give it a shot, experts recommend 40 to 60 milligrams, three to four times daily for the best results. The effects may take about a month to show up.

Be careful, however, if you're already taking aspirin or warfarin since combining them with ginkgo could lead to bleeding problems. It doesn't mix well with blood pressure medicines either. Japanese researchers found taking ginkgo along with nifedipine, a calcium-channel blocker, caused severe headaches, dizziness, and hot flashes.

Let Medicare foot the bill

Early detection of Alzheimer's is critical to starting a drug treatment program that will help hold off the disease. Unfortunately, it's very hard to identify in its initial stages. Enter the PET — positron emission tomography — scan. This powerful brain scan correctly diagnoses Alzheimer's about 90 percent of the time. The problem is one scan can cost up to $1,500. But if you know someone whose dementia has been getting worse for six months, Medicare will cover the cost. Check it out because private health insurance companies may already be following suit.

Support eases caregiving burden

No man is an island. Taking care of someone with Alzheimer's disease is a big job and can become overwhelming if you take it on by yourself.

A recent study shows that when family caregivers work as a team to look after an Alzheimer's patient, it not only helps the caregiver feel less stressed, but also improves dementia symptoms in the patient. Another study found that symptoms were also better in patients whose caregivers felt less depressed and burdened. It's OK to ask for help and support. You're doing the patient a favor by taking care of yourself as much as you take care of them.

If you need a break to recharge, take advantage of a respite program — a service provided by organizations to help people who provide care to chronically ill senior citizens. Sometimes they'll give you free care services or grants, or they'll at least put you in contact with services you fund yourself. Use the Eldercare Locator to find a respite program near you. Go online at *www.Eldercare.gov* or call 800-677-1116.

Geriatric care managers are another option. They help people make sense of nursing homes, insurance policies, legal issues, medications, and other confusing aspects of home care.

Healthy teeth and gums may mean more than a nice smile. Researchers have found that inflammation and infection caused by loose teeth can quadruple your risk of Alzheimer's disease.

Compare costs of Alzheimer's drugs

Brand/dosage	Average retail price for monthly supply
Cholinesterase inhibitors (for mild to moderate AD)	
Aricept (5 mg @ 1/day)	$170.19
Razadyne (4 mg @ 2/day)	$173.35
NMDA receptor antagonists (for moderate to severe AD)	
Exelon (1.5 mg @ 2/day)	$187.77
Namenda (10 mg @ 2/day)	$150.58

To find a qualified geriatric care manager in your area, visit the National Association of Professional Geriatric Care Managers' Web site at *www.findacaremanager.org* or call 520-881-8008.

Simple test an early clue to Alzheimer's

People in the early stages of Alzheimer's disease have trouble recalling certain words. In a study at the University of York in Great Britain, participants were asked to name as many animals as they could in one minute. Researchers discovered that the Alzheimer's victims remembered words learned early in life, like dog and cat, but had difficulty recalling words learned later, like leopard.

This simple test could help determine if someone is suffering from a memory lapse or Alzheimer's disease.

Dollars&Sense
9 smart ways to slash health-care costs

Health-care costs have been rising five times faster than salaries. Use these tips to help shrink your spending and get more bang for your medical buck.

Save at in-store clinics. These walk-in clinics are opening up at Wal-Marts, drugstores, and other retailers. They're much cheaper than doctors' offices — some say half as much — and significantly less than the emergency room. Many of these clinics only treat minor illnesses, but their nurse practitioners can refer you to a doctor if you need further care.

Get health-care assistance. If you have no insurance or can't pay for health care, visit *http://ask.hrsa.gov/pc* or call toll-free 888-ASK-HRSA (888-275-4772.) You'll learn about centers that offer low- or no-cost emergency exams, lab tests, X-rays, and immunizations. This program does not cover medication costs.

Choose insurance wisely. Don't pick an insurance plan solely because the premiums are low. Co-payments and deductibles can cost you a lot. So can choosing a plan that doesn't match your needs. For example, a PPO-style plan is often more economical for people who expect to use specialists or out-of-network doctors. But if your family rarely gets sick and only needs check-ups and preventive care, an HMO-style plan may be best.

Pay with tax-free dollars. Stash them in a flexible spending account (FSA.) New rules give you 10 extra weeks after December 31 to use up each year's contributions to your account, so you're less likely to forfeit leftover money at deadline time. And now you can spend FSA dollars on nonprescription drugs, insurance deductibles and co-payments, flu shots, and more. Ask your plan administrator which expenses qualify.

Avoid preventable costs. Specialists like allergists or gastroenterologists can be expensive on some insurance plans. Before you visit a specialist, call and check with your family doctor first. She can help you determine whether the extra cost of a specialist is necessary.

Screen your medical tests. The U.S. Preventive Services Task Force says some screenings and tests should not be given to healthy people unless a doctor has reason to suspect disease. These tests are less likely to uncover hidden disease in symptom-free people and more likely to produce inaccurate results that require more testing. But new research shows that doctors still order these tests. Before agreeing to a test, ask why you need it and how it will affect treatment decisions. You may discover the test isn't necessary.

Choose outpatient surgery. You could save hundreds by avoiding an overnight hospital stay. Ask your doctor about the risks and benefits of outpatient surgery.

Catch billing errors. Most medical bills contain at least one error. While you're in the hospital, ask family members to help you keep a log of all tests, medication, and procedures that you're given. Then request an itemized bill from the hospital. Compare it with your log, and check for double billings, items you didn't get, or inaccurate dates. If you find a problem, notify both your insurance company and a hospital billing department supervisor.

Volunteer for a clinical trial. You can try new medicines and treatments that may not be available otherwise. The treatment under study is generally free, but ask to make sure. You can find industry-funded clinical trials in your area online at *www.centerwatch.com*. To learn about government-sponsored clinical trials, visit *www.clinicaltrials.gov*, or ask for help at your doctor's office or local clinic. Visit *www.cc.nih.gov* or call the Patient Recruitment Office at 800-411-1222 for studies at the National Institutes of Health Clinical Center in Bethesda, Maryland.

Anxiety
Low-cost ways to calm jangled nerves

Everyone worries occasionally. Your family, health, and financial situation — to name just a few aspects of everyday life — can cause plenty of legitimate concerns. But some people worry almost all the time. For people with generalized anxiety disorder (GAD), the most common form of anxiety, life can be overwhelming.

Excessive worrying, tension, and feelings of dread accompany your day-to-day decisions. You probably realize your worrying is way out of proportion to the situation, but you can't help agonizing over it. This constant feeling of being on edge takes its toll on your quality of life. In fact, anxiety often leads to physical symptoms, like headaches, sweating, palpitations, nausea, restlessness, and sleep disturbances.

When you are anxious, you have enough worries. One thing you shouldn't have to worry about is your treatment. Find out how to save money on the medication you need, avoid dangerous side effects, and calm yourself without drugs.

Escape the benzodiazepine menace

If you're taking benzodiazepines, such as Valium or Xanax, to manage your anxiety, you're also taking a big risk.

Benzodiazepines do help you cope with anxiety, but they come with major problems. First, you develop a tolerance to them. That means you eventually need more and more of the drug to get the same effect. They may also lead to addiction. In fact, withdrawing from benzodiazepines has been compared to trying to quit heroin.

Seniors and women are especially vulnerable to dependency. Seniors are also more likely to experience side effects, including daytime drowsiness and impaired coordination.

Your doctor may opt to prescribe certain antidepressants, such as selective serotonin reuptake inhibitors (SSRIs), instead. These drugs are not habit forming. If you do need benzodiazepines, which work more quickly than antidepressants, they should not be a long-term solution.

Take precautions when storing benzodiazepines. Keep your medication locked up to keep it out of the hands of curious youngsters.

> What time is it? Time to ease your tension. Stressed-out British politicians found that wearing a magnetic wrist-watch helped relieve anxiety and improve their sleep.

Why generics aren't always the best deal

You can save money by opting for generic drugs rather than brand name pills. The active ingredients are supposed to be the same, so they should have the same effect. But do they?

Some experts think not. When it comes to anxiety medication, generic drugs may not have the same calming effect because the body doesn't seem to absorb them as well. Doctors often have to increase the dose of a generic drug — by as much as 50 percent — to get the same effect as a brand name drug. On the other hand, maybe the power of suggestion makes you think the cheaper drug isn't as good. It's like the placebo effect, in reverse.

If you do want to try generic drugs, you don't have to go to Canada to find them. U.S. generics are, in fact, cheaper. Whether they are as effective as their brand name counterparts, however, remains to be seen.

Seek expert help to get back on track

Drugs certainly have their place in treating anxiety. The right prescription can help you function and feel like yourself again.

But maybe you don't need drugs at all. Instead of relying on a "magic pill" to make you feel better, try getting to the root of your problems with therapy.

Cognitive behavioral therapy, with its focus on helping you change how you think about and react to stressful situations, is considered the best option for generalized anxiety disorder. Look for a qualified therapist. You may want to ask your doctor for a recommendation.

Remember, drugs and therapy are not mutually exclusive. You don't have to choose one or the other. In fact, combining your medication with therapy can make your treatment even more effective.

Holding hands helps lower anxiety. In a recent study, brain scans of women anticipating an electric shock showed a soothing effect when their husbands held their hands.

Just talking about your problems with other people, perhaps in a support group, can also help. Thanks to the Internet, you can even chat with a therapist online.

Melt your cares away with a massage

Take a hands-on approach to relieving your anxiety — get a massage. There's nothing like a good rubdown to eliminate tension and stress.

Swedish massage is the most common type, and a typical massage can cost $45 to $85 an hour. Sometimes your insurance will even cover the cost if it's for medical reasons.

Massage is an effective alternative treatment. Just make sure you find a qualified massage therapist. You can do that at the American Massage Therapy Association Web site at *www.amtamassage.org*.

Researchers are testing the illegal drug ecstasy to treat post-traumatic stress disorder. This drug, whose technical name is methylene-dioxymethamphetamine (MDMA), may also help relieve anxiety in the terminally ill.

Hands-on therapies, like massage, might not be best for everyone, including people who suffer from panic attacks.

Another good way to relieve mild anxiety is through aromatherapy. Often used in conjunction with massage, aromatherapy involves soothing scents from essential oils. Some favorites include lavender, chamomile, and jasmine.

Straight talk about natural alternatives

Herbs and supplements provide natural alternatives to prescription medication. But natural does not always mean safe.

For example, the herb kava does help relieve anxiety. But it also comes with some risks, including the possibility of liver damage. So while it might be effective, it may not be the best option.

Explore the world of unusual phobias

Phobia, the excessive and persistent fear of a specific object or situation, is a common anxiety disorder. You've probably heard of agoraphobia, the fear of open spaces, or xenophobia, the fear of foreigners or strangers. But what about arachibutyrophobia? That's the fear of peanut butter sticking to the roof of your mouth. Pogonophobia is the fear of beards, while syngenesophobia is the fear of relatives. For more interesting phobias, check out the Phobia List at *www.phobialist.com.*

Other herbs that have been used to treat anxiety include passion flower and gotu kola, but more research needs to be done before they can be recommended. For mild stress relief, you can also turn to valerian, ginseng, or chamomile. Supplements that may help your body deal with stress include vitamin C, B vitamins, and magnesium.

Unlike prescription drugs, the Food and Drug Administration (FDA) does not regulate herbs and supplements. That means you do not always know exactly what you're getting. Always tell your doctor what herbs you're taking. Certain herbs may dangerously interact with drugs.

Smart way to calm an anxious mind

What you put on your plate may affect what goes on in your mind. That's why a healthy diet may play a role in overcoming anxiety.

In times of stress, your body especially needs protein. Complex carbohydrates, vitamin C, B vitamins, and minerals like zinc, iron, and selenium will also serve you well.

Anti-anxiety drug alerts

Drug class	Generic (Brand)	Consumer alerts
Benzodiazepines	alprazolam (Xanax) clonazepam (Klonopin) diazepam (Valium) lorazepam (Ativan)	May lead to dependency. Not covered under recent Medicare Modernization Act.
Selective serotonin reuptake inhibitors (SSRIs)	citalopram (Celexa) escitalopram (Lexapro) fluoxetine (Prozac) fluvoxamine (Luvox) paroxetine (Paxil) sertraline (Zoloft)	Fatal reaction may occur if taken with monoamine oxidase inhibitors, another type of anti-depressant.
Serotonin-norepinephrine reuptake inhibitors (SNRIs)	venlafaxine (Effexor) duloxetine (Cymbalta)	Extended-release venlafaxine may trigger high blood pressure.
Tetracyclic	mirtazapine (Remeron)	May cause blurred vision.
Tricyclics	clomipramine (Anafranil) imipramine (Tofranil) nortriptyline (Aventyl)	May interfere with some blood pressure lowering drugs.
Azapirone	buspirone (BuSpar)	Fewer side effects than benzo-diazepines, but may also be less effective.

One study found that eating gazpacho, a cold vegetable soup, helped lower stress chemicals in the body. Other specific foods that may help reduce stress include asparagus, broccoli, kale, and spinach, which are chock-full of B vitamins. Warm milk may also calm your nerves.

Omega-3 fatty acids, found in fish, walnuts, and flaxseed, can have a calming effect, especially if you also cut down on omega-6 fatty acids, which appear in vegetable oils and deep-fried or processed foods.

Avoid caffeine and alcohol, which can adversely affect your mood and leave you jittery or depressed. They can also lessen the effects of some anxiety medications.

Simple steps to squash stress

They may not be as powerful as prescription drugs or therapy, but these simple lifestyle strategies can help reduce your stress.

▶ **Get plenty of sleep each night.** Your body needs to recharge.

▶ **Laugh more.** Watch a funny movie or visit a humorous friend or relative. Studies show laughter lowers stress.

▶ **Exercise regularly.** You'll sleep better, feel better about yourself, and reduce anxiety symptoms.

Antibiotic helps people overcome fear

A drug that fights bacteria may also help fight fear. In recent studies, the antibiotic D-cycloserine has helped people overcome their fear of heights and public speaking. When used with behavioral therapy, it works by speeding up the effects of the therapy. This combination may work for social phobia and other anxiety disorders.

▸ **Spend time in your garden.** It's a peaceful way to get some exercise.

▸ **Play some music.** Whether you tickle the ivories on your piano or just turn on the radio, music helps you relax.

▸ **Hold no grudges.** Forgiveness helps lower stress — and the health problems that come with it.

▸ **Affirm your values.** A recent study of college students found that those who reflected on values important to them, such as religion or social issues, before undertaking a stressful task had lower levels of the stress hormone cortisol.

▸ **Take a vacation.** It may seem obvious, but just getting away for a vacation will do wonders for your health.

Asthma

How to control symptoms — and cost

About 20 million Americans have asthma, and thousands — many of them elderly — die from it every year. About 10 percent of all people who have asthma are over 65, when asthma attacks can combine with other health problems to make things worse.

Asthma is a chronic inflammation of your airways that tightens up your bronchial tubes and fills them with mucus. Unfortunately, it has some of the same symptoms as several other diseases, including heart attack. You need a doctor's diagnosis to be sure of what you have.

Once you know you have asthma, get the most for the money you spend on treatment by working closely with your doctor to get the right dosage of the right medicine. You'll find cost-cutting asthma-fighting tips throughout this chapter.

Easy way to lower expenses

The best way to keep asthma's expenses under control is to use your medicine exactly the way your doctor tells you. He will likely prescribe a quick-acting bronchodilator inhaler for relief from acute asthma attacks. For longer relief and to prevent attacks, you will need corticosteroids, which are also inhaled.

A 2006 study shows asthma sufferers who took the antibiotic telithromycin had milder attacks and quicker recovery than those who didn't.

They control the inflammation that causes your bronchial tubes to swell and fill with fluid.

Albuterol, a short-acting beta2 agonist, is the standard U.S. bronchodilator, but it only relaxes the muscles surrounding your bronchial tubes. It does nothing to stop inflammation and actually becomes less effective the more you use it because you develop a tolerance. So an extra shot of albuterol when you don't think it's working fast enough both wastes and weakens the medicine.

On the other hand, you may think you're saving money by using your long-term inhaler less when you're feeling fine — or using the cheaper albuterol instead. In reality, you're letting the inflammation build up to a point that your next attack could be one that brings huge emergency room and hospital bills.

Beware the danger of top asthma drug

One of the most-prescribed long-term asthma medicines may not be so good for you after all. The U.S. Food and Drug Administration (FDA) has warned that Advair should only be prescribed as a last resort.

The problem is with one of the drugs in Advair — salmeterol, a long-acting beta2 agonist (LABA) bronchodilator. Like their cousins the short-acting beta2 agonists, LABAs don't work as well when you use them too often. They can even lead to more severe attacks and have been associated with a higher number of asthma deaths.

LABAs combined with corticosteroids have become a favorite long-term asthma treatment. The steroids reduce inflammation while the LABAs keep the airways open and help your lungs work better over time. Sometimes physicians prescribe separate doses of a LABA and a steroid. Advair is a single medicine that combines salmeterol and the corticosteroid fluticasone.

The FDA warnings also apply to Serevent, which is salmeterol by itself, and Foradil, which is the related LABA formoterol. It says other drugs should be tried first to control asthma. If they don't work, then the LABAs should be used only in combination with another asthma treatment drug.

Don't stop taking these medicines if your doctor has prescribed them, but check with him to make sure you're taking them properly and not overusing them.

The little pill you should never take

You may reach for aspirin when you're in pain, but research shows that may not be a good idea if you're asthmatic. Over-the-counter (OTC) pain relievers will set off an attack in about one of every five adult asthma sufferers.

Experts call it aspirin-induced asthma, but it includes other nonsteroidal anti-inflammatory drugs (NSAIDs) like ibuprofen and naproxen as well. If you think this has happened to you, you should

Help yourself during an attack

Pursed-lip breathing can help keep your airways open during an asthma attack. Breathe in through your nose and out through your mouth with your lips in a whistling or kissing position. Take two seconds to inhale and four to six seconds to exhale.

Avoid lung-damaging aroma

Stop buying mothballs, air fresheners, and toilet bowl deodorizers. You'll not only save money, you may save your lungs. Scientists have found that the chemical you smell in mothballs affects lung function, which can be serious if you have asthma. The volatile organic compound 1,4-dichlorobenzene (1,4-DCB) is a prime ingredient in many sanitizing products. Control the risk from 1,4-DCB by limiting your use of these items.

switch to the non-NSAID painkiller acetaminophen, some experts say. Unfortunately, research also links the regular use of acetaminophen with increased asthma risk, so it's possible that could cause problems as well.

Cold remedies and even heartburn medicines often contain pain relievers, too. Read the labels of all over-the-counter medicines and know exactly what you are taking. Don't forget to tell your doctor about all the medicines, herbs, and supplements you take whenever you get a new prescription.

Remember, too, that pills aren't the only answers for aches and pains. You can avoid both the side effects and expense of painkilling drugs by first trying ice packs, heating pads, physical activity, or relaxation.

5 ways to guard against EIA

Don't be afraid to exercise if you have asthma. Working out can boost your breathing capacity and cut back on asthma symptoms. Even the American Thoracic Society recommends moderate aerobic exercise for

Benefits and risks of asthma drugs

Drug	Generic (Brand)	Purpose	Concerns
Bronchodilator – relaxes smooth muscles around your bronchial tubes to open up your airways			
Inhaled, short-acting beta 2 agonist	albuterol (Proventil) pirbuterol (Maxair)	Provides immediate relief for all types of asthma, but no long-term benefits	Frequent use lowers their benefit. Overuse can turn them into a trigger.
Inhaled, long-acting beta 2 agonist	salmeterol (Serevent) formoterol (Foradil)	Preferred treatment for moderate to severe asthma when used with inhaled corticosteroids	Never use alone. If inflammation isn't treated at the same time, overuse can lead to serious consequences.
Anti-inflammatory – controls the inflammation that promotes mucus buildup and swelling			
Inhaled corticosteroid	fluticasone (Flovent) budesonide (Pulmicort) flunisolide (AeroBid)	Prevents asthma attacks and relieves chronic symptoms	Minimal side effects since little inhaled medication reaches bloodstream.
Oral steroid	prednisone (Deltasone, Sterapred) methylprednisone (Medrol)	Reduces inflammation	Long-term use can produce serious side effects.

asthmatics. But don't go overboard. Before you start training, take steps to guard against the possibility of exercise-induced asthma (EIA).

Vigorous physical activity triggers asthma attacks in more than 90 percent of people who have asthma. About 10 percent of the

Protect health with an ozone-free home

An air purifier in your home might be just the ticket if airborne allergens are a major factor in triggering your asthma. They can filter out triggers like pollen, mold, dust, and animal dander. But avoid air cleaners that produce ozone — either on purpose or incidentally. While ozone is great for purifying water or blocking ultraviolet rays, it is also the primary ingredient of smog and can make your asthma much worse. See the *Allergies* chapter to learn more about choosing the best type of air cleaner for your condition.

general population, some of whom don't normally have asthma, also suffer attacks. EIA may be even more common among serious athletes. Studies of Olympians have shown up to 40 percent suffer EIA symptoms.

These steps will help you avoid this potentially serious problem.

▸ Make sure you have your overall asthma under control.

▸ Take a dose of your albuterol inhaler 15 to 30 minutes before you work out.

▸ Exercise in a warm, humid environment.

▸ Include warm-up and cool-down periods in your workout.

▸ Avoid salt in your diet, and eat plenty of foods with antioxidants and omega-3 fatty acids. Caffeine also helps reduce the severity of EIA.

Top foods that fight asthma

Studies show that people who eat a lot of the right kind of foods are less likely to have asthma. Vegetables, fruit, and fish are all part of a good defense against breathing problems.

Go to the garden for vitamins. Carrots, tomatoes, and leafy greens like lettuce and spinach are rich in carotenoids. These phytonutrients convert to vitamin A, which helps regulate your immune system and keep the lining of your respiratory tract in shape.

Sweet peppers, especially the red ones, are another good asthma-fighting vegetable. They have lots of vitamin C, the major antioxidant in the surface of the lungs. Just one cup of red peppers will give you 283 milligrams of vitamin C — more than three times your daily requirement. Oranges and other citrus fruits are also good choices for this important nutrient.

Eat apples to avoid asthma. They're red and delicious, and they top the list of fruits that may ease asthma. Apples are full of quercetin and other flavonoid antioxidants that fight the free radicals produced by your inflamed airways. Apple peelings have even more quercetin than the flesh, so be sure and eat all the apple.

Build up your lungs with fish. Researchers think the omega-3 fatty acids in fish oil may help your lungs by suppressing inflammation. Studies have shown that eating fish seems to help more than taking fish oil supplements. Experts recommend eating fish three or more times a week as part of a well-balanced diet that keeps up your levels of omega-3.

> Asthmatics may soon benefit from their own "music therapy." Researchers are studying how playing wind instruments like flutes and horns can increase lung capacity.

Natural solutions keep asthma at bay

You can help yourself avoid asthma attacks naturally. Try boosting your breathing with these nutrients and herbs.

Magnesium is a natural bronchodilator. It helps open up your airways and ease the muscle spasms of asthma attacks. You can keep up the magnesium level in your body by eating avocados, oysters, beans, and broccoli.

Rosemary is an herb used for flavoring food and beverages, but it has also been used in folk medicine as an antispasmodic. It relaxes the smooth muscles of the trachea and reduces the production of leukotrienes that cause inflammation. Research shows that a mixture of Chinese herbs called anti-asthma herbal medicine intervention (ASHMI) may be as safe and effective in treating moderate asthma as the corticosteroid prednisone — without the side effects.

Laughter is a more common asthma trigger than even dust mites and mold. Experts think it may have to do with hyperventilation.

Butterbur extract helps control asthma and hay fever by acting as an antihistamine and improving lung function. Certain parts of this plant can be harmful, but the extracts used in research had no toxins. Be careful though. Butterbur is primarily a European medicine that is not regulated in the United States, so some products on the market may not be safe to use. It's best to talk to your doctor about any herbal remedies you would like to try.

Back pain
Right techniques promise real relief

There are two kinds of people — those with back problems and those without. In the United States alone, back injuries cost more than 80 billion dollars a year in medical expenses and lost work.

Roughly four out of five people will suffer with back pain at some point during their lives. Too often, doctors don't know why. In an effort to end your pain, they may prescribe surgery you don't need or pain medications that cause serious health problems.

But here is something you may not know — in nine out of 10 cases, back injuries heal on their own within six weeks. Ahead, you'll discover easy-does-it secrets to help you escape back pain and — surprise — none of them calls for surgery, drugs, or extra time in bed.

Dodge deadly dose of common pain reliever

Over-the-counter pain relievers, or analgesics, often form the first line of defense against back pain. Acetaminophen is considered safer than most, but the hidden danger can be deadly.

Overdosing on acetaminophen is the most common cause of acute liver failure, and it's easier to do than you may think. Researchers at the University of Washington Medical Center studied more than 600

people with acute liver failure and found most had been taking acetaminophen for pain. More than a third were taking two or more
medicines that contained the ingredient.

The biggest problem is that most people don't realize how many
drugs contain acetaminophen. It's in everything from TheraFlu,
Tylenol, and Alka-Selzer Plus cold medicines to Vicodin and Percocet.
Read the Active Ingredients label on all over-the-counter and prescription drugs carefully, and avoid taking those containing the same active
ingredients unless your doctor approves. Limit your total acetaminophen intake to less than 4,000 milligrams (mg) daily. Call Poison
Control immediately at 800-222-1222 if you suspect an overdose.

Say 'no' to save your heart

Propoxyphene (Darvon, Darvocet) is one of the five most commonly
prescribed narcotic pain relievers, despite the fact that it is only mild-
ly effective. What many doctors don't realize is that pain experts no
longer recommend propoxyphene as a first-line treatment.

Propoxyphene produces a chemical in your body as it breaks
down called norpropoxyphene, which can trigger heart arrhythmias.
For this reason, elderly people in particular should avoid taking it.
Doctors may also prescribe acetaminophen to boost its weak
painkilling power. However, one brand of propoxyphene called

Check your medicine cabinet

The drugs you take could be causing your back pain. For example, Omacor and verteporfin both have side effects that mimic
back pain. Cialis may cause back pain in as many as 20 percent
of men taking it. If your back bothers you, talk to your doctor
about whether medication could be responsible.

Darvocet already contains 650 milligrams of acetaminophen. Adding more for breakthrough pain puts you at risk of a toxic acetaminophen overdose.

Narcotic pain medicines like this one can also be addictive. Plus, they can suppress your immune system, making you more vulnerable to infection and disease. However, taken exactly as your doctor prescribes, narcotics may help manage severe pain.

Do not stop taking propoxyphene without your doctor's permission. Instead, talk to him about switching to a less dangerous, more effective painkiller.

Surgery: a last resort for bad backs

Few people truly need back surgery. In fact, some experts say less than 1 percent of people with back pain need aggressive surgery. In most cases, natural alternatives like exercise, physical therapy, and applying heat and cold help heal the injury. If your doctor tells you that you need surgery, get a second opinion.

If you suffer with sciatic pain, worsening weakness in the legs, or a herniated disc or spinal stenosis (narrowing of the spine) causing bowel or bladder control problems, you may need surgery if medicines and natural options don't help after six weeks. Discuss your particular case with a doctor you trust, and choose a surgeon who has lots of experience performing the procedure you need. Remember, surgery is not always successful, it may take months to fully heal, and you may never regain full flexibility.

Your back is particularly vulnerable when you first get out of bed. Go easy on it. Roll onto your side, bend your knees, push yourself upright with your arms, and lower your legs over the bedside.

The inside story on back pain drugs

Drug class	Generic (Brand)	Concerns
	acetaminophen (Tylenol, Excedrin, Goody's)	High dosages taken long-term can damage liver and kidneys.
Over-the-counter NSAIDs	aspirin (Bayer) ibuprofen (Advil, Motrin IB) naproxen (Aleve)	Used for short-term injuries; may not effectively control chronic pain. Can lead to ulcers and bleeding along digestive tract.
Prescription-strength NSAIDs	ibuprofen (Motrin) naproxen (Naprosyn, Anaprox) diclofenac (Voltaren) ketoprofen (Orudis)	Can cause kidney damage and raise blood pressure in high dosages.
COX-2 inhibitors	celecoxib (Celebrex)	Causes no gastrointestinal side effects but could more than double risk of heart problems.
Muscle relaxants	diazepam (Valium) cyclobenzaprine (Flexeril) carisoprodol (Soma)	Can cause drowsiness, dizziness, dry mouth, and nausea. Can be addictive; do not take longer than two weeks at a time.
	tramadol (Ultram, Ultracet)	May trigger seizures. Taking antidepressants or antipsychotic drugs increases this risk.
Narcotics (opioids and opiates)	hydrocodone (Vicodin) morphine (MSIR, MS Morphine) oxycodone (Percocet, Percodan, OxyContin) meperidine (Demerol) propoxyphene (Darvon)	Can be highly addictive and may cause constipation, drowsiness, confusion, nausea, and trouble emptying bladder. Older adults may need extra fiber or laxatives while taking narcotics.

Try some free (and fun) therapy

Physical therapy can help you get on your feet after a lingering back injury, but emerging evidence suggests you can save money and get the same pain-busting benefits with do-it-yourself workouts.

Ask for advice. Your doctor may refer you for physical therapy if your pain lasts longer than three weeks. Instead of signing up for weeks of costly therapy, ask about a one-time session for exercise advice. In a study published in the prestigious *British Medical Journal,* advice from a physical therapist on how to stay active helped people with mild to moderate low back pain as much as four or more weeks of physical therapy.

Make fitness fun. Leisurely, low-impact workouts like walking and swimming seem to relieve low back pain better than specific back exercises. Fun activities like these also lighten psychological stress. In fact, researchers from the University of California and University of Michigan say walking briskly about half an hour each day is enough to reap these pain-reducing, mood-boosting benefits. Doing specific back exercises, on the other hand, may worsen both back pain and stress.

Turn up the heat. Applying heat with a Thermacare patch, heating pad, or hot, moist compress can cut pain even more. Exercising and wearing a continuous low-level heat wrap for five days packed more pain relief and improved function better than exercise or heat wraps alone in a study of 100 people with acute low back pain. What's more, 72 percent of those who used this combo treatment regained full mobility just one week after starting it.

If you have constant back pain, ask your doctor about sustained-release drugs. They may manage your pain better than short-acting medications, and you may find yourself taking fewer doses to get the same relief.

After a back injury, you should try to return to your

normal activities as soon as possible, as much as your pain allows. Simply start out slow to give damaged muscles time to rebuild.

End pain through proper posture

Here is a free, easy way to relieve back pain — improve your posture. Bad posture can worsen existing pain, but how you stand, sit, and even sleep could put the skip in your step again.

Stand tall. When standing, raise your head so your chin is parallel to the floor, and use your abdominal muscles to pull in your stomach. Don't stand "at attention," with shoulders pulled back and chin thrust out. This position only adds to back strain. Instead, keep your ears, shoulders, hips, knees, and ankles in line with each other. Try not to stand for long periods of time. If you do, take turns resting each foot on a nearby footstool.

Sit pretty. Sitting puts the most strain on your back, so get up and move every half hour. Choose straight-backed chairs or those with low-back support, and sit with your shoulders touching the chair back. Keep your upper back straight and chest lifted. If you spend lots of time at a desk, get a swivel chair that lets you turn without twisting at the waist. Look, too, for one with armrests and an adjustable back. You can place a rolled-up towel in the small of your back for added lumbar support. Sit with your knees slightly higher than your hips, and prop them on a footrest if needed.

To protect your stomach, look for buffered over-the-counter medications, and take them with food or milk.

Sleep smarter. Strategically placed pillows help support your back while you sleep. People with back pain should sleep on their side in a fetal position with a pillow between their knees to maintain the spine's natural curve. Back-sleepers, on the other hand, should put a pillow under their knees to support their lower back. Sleeping on your stomach is the worst position for a bad back and can trigger pain and prolong recovery. If you just can't break the habit, at least place a pillow under your stomach or chest to keep your spine aligned.

Sleep your way to a better back

Doctors have long told people with bad backs to sleep on a hard mattress — but no more. Spanish researchers replaced the mattresses of 313 people with chronic low back pain with either soft, hard, or medium mattresses. Those who slept on the medium mattress for 90 days felt less pain and needed less pain medicine than those sleeping on a hard mattress.

That still leaves you lots of choices when bed shopping. Try this advice to narrow the field.

- **Don't trust tags.** They won't tell you how firm a mattress really is. One manufacturer's "firm" may be softer or harder than another's. Test each bed yourself by lying on it.

- **Buy the right size.** Single sleepers can make do with a twin bed, but couples need at least a queen-size so both people can move freely at night.

- **Don't go by price alone.** Buy the best quality mattress you can afford for longer-lasting sleep comfort.

- **Extend the life of your mattress.** Slip a piece of plywood between a too-soft mattress and its box spring. That will hold you over until you're ready to buy a new one.

Get crackin' to beat back problems

Chiropractic therapy, otherwise known as spinal manipulation, may help back pain that has lasted less than a month. Previous studies on its

Short-term back pain is called acute. Pain that lasts longer than three months is considered chronic.

effectiveness have shown mixed results — it seems to help some people but not others. Now researchers think they have the answer why.

Army and Air Force physical therapists randomly assigned people with low back pain to either exercise therapy or spinal manipulation. Researchers also kept track of who improved with chiropractic treatment. People who met four out of five of these criteria were most likely to benefit.

▶ pain for fewer than 16 days

▶ only pain above the knees, not below

▶ not afraid of physical activity causing pain

▶ at least one stiff segment of the spine

▶ normal range of motion in at least one hip

Researchers say as many as 92 percent of people who meet four of the five criteria could improve after just one week of chiropractic treatment. Plus, six months later, people in the exercise-only group were taking more medicine, seeking more medical help, and had lost more work days due to back pain than those in the chiropractic group.

The sooner you seek help, the better. These experts say the single most accurate prediction of who would benefit from manipulation was how long their back pain had lasted.

A good doctor or chiropractor will first take X-rays and examine you for osteoporosis, herniated discs, spinal stenosis, and other nerve, bone, or joint disorders. People with these conditions are not candidates for chiropractic therapy.

Shockingly simple way to ease pain

Gentle jolts of electricity can help relieve pain. At least, that's the theory behind TENS (transcutaneous electric nerve stimulation) devices.

Visit a physical therapy clinic, and chances are you'll find one of these machines. TENS units have small electrodes that attach to your skin at or near the site of pain. The unit sends gentle electrical impulses that seem to block pain signals traveling to your brain, at least temporarily. It may also trigger your body to release natural feel-good chemicals called endorphins.

You can get TENS treatments in physical therapy or chiropractic offices, but buying or renting your own machine could save you a bundle, especially if you suffer with chronic back pain. In most cases, Medicare or insurance will help cover the cost.

Discuss TENS treatment with your doctor, and consider renting one first to see if it helps. Some devices are available for over-the-counter sale, but you will need a prescription to get Medicare or insurance coverage. Your doctor or physical therapist will also need to show you where to place the electrodes, how to operate the machine, and what settings to use for your pain.

Not all experts recommend TENS therapy, and it alone may not be enough to control back pain. It tends to work best in combination with other therapies, like pain relievers.

Beware of addictive drugs

Narcotic pain relievers such as OxyContin and Vicodin can work wonders for pain but can be addictive because they affect the same places in the brain as the street drug heroin. Take them exactly as prescribed and only under your doctor's close supervision.

Dollars&Sense
6 myth-busting truths about generic drugs

You can save up to 70 percent by choosing generic drugs, but are they as good or as safe as brand-name drugs? Here is what you need to know to separate fiction from fact.

Myth: Generics are not as safe as brand names.

Truth: Generic drugs must meet the same FDA safety standards as their brand-name equivalents. In fact, *Consumer Reports* and health watchdog *Public Citizen* say some generics may be safer than new brand-name drugs prescribed for the same condition. Here's why. From time to time, a few health dangers of a new drug are not discovered before FDA approval. But such problems are usually found before the drug is old enough to be available as a generic. Consequently, generic drugs are less likely to be pulled off the market or have extra warnings and restrictions added to their labels for safety reasons.

Myth: Generics are not as good as brand names.

Truth: To win FDA approval, a generic drug must meet the same guidelines for quality, purity, strength, and effectiveness as its brand-name equivalent. It must also use the same active ingredients, act just as fast, and work the same way in your body. The only difference is generic drugs can include other fillers and inactive ingredients, and these may cause an allergic reaction in some people. If you find this happens, you will have to avoid drugs that contain the problem ingredient.

Myth: The lower price means corners were cut.

Truth: Generics are cheaper simply because their makers don't have all the costs associated with creating a new drug. Any drug company that patents a new drug is granted a period of time to earn back the millions spent to create and test that drug.

When the patent period ends, other companies can copy and sell the drug for less money than it took to create it. They pass along that savings to you.

Myth: Brand-name drug costs don't rise much.

Truth: AARP reports that prices of brand-name drugs have been rising faster than inflation — sometimes twice as fast. Yet generic prices have lagged well behind inflation. And now, thanks to a new Wal-Mart program, you may soon pay the low price of $4 for a month's supply of many generic drugs. Ask about this program at your local Wal-Mart pharmacy.

Myth: Canadian drugs are cheaper than generics.

Truth: The seven best-selling generic drugs for chronic conditions in the United States are also available in Canada, so the FDA compared the costs. For five of the drugs, you would save by choosing the American generics instead of their Canadian brand name or generic versions.

Myth: All drugs have generic equivalents.

Truth: Some drugs are too new to have generic equivalents, but you might still find a generic drug with these tips.

▸ Ask both your doctor and pharmacist if your prescription has a generic equivalent. Your pharmacist may know about a generic drug that your doctor doesn't. If so, the pharmacist can consult with your doctor about changing your prescription.

▸ If your drug has no generic, ask your doctor if there are similar medications you can take that do have generic versions.

▸ Keep checking. Patent periods end every year. In fact, a high number of patent periods are set to expire before 2010, so many new generics will soon be on the shelves.

BPH

Top healers and helpers for enlarged prostate

For most men, the prostate gland gets larger with age, a condition known as benign prostatic hyperplasia (BPH). About 50 percent of men ages 51 to 60 have enlarged prostates, and almost 90 percent over age 80.

BPH is not cancerous, but it can certainly crimp your lifestyle. Enlarged prostates put the squeeze on your urethra, the tube carrying urine from the bladder out of the body. Men with BPH may have trouble urinating; feel the need to urinate often, especially at night; develop urinary tract infections; or become incontinent.

Fortunately, not all men with BPH have symptoms. In fact, doctors only recommend you seek treatment if symptoms become bothersome, or if you get frequent urinary tract infections. Luckily, men with this condition have lots of options, from natural herbs to effective drugs, and even high-tech laser surgeries.

When 'watchful waiting' makes good sense

Having BPH doesn't doom you to a life of expensive medication or surgeries. In fact, many men live fulfilling lives without any treatment. Experts call this approach "watchful waiting." It involves

lifestyle changes to boost prostate health and an annual exam —
and it could be right for you.

Benign prostatic hyperplasia can cause annoying urination problems, but rarely does it lead to serious complications, like kidney
damage. Whether you choose to take medication, undergo surgery,
or do nothing and wait mostly depends on the severity of your
symptoms and how much they affect your life.

To gauge your symptoms, your doctor will examine you and ask
a set of questions called the International Prostate Symptoms Score
(IPSS) questionnaire. Your answers will help you and your doctor
decide whether to choose watchful waiting, medication, surgery, or
another procedure.

IPSS score	Rating	Treatment options
0 – 7	Mild	Consider watchful waiting if unbothered by minor symp-toms, even if prostate is enlarged. Roughly 15 percent of "waiters" eventually need treatment.
8 – 19	Moderate	Decide whether symptoms are bothersome enough to merit treatment. Weigh complications, side effects, and cost against severity of symptoms.
20 – 35	Severe	Will most likely need medication or surgery.

Men who choose watchful waiting can take active steps to ease
their symptoms and prevent them from getting worse.

▸ **Make it through the night.** Stop drinking fluids at 7 p.m. to
cut down on nighttime bathroom trips.

▸ **Seize the opportunity.** Visit a restroom whenever you can,
even if you don't feel the urge to go.

▸ **Cut out caffeine, especially coffee.** It's linked to a higher risk of BPH.

▸ **Limit alcohol.** Heavy drinking can aggravate your lower urinary tract.

▸ **Be choosy when picking a seat.** Take an aisle seat on airplanes, in theaters, and during other events.

▸ **Keep warm.** Cold weather improves muscle tone within the prostate, putting a stronger squeeze on your urinary tract and worsening common BPH symptoms.

▸ **Stay active.** Being immobile worsens urinary retention, while moderate exercise reduces urinary tract problems.

▸ **Squeeze in some Kegels.** These exercises strengthen your pelvic floor muscles, the ones you squeeze to stop urinating, and can boost bladder control. Squeeze them and hold for three seconds, then release for three seconds. Do this 15 times, three times a day. Do one set standing, one while sitting, and the last lying down.

▸ **Say "no" to Sudafed.** Cold remedies that contain decongestants like pseudoephedrine can keep the muscles in your prostate and bladder from relaxing, making it more difficult to urinate.

▸ **Avoid allergy drugs.** Antihistamines, such as diphenhydramine (Benadryl), can slow urine flow in some men with BPH.

▸ **Be smart about diuretics.** They increase urination, a problem for men with BPH. Yet, they can also save your life if you have high blood pressure, so don't stop using them without your doctor's permission.

The latest scoop on saw palmetto

As many as 2.5 million Americans take saw palmetto supplements, and European doctors routinely prescribe it for BPH. But does it really work? New studies raise questions and shed doubt on this popular herbal remedy.

Help your heart along with your prostate

If you have high blood pressure or cholesterol, you may want to ask your doctor about taking certain alpha-blockers. Terazosin (Hytrin), doxazosin (Cardura), and alfuzosin (Uroxatral) can lower pressure and cholesterol while preventing the growth of prostate cancer cells. That makes them a good choice for men with severe urinary problems along with high blood pressure, high cholesterol, or both.

European researchers analyzed the results of 17 studies on Permixon, a high-quality saw palmetto supplement for BPH. Overall, results were similar to those with alpha-blockers, the most common drugs for BPH. Permixon improved men's IPSS nearly five points, and it eased urinary problems in every study. Another analysis of 21 studies involving more than 3,000 men with BPH found saw palmetto supplements were about as effective as the BPH drug finasteride (Proscar) and caused fewer side effects, such as erectile dysfunction.

But experts have never whole-heartedly endorsed this herb. They point out that most trials have included too few people, didn't last long enough, and had no standard measure for success.

To better test this popular supplement, researchers at the University of California conducted a randomized, placebo-controlled, double-blind trial — the "gold standard" of clinical studies. Out of 225 men with moderate to severe BPH, some took 160 milligrams (mg) of saw palmetto twice a day, and some took a placebo, or fake pill. After one year of treatment, the herb showed no more effect than the fake pills on urine flow, prostate size, ability to empty the bladder, or the men's quality of life.

That's bad news for a promising herb, but experts haven't given up on it just yet. The National Institutes of Health (NIH) has a major

Get a definite diagnosis from your doctor before self-treating with saw palmetto or other supplements. Serious conditions such as prostate cancer can cause symptoms similar to BPH.

study underway pitting saw palmetto against another herb, *Pygeum africanum*, and the BPH drug tamsulosin (Flomax) in almost 3,000 men. Unfortunately, results won't emerge until 2012. In the meantime, discuss the evidence with your doctor.

If you decide to try saw palmetto, look for high-quality supplements, like those shown to work in clinical trials. You'll need an extract containing at least 85 percent fatty acids and 0.2 percent sterols. A 160-milligram (mg) capsule should pack 136 mg of fatty acids and 0.32 mg of sterols. Saw palmetto may keep your blood from clotting properly, so tell your doctor if you take it. If your symptoms don't improve in two months, stop taking the supplement.

Straight talk on prostate drugs

Eventually, some men need medication to control their BPH symptoms. They can choose from two types of drugs — alpha-1-adrenergic blockers (alpha-blockers) and 5-alpha-reductase inhibitors.

Alpha-blockers work for many men, have no sexual side effects, and are cheaper than reductase inhibitors. For that reason, some experts recommend them as a first line of treatment for moderate to severe BPH. But the two work differently, and certain men respond better to reductase inhibitors.

The drugs listed on the following page are the most common treatments for controlling BPH. Your should work with your doctor, weighing the benefits, risks, and costs, to find the best treatment for you.

Top drugs to treat BPH

Drug class	Alpha-1-adrenergic blockers	5-alpha-reductase inhibitors
Generic (Brand)	tamsulosin (Flomax), doxazosin (Cardura, Cardura XL) alfuzosin (UroXatral) terazosin (Hytrin)	finasteride (Proscar) dutasteride (Avodart)
Who benefits most	Men with small prostates	Men with large prostates (1.5 ounces or larger)
How they work	Relax smooth muscle tissue in prostate and bladder, improving urinary BPH symptoms.	Prevent body from turning testosterone into dihydrotestosterone, the hormone that triggers prostate growth. Can shrink prostate 20 to 30 percent.
When you'll see results	Weak urine flow, frequency, urgency, and nighttime urination improve within days.	May take one year to see full benefit.
Consumer concerns	Can trigger sudden drop in blood pressure when standing. Take at night to lower this risk.	Can cause erectile dysfunction and decreased sex drive.

Get twice the protection from drug combo

You've heard the saying "two heads are better than one." In this case, two drugs may be better than one. The National Institutes of Health recently finished a 4 1/2-year study involving more than 3,000 men. The goal — to see if taking both an alpha-blocker and reductase inhibitor battled BPH better than taking either drug alone.

The combination seemed to work. Men getting only doxazosin (Cardura) or finasteride (Proscar) were almost twice as likely to see their BPH progress as men taking a combination of both drugs. Sounds great, but is it worth it? Reductase inhibitors like finasteride cost more than alpha-blockers, and together the two prescriptions can run a pretty penny.

> The alpha-reductase inhibitor finasteride (Proscar) stops hair loss caused by male hormones. It may even trigger hair growth in men with mild to moderate male pattern baldness.

Experts are quick to point out that most men do just fine on one medication. However, men with large prostates, high prostate-specific antigen (PSA) levels, and bothersome urinary problems may benefit from the combination. Discuss it with your doctor, and find out if your insurance or prescription drug plan will cover the cost.

Beware of drugs that cool off sex life

Finasteride (Proscar) isn't the only romance-robbing drug that can ruin your sex life. Many other medications can lower the boom on your libido or lead to impotence, including these.

- cimetidine (Tagamet)
- famotidine (Pepcid)
- nizatidine (Axid)
- citalopram (Celexa)
- fluoxetine (Prozac, Sarafem)
- fluvoxamine (Luvox)
- paroxetine (Paxil, Pexeva)
- sertraline (Zoloft)
- venlafaxine (Effexor, Effexor XR)
- mirtazapine (Remeron)

Remember — the benefits of a drug may outweigh its risks, so never stop taking it without your doctor's permission. If you think a medication is affecting your sex life, talk to your doctor about switching to a different drug.

More options for BPH sufferers

As many as one-third of men with BPH who decide to watch and wait choose to take supplements, such as saw palmetto. But other herbs and extracts are making news these days, too, for their potential to boost prostate health. Talk to your doctor about whether these therapies could be right for you.

Beta-sitosterol. Several studies suggest this mixture of plant compounds improves urine flow and other BPH symptoms, but it may also lead to erectile dysfunction and decreased sex drive. Some beta-sitosterol supplements are made to lower cholesterol. Be sure to buy those specifically made for BPH — the dosages and instructions differ greatly. Look for a brand that lists the specific amount of beta-sitosterol it contains, not just the total sterols, and take it on an empty stomach.

Stinging nettle. The root, not the leaves, of this prickly weed may put an end to enlarged prostates. Extracts made from stinging nettle roots also pack the steroid beta-sitosterol. Try the powdered root as a tea three to four times daily, or as a supplement. Experts typically suggest 4 to 6 grams of dried root daily for BPH.

Red clover. This common weed could one day prevent BPH and even prostate cancer. Two recent lab experiments found feeding mice a diet supplemented with red clover extract prevented the out-of-control growth of prostate cells that marks both BPH and prostate cancer. Scientists think compounds in red clover called isoflavones could be the key. If you decide to try red clover isoflavone supplements, take half the daily dose in the morning and half in the evening. Taking it with food rich in carbohydrates, like bread, beans, pasta, or potatoes, may help you absorb more isoflavones.

Lower your risk of surgical complications

Sometimes drugs and lifestyle changes aren't enough to control BPH, and you find yourself facing surgery. The most common and effective procedures for enlarged prostates are the most invasive — transurethral resection of the prostate (TURP) and open prostatectomy. They also carry the highest risk of complications, including bleeding, incontinence, and impotence.

Holmium laser resection of the prostate (HoLRP) offers a promising, less-invasive alternative. It has very little risk of bleeding, so it may be perfect for men taking blood thinners. Two- and four-year studies show it works as well as TURP at improving urinary symptoms and may carry less risk of incontinence and impotence, making it a good option for younger men. It's also done on an outpatient basis, which means no costly hospital stay, unlike TURP. And as with TURP, urinary symptoms improve almost immediately for most men.

Another version of this procedure, called Holmium laser enucleation of the prostate (HoLEP) may actually remove very large prostates better than TURP or open prostatectomy. Another exciting laser treatment, PVP (photoselective vaporization of the prostate), may also prove to be as effective as TURP — and safer.

Surgeons must be specially trained to operate a laser, one reason TURP is still more common. Look for a surgeon who has done at least five to 10 procedures.

Cancer

Natural strategies to combat cancer

A few simple changes can improve your chances of staying healthy and cancer free, and all without drugs. The American Cancer Society says following these simple guidelines could prevent more than half of all cancer deaths.

▶ Stop smoking.

▶ Eat at least five servings total of fruits and vegetables every day.

▶ Buy foods made with whole grains instead of refined grains and sugar.

▶ Choose low-calorie, filling foods to maintain a healthy weight.

▶ Get moderate exercise 30 minutes a day, five days a week.

▶ Limit the red and processed meats you eat.

▶ Go in for regular cancer screenings.

The next few pages give you insider tips to ward off cancer, catch it early, and get the best treatment, while avoiding the financial nightmare of this long-term disease.

Drink your way to better health

What is in your cup could help decide whether or not you develop cancer. Best of all, you probably enjoy some of these everyday beverages already. If not, maybe it's time to start. So raise your glass to the latest research, and toast to longer life.

Fight back with this brew. Tea, red wine, soybeans, fruits, and vegetables are loaded with flavonoids, a class of cancer-fighting compounds with anti-inflammatory and antioxidant powers. Out of 66,000 women in the Nurses' Health Study, those who got the most kaempferol, a flavonoid found mostly in tea, broccoli, and kale, sliced their chance of ovarian cancer nearly 40 percent. Experts say four daily cups of black or green tea, or two cups of broccoli, pack enough kaempferol to drop your risk, too.

Another study of 3,000 women living in Long Island found the flavonoids in tea, tomatoes, green salad, and apples lowered the boom on breast cancer risk in post-menopausal women as much as 46 percent. Other research suggests green tea, in particular, could help prevent invasive prostate cancer as well as gallbladder, colon, stomach, pancreatic, and esophageal cancers.

Don't buy into deadly 'cure'

Scam artists claim that super-strong, 35-percent hydrogen peroxide can treat cancer, emphysema, AIDS, and other deadly illnesses. Don't be fooled. The Food and Drug Administration (FDA) has never approved high-strength hydrogen peroxide for internal use, and absolutely no research backs its curative claims. Even handling it is dangerous.

High-strength hydrogen peroxide is 10 times stronger — and more corrosive — than the over-the-counter kind used to clean wounds. Drinking it can irritate the stomach lining and cause ulcers. Taking it intravenously can inflame blood vessels, create gas bubbles in the blood, and lead to deadly allergic reactions.

'Mooove' in on cancer. Getting more low-fat dairy in your diet could crush your risk of breast cancer. That's the finding from a nine-year study of more than 68,000 women. Women who ate at least two servings of dairy a day — including milk, yogurt, and cheese — were 19 percent less likely to develop breast cancer after menopause. Likewise, women who got the most calcium in their daily diet, at least 1,250 mg, dropped their risk 20 percent. Supplements of calcium and vitamin D, however, didn't do the trick in this study.

Dairy may be just as important for men. In a new Swedish study, men who got the most calcium from food significantly cut their risk of colon and rectal cancers. Those who ate seven or more servings of dairy daily slashed their risk in half compared to men eating less than two servings a day.

Calcium may be just one of the protective ingredients. Dairy foods also contain conjugated linoleic acid, sphingolipids, and milk proteins, which are all linked to lower rates of colon cancer in animal studies. Milk by far packed the most preventive power, but hard cheese, sour cream, and regular cream also seemed to lower colon cancer risk. Discuss these results with your doctor before making big changes in your diet, though — some research links high-calcium diets to increased risk for advanced prostate cancer.

Wake up to a lower risk. That cup of joe could give you even more reason to get up in the morning. Among 90,000 Japanese, those who drank coffee every day had half the risk of liver cancer as people who rarely drank coffee — and the more cups, the lower their risk. A Canadian study, on the other hand, found coffee drinkers with BRCA gene mutations slashed their breast cancer risk as much as 70 percent. Again, the more cups they drank a day, the better. The caffeine in coffee may offer protection, but this wake-up brew is also packed with antioxidants — potential cancer-fighting compounds that may squash the development of tumors.

Enjoy an exotic juice. Drinking just 8 ounces of pure pomegranate juice a day could slow the growth of prostate cancer and curb the need for drastic treatments like hormone therapy or chemotherapy. Researchers at the University of California tested the juice on 46 men with prostate cancer. In four out of five men, PSA levels — a marker of prostate cancer progression — remained stable up to 4 1/2 years, nearly four times longer than normal. Men in this study drank the POM Wonderful brand of juice sold in supermarkets, but you can also make your own. Simply roll a pomegranate on the counter to soften it, poke a hole in the top, insert a straw, and drink to your health.

Sip this sweet treat. An extract made from store-bought apple juice stopped the growth of colon cancer cells in the lab. Scientists suspect the juice's healing powers belong to two antioxidants — proanthocyanidins and quercetin. However, a man-made extract of these compounds didn't work nearly as well as the whole juice in halting the growth of cancer cells, leading experts to believe apples may hold more mysterious cancer-fighters.

7 food secrets to sidestep cancer

Load your diet with these tasty foods, and you'll lower your risk of many types of cancer, including breast, prostate, colon, and lung cancers.

Start off with oatmeal. The soluble fiber in oatmeal is famous for banishing colon cancer, not to mention lowering cholesterol. Count on beans, oats, and many fruits and vegetables for this special fiber.

Turn it up with turmeric. Add a dash of curry to your next stir-fry. It's made with turmeric, a sizzling spice that may help prevent nine different cancers — prostate, breast, colon, skin, liver, stomach, mouth, blood, and lung. Topping cruciferous vegetables with turmeric could even fight existing prostate cancer.

Eat more legumes. If you eat beans or lentils less than once a month, you could be cheating yourself out of some hefty cancer protection. Studies have shown that eating these tasty legumes twice a week could lower your breast cancer risk 24 percent and help fend off colon, lung, and prostate cancers. A compound in legumes known as inositol pentakisphosphate may stop cancer cells from growing and could boost the effectiveness of anti-cancer drugs.

Savor tasty tomatoes. Thanks to whopping amounts of lycopene, tomatoes are potent against prostate and pancreatic cancers. Cook them in olive oil to double the lycopene you absorb, and eat cooked tomato products like sauces, which pack more lycopene than raw tomatoes.

Pour on olive oil. It's full of healthy fats, one of which — oleic acid — targets the gene that promotes breast cancer, while other compounds called phenols protect against colon cancer.

Pick a pail of berries. Berries pack a three-part punch against cancer. Studies have shown that blueberries keep colon cancer cells from growing; the ellagic acid in raspberries and strawberries kills cervical cancer cells; and cranberry juice seems to stop cancer from spreading throughout the body.

Go nuts for selenium. Selenium-rich foods could help prevent cancer of the colon, rectum, stomach, esophagus, and lung. Just six to eight Brazil nuts give you 543 micrograms of selenium, nearly 10 times the amount you need each day.

Beware of fruit juices and dried fruits that claim to treat or prevent cancer. No studies prove these claims. The FDA has warned companies to stop making promises or face bans and criminal charges.

Focus on prostate cancer

Ease recovery with new therapies

Finding out you have cancer can be frightening, and many men decide to treat their prostate cancer aggressively with surgery and radiation. These therapies may wipe out the cancer, but they can drastically affect your quality of life, causing urinary, bowel, or sexual problems. Experts say more men should consider less-invasive, and less-radical, options. Talk to your doctor and see if one of these is right for you.

Expectant management. One in every six men gets prostate cancer but very few die from it. Unlike other cancers, prostate tumors tend to grow slowly. Men between the ages of 70 and 80 diagnosed with early prostate cancer are more likely to die from other conditions, like heart disease or stroke.

Once known as "watchful waiting," expectant management means monitoring the cancer closely instead of treating it immediately. Men visit their doctor at least twice a year for PSA testing, biopsies, and other screenings to check the cancer's progress. If the doctor notices changes, he then discusses treatment options.

This choice makes the most sense for men 70 years and older with early-stage, slow-growing prostate cancer. According to experts at Johns Hopkins University, the best candidates for expectant management have:

▸ small tumors that cannot be felt during a digital rectal exam.

▸ Gleason scores of six or lower.

▸ PSA density of less than 0.15.

▸ no more than two biopsy samples with signs of cancer.

▸ cancer cells in less than half of any single biopsy sample.

Proton-beam therapy. This cutting-edge therapy uses a beam of atomic particles called protons to zap tumors. But unlike traditional radiation beams, proton beams deposit all their radiation in the tumor, sparing the healthy tissue.

You will have daily treatments as an outpatient procedure for several weeks, depending on the size of your tumor. Proton-beam therapy costs less than surgery but more than traditional radiation treatments. However, Medicare and most health insurance will cover the cost.

This treatment works best for localized tumors that have not spread outside the prostate. Your doctor may also recommend proton-beam therapy to boost the effectiveness of surgery or traditional radiation.

Only a few proton treatment centers exist in the United States. Ask your doctor for a referral to one of these.

▶ Loma Linda University Medical Center in southern California

▶ Midwest Proton Radiotherapy Institute at Indiana University in Bloomington, Ind.

▶ Northeast Proton Therapy Center at Massachusetts General Hospital in Boston, Mass.

▶ M.D. Anderson Cancer Center in Houston, Texas

▶ The University of Florida Proton Therapy Institute in Jacksonville, Fla.

Brachytherapy. Another type of radiation treatment, brachytherapy, involves planting radioactive "seeds" or pellets in the prostate. As a one-time, outpatient procedure, it is less hassle than proton-beam therapy, costs less, is more widely available, and seems equally effective against prostate cancer. It also carries less risk of urinary incontinence than other radiation treatments and a lower risk of impotence than surgery.

Men who have had TURP for an enlarged prostate are not good candidates for this treatment, but it may be a good choice for men with:

▶ relatively small prostates (prostate volume less than 60 mL).

▶ early-stage (T1) cancer.

▶ a score of 6 or less on the Gleason scale.

▶ PSA levels less than 10 ng/mL.

▶ inflammatory bowel disease (IBD) or prostate cancer close to the bowel.

Look for a specialist with lots of experience in brachytherapy to lower your risk of complications and boost your chance of success.

Make sure you avoid holding children or pets on your lap for a few months after undergoing brachytherapy, as the radioactive seeds pose some risk to others.

Robotic prostatectomy. Radical prostatectomy — removal of the prostate gland — remains one of the most common treatments for prostate cancer. But traditional prostatectomy involves a lengthy hospital stay and recovery.

The da Vinci procedure is changing that. In this new procedure, the surgeon controls a robot with several "arms" and instruments that removes the prostate laparoscopically, which is less invasive than regular surgery. Long-term studies are still needed, but current evidence shows da Vinci has similar success at removing cancer as traditional techniques, along with similar rates of incontinence and impotence. The biggest benefit — people who choose da Vinci typically report faster recovery, a shorter hospital stay, and less discomfort. Men with large tumors or advanced cancer (grade T3) may still do better with traditional surgery.

Ask your doctor for help finding a specialist trained in robotic prostatectomy, or visit the Web site *www.davinciprostatectomy.com* and click on "Find a hospital or doctor."

Crunch down on cancer with crucifers

If Superman were a food, he'd be a cruciferous vegetable. Crunchy munchies like broccoli, cabbage, cauliflower, and watercress really know how to knock out cancer.

Cruciferous vegetables contain large amounts of glucosinolates (GLS). When you chew, chop, or otherwise prepare these veggies, the GLS break down into potent cancer-fighting chemicals including isothiocyanates (ITCs) and indoles. These compounds have been shown to prevent and slow the development of cancer in lab and animal experiments.

One type of ITC known as phenethyl-ITC (PEITC) and sulforaphane, a compound found in broccoli, seem especially promising. Experts think eating vegetables rich in these compounds could help prevent cancer as well as slow the growth of existing tumors, even in people genetically prone to certain cancers. So if you want to cut your risk of cancer and avoid drugs and surgery, give a helping hand to your immune system with these delicious foods.

Beat the odds of breast cancer. The BRCA gene makes two proteins, BRCA1 and BRCA2, that repair damaged DNA. People with a faulty BRCA gene have a harder time repairing DNA and, as a result, face a greater risk of certain cancers, including breast, ovarian, and prostate. Lucky for them, an indole known as indole-3-carinol (I3C) in broccoli, cauliflower, and cabbage boosts levels of BRCA repair proteins. These three vegetables seem to be particularly potent against breast cancer.

▸ Italian researchers discovered that juice squeezed from cauliflower leaves prevented the growth of both estrogen (ER)-positive and ER-negative breast cancer cells. Lightly cook or eat cauliflower raw, since cooking destroys most of the anti-cancer compounds.

▸ In Europe, Polish women tend to face low rates of this disease, so researchers compared Polish natives to Polish-American immigrants. The women who ate three or more servings of raw or lightly cooked cabbage each week during their teenage years reaped a powerful benefit. Their breast cancer risk was a staggering 72 percent less than women who had eaten fewer than 1.5 servings weekly.

▶ A new lab study finds sulforaphane, broccoli's powerful anti-cancer compound, may not only help prevent the mutations that turn normal cells cancerous, it also keeps existing breast cancer cells from growing and spreading.

Put the squeeze on prostate cancer. Eating cruciferous vegetables, especially broccoli, at least twice a month could cut your risk of prostate cancer, say researchers at Mt. Sinai School of Medicine in New York. In a related lab experiment, mice with

Supplements sabotage cancer therapy

Cancer patients often take antioxidant supplements like vitamin C alongside regular radiation or chemotherapy. Unfortunately, popping antioxidant pills could actually sabotage these treatments.

Radiation and chemotherapy kill cancer cells by creating free radicals — the same compounds antioxidants disarm. Plus, cancer cells absorb more vitamin C than healthy cells, boosting their defenses against treatment. At least one study found women with breast cancer who took antioxidant vitamins and minerals alongside standard cancer treatment had lower survival rates than women who opted for standard therapy alone.

While eating antioxidant-rich foods could help prevent this disease, numerous clinical trials show supplements do not and may, in fact, raise some people's cancer risk. Save your money and stick with natural food sources.

prostate cancer that ate a small amount of PEITC daily for a month had half as many tumors as those that didn't get the extract. How many greens does that mean? A single ounce of watercress yields five times the amount of PEITC needed to slow the growth of prostate tumors in these mice. Serve up a side and dig in.

Lower your risk of lung cancer. What's more, animal research shows PEITC and sulforaphane could help prevent lung cancer in smokers and former smokers. And a study recently published in *The Lancet* found non-smokers who ate cabbage or a combination of broccoli and brussels sprouts at least once a week enjoyed the lowest risk for lung cancer, thanks to those famous isothiocyanates.

> Often sold as an herbal treatment for cancer, bitter apricot kernels produce cyanide and can be poisonous at high doses.

Cut cancer risk without spending a dime

Skip the supplements and save your money by taking advantage of the cheapest medicine on earth. Read on for these life-saving, cancer-busting secrets.

Get up and get moving. You don't have to be a fitness fanatic, but you do need some exercise every day. Although it won't guarantee you a cancer-free life, it just might help you beat the odds.

▶ Overweight women who start exercising could significantly drop their breast cancer risk. Scientists believe the amount of fat in your body influences the amount of estrogen in your system. High levels of estrogen in postmenopausal women point to increased risk of breast cancer. Based on a recent study, exercising moderately 45 minutes a day, five days a week can help you lose enough fat to lower estrogen levels and slice cancer risk.

But dieting isn't enough. Women who dropped pounds but did not exercise actually saw their estrogen levels rise over the course of a year.

▸ A Canadian study links recreational activity with a drop in ovarian cancer rates in both pre- and postmenopausal women. The more exercise, the lower their risk. Being sedentary more than six hours daily may boost women's risk.

▸ Australian researchers found that moderate exercise protected against prostate cancer, while Harvard scientists discovered regular, vigorous exercise slowed the progression of prostate cancer in men over 65.

▸ Lab studies show exercise can prevent the development of skin cancer and slow the growth of existing skin tumors in mice.

Learn to relax. Experts suspect chronic stress suppresses the immune system and affects cells' ability to repair damage, which can set the stage for some cancers. Johns Hopkins researchers put an unlucky group of mice under constant stress. The results — compared to relaxed mice, the stressed-out mice were five times more likely to get skin cancer, and their cancers developed nearly three times faster.

These experts suggest people at high risk of skin cancer consider taking classes in stress reduction, but you could manage without spending money. You'll get a good laugh out of this easy way to relieve pain, lower stress, and boost immunity. Researchers have learned laughter can fight the immune-suppressing effects of stress. Women who laughed out loud at a funny video gave a big boost to their immune system. Simply watching a humorous show didn't do the trick, though — only women who laughed aloud saw a benefit.

Stop smoking. Women smokers are twice as likely as men to develop lung cancer, even when they smoke less — perhaps because women are more susceptible to the cancer-causing chemicals in cigarettes. Secondhand smoke is no better. According to a new

Surgeon General's report, there are no safe levels of secondhand smoke. Breathing even small amounts at work or home increases your risk of lung cancer as much as 30 percent, plus boosts your risk of heart disease and heart attack.

Keep a lid on cholesterol. A history of high cholesterol or gallstones may increase your risk for prostate cancer. In fact, the earlier in life you develop high cholesterol, the greater your risk. Similarly, research shows overweight, postmenopausal women who have low levels of "good" HDL cholesterol have a higher risk of breast cancer.

Experts say low HDL can signal high levels of cancer-causing hormones including estrogen, androgens, and insulin. This might explain why some studies show cholesterol-lowering statin drugs seem to ward off prostate cancer. The jury is still out on this protective effect. In the meantime, follow your doctor's orders and check the *High cholesterol* chapter for advice on keeping these important numbers under control.

Count on friends. Making time for friends and family could help you survive ovarian cancer. Researchers found women with the disease who had a strong social support system also had lower levels of IL-6, a pro-inflammatory compound linked to the spread of ovarian cancer. Don't wait until illness strikes to reach out to loved ones. Strengthen the bonds of friendships and family, and you just might live a lot longer.

Beat disease with fun in the sun

Everyone knows too much time in the sun can cause cancer, but — surprise — so can too little. Your skin turns sunlight into vitamin D, and new studies link vitamin D deficiencies to 13 different cancers, including prostate, colon, breast, and ovarian.

Ultraviolet B (UVB) rays from the sun react with a compound in skin to produce vitamin D. The liver and kidneys process this vitamin but so do cells in other parts of the body, such as the prostate and colon. In these areas, vitamin D stops cancer cells from multiplying and spreading and triggers them to self-destruct.

Vitamin D in food and supplements is measured in either IU (international units) or micrograms of calciferol. One microgram equals 40 IU.

Many new studies link high levels of D in the blood with a drop in cancer risk. One study found people who got the equivalent of 1500 International Units (IU) of this vitamin daily slashed their risk of getting any cancer by 17 percent and were a whopping 45 percent less likely to die from digestive cancers.

Unfortunately, vitamin D deficiency increases your risk, and it is amazingly common. People who live in the northeastern United States, dark-skinned people, and seniors all face a potential shortage.

▸ People in the Northeast don't get enough UVB rays from November through March to make vitamin D.

▸ The pigment melanin in skin acts like a sunscreen, so darker-skinned people absorb less UVB and make less vitamin D than lighter-skinned people. In fact, one survey found 42 percent of black women were deficient.

▸ Everyone absorbs less vitamin D with age, so older adults need even more of it.

The National Academy of Sciences recommends people ages 50 to 70 get 400 IU daily, and seniors over 70 get 600 IU daily. But other experts say that's not enough to fight cancer or prevent deficiencies, especially in northeastern areas. Some experts suggest aiming for 1,000 IU of vitamin D each day.

In most parts of the United States, that means a stroll with the sun on your neck, shoulders, and back (without sunscreen) each day between 11 a.m. and 2 p.m. — 15 minutes a day in summer and 20 minutes a day in early fall and late spring. Black people need twice as much sun. Other experts, including dermatologists, argue inexpensive vitamin D supplements are the safest way to boost blood levels.

Discuss your options with your doctor and ask how much of this nutrient he thinks you need based on your age, location, and skin tone. Then follow these tips to get the "sunshine vitamin" safely.

▸ Avoid burning. The same UVB rays that make vitamin D also cause skin cancer. Limit your sun exposure to 20 minutes a day if you burn easily and tan poorly. More than that will not noticeably increase your D levels.

▸ Hold off showering, bathing, or swimming for an hour after being in the sun to give your body time to absorb the vitamin.

▸ Get your daily D from supplements if you have fair skin, are sensitive to sunlight, or take medications that cause light sensitivity.

▸ Shop for cereals, milk, butter, and margarine fortified with vitamin D.

▸ Angle to occasionally eat fatty, coldwater fish such as tuna, sardines, herring, and mackerel, all rich in this nutrient.

▸ Discuss vitamin D supplements with your doctor first if you take calcium-channel blockers or thiazide diuretics.

▸ Avoid getting more than 2,000 IU of vitamin D from food and supplements in a single day.

Catch cancer early with home tests

Colonoscopies, annual mammograms, Pap smears, and more — cancer screening may be important, but it's rarely quick or easy. Until now. These simple do-it-yourself tests can help uncover

cancer-causing agents in your own home and catch tumors early —
before they turn deadly.

Expose hidden cause of lung cancer. One in 15 homes contains dangerous levels of radon, an invisible, odorless, radioactive
gas released from the earth as natural uranium decays. Radon
exposure is the leading cause of lung cancer among nonsmokers,
responsible for 20,000 lung cancer deaths each year in the
United States.

You can quickly test radon levels in your home with an afford-
able kit sold in local hardware stores. If you get a reading higher
than 2 pCi/L, you need to improve your home's ventilation system
to lower radon levels. Contact your state's radon office, and ask
them to recommend contractors who specialize in lowering home
radon levels. Then retest every two years.

Simplify colon cancer screening. A new take-home test
could catch colon cancer with less risk, expense, and hassle than
colonoscopy. Fecal occult blood tests (FOBTs) check for blood in
stool samples, a common sign of cancerous changes in the colon.
But old FOBTs return lots of false-positive results, which means
unnecessary worry and follow-up colonoscopies.

Beware: Laxative can harm kidneys

The FDA warns that oral sodium phosphate (OSP) solutions
(Visicol, Fleet Phospho-soda, Fleet Accu-Prep) used to flush out
bowels before a colonoscopy can lead to kidney failure in some
people. Ask your doctor to prescribe a non-sodium phosphate
laxative before a colonoscopy if you are on a low-salt diet, use
diuretics, take drugs for high blood pressure or arthritis, or have
a history of kidney problems. Also, tell your doctor if you have
taken a laxative for constipation in the last week.

The fecal immunochemical test (FIT), a new stool test, is more accurate than the FOBT and easier to take. It returns fewer false-positives, finds cancer better, creates less mess, and lets you eat normally and take your regular medications before testing, unlike FOBTs. Your doctor will give you a take-home test kit, and a lab expert will analyze the samples you return. If any are positive, the doctor will ask you to come in for further tests. Because colon cancers don't bleed during every bowel movement, you need to take the FIT annually to boost your chances of finding cancers.

Find bladder cancer faster. Bladder cancer is the fourth most common cancer in men and is hard to treat once it develops. A new study found the at-home test strips Ames Hemastix can detect bladder cancer early while it's still treatable, greatly increasing your chance of survival. These strips test for hematuria, or blood in the urine, the most common sign of bladder cancer.

Most cases of hematuria are not caused by cancer, which means at-home tests often give false-positive results and lead to riskier, more invasive testing. For this reason, the National Cancer Institute and the American Cancer Society recommend that only people at high risk for bladder cancer consider regular screening. If you have a family history of the disease, suffer recurring bladder infections, or work around chemicals, then talk to your doctor about whether Hemastix screening is right for you.

Popular drugs dash disease risk

Until recently, popular statin drugs used to lower cholesterol showed lots of promise for protecting people from cancer. Most new research doesn't find a benefit, but drugs for common conditions like high blood pressure, osteoporosis, and depression are also stepping up to bat against cancer.

Doctors aren't ready to prescribe these medicines specifically for cancer, but keep their potential protection in mind when considering them for other conditions.

Fight back against breast cancer. The osteoporosis drug raloxifene (Evista) may prevent breast cancer in high-risk women about as well as tamoxifen (Nolvadex) and with fewer dangerous side effects. FDA experts need to review the evidence and safety of raloxifene, but women at high risk may soon have another weapon against breast cancer.

Dodge digestive cancers. Angiotensin coverting enzyme (ACE) inhibitors may protect people with high blood pressure from several deadly digestive cancers. Out of more than 480,000 veterans, those taking ACE inhibitors slashed their risk of colon, rectal, and pancreatic cancers nearly in half and faced 55 percent less chance of esophageal cancer. Scientists suspect these drugs keep tumors from growing and are trying to discover how long and at what dose people must take them to gain this benefit.

New vaccine stops cervical cancer

Most cases of cervical cancer are caused by the human papillomavirus (HPV). About half of all sexually active people will be exposed to some strain of HPV during their lives.

For the first time, scientists have a way to stop the spread of this disease and save thousands of lives. A new vaccine, Gardasil, guards women from getting four strains of HPV, including two that cause 70 percent of cervical cancers. The FDA has approved the vaccine for use in girls ages 9 to 26. Safety studies are underway in men and older women, which means the vaccine could soon be more widely available.

Get the drop on colon cancer. A type of antidepressant known as selective serotonin reuptake inhibitors (SSRIs) could put the brakes on colon cancer. New findings show people taking high doses of SSRIs such as citalopram (Celexa) and fluoxetine (Prozac) may reduce their risk of colon cancer 30 to 40 percent.

SSRIs keep your cells from absorbing serotonin, a chemical that helps regulate mood. Scientists think cancerous tumors use serotonin to grow and spread. Since they block cells from absorbing this chemical, SSRIs may also stunt the growth of cancer, especially in serotonin-rich areas like the colon. Other research suggests SSRIs keep your body from secreting IGF-1, a growth hormone thought to fuel the development of tumors in the breast, prostate, and colon. More studies are needed but, either way, these drugs could one day be used to help prevent colon cancer.

Find free, top-notch treatment for cancer

Taking part in a cancer study can be a good way to get top-notch care and cutting-edge treatment you may not otherwise be able to afford.

Only five to 10 percent of adults with cancer take part in clinical trials. Current studies face a serious volunteer shortage, especially among seniors. Most people diagnosed with cancer are over the age of 65, but most people who volunteer for cancer studies are not. Researchers worry new treatments aren't being tested in the people most likely to need them.

Unlike other clinical trials, cancer studies never give people with cancer a fake treatment (placebo) in place of the real thing. Instead, you'll get either the experimental therapy or the current standard treatment for your condition. Plus, you'll be treated by top cancer experts.

Medicare pays for most tests, doctor visits, hospital stays, and surgery related to a clinical trial, as long as the study is funded by

> The latest studies suggest estrogen-only therapy is safe up to 15 years in women who have had a hysterectomy. After that, the risk of breast cancer begins to rise.

the National Cancer Institute or another federal agency. Many private insurers cover study costs, too, although co-payments and deductibles may still apply. Some trials even cover travel expenses and hotel stays.

Still, studies aren't for everyone. You do face risks. For instance, you have no guarantee the experimental treatment will help more than the standard therapy or that a new pill will actually cut your risk of cancer recurrence. And experimental treatments can carry serious side effects. Your doctor can help you decide if, in your case, the benefits of a trial outweigh the risks.

People with cancer can find trials for every stage of their illness, but you needn't have cancer to take part. Many studies focus on preventing cancer in regular and high-risk people, while others study cancer survivors. Don't count on your doctor to know about all the clinical trials available. Do your own sleuthing, starting with these organizations.

American Cancer Society (ACS). Call 800-303-5691 and ask about the free Clinical Trial Matching and Referral Service. Or go online to *www.cancer.org* and click on "Find a clinical trial."

National Cancer Institute (NCI). Contact the Cancer Information Service at 800-4-CANCER, and ask them to search the PDQ database for trials you are eligible for. You can search it yourself by visiting the Web site *www.cancer.gov* and clicking on "Clinical Trials."

Coalition of Cancer Cooperative Groups. The Coalition helps put people in touch with cancer trials and important information. Search its database online at *www.trialcheck.org*.

Local cancer centers. Sometimes local cancer treatment centers can tell you about new trials they're doing before ACS or NCI hear about them. Call the NCI at 800-4-CANCER, and request contact information for cancer treatment centers in your area.

Pharmaceutical Research and Manufacturers of America (PhRMA). Contact them at 202-835-3400 to ask about new drugs being tested for your type of cancer.

CenterWatch. This company keeps a thorough list of clinical trials for many conditions. Search its listings online at *www.centerwatch.com*.

Save money: say no to cancer insurance

Supplemental insurance for serious, costly conditions like cancer sounds like a good idea, until you read the fine print. Critical illness and cancer insurance policies often carry severe limitations.

Save your money and buy a policy that offers you real protection. Seniors with Medicare should consider a comprehensive Medigap policy. You can choose from 12 different Medigap policies, ranging from basic to comprehensive coverage. Experts say low-income people on Medicaid do not need extra insurance.

Too young for Medicare? Make sure you have good, general health insurance, either through your employer or an individual policy. You'll get more use and better value from a comprehensive health policy than from narrow, specific coverage like cancer insurance.

If you're still sold on cancer and critical-illness policies, be sure to read the fine print and avoid these hidden limitations.

Exclusions. A cancer policy may not cover all types or stages of cancer. For instance, it may cover melanoma but not basal cell carcinoma, a skin cancer and the most common of all cancers.

Though seldom deadly, it can cause serious disfiguration and require costly surgery.

Inpatient only. Older policies may only pay for hospital, or inpatient, services. However, the average cancer patient spends just 13 days in the hospital. These days, everything from chemotherapy to radiation and even some surgeries are done on an outpatient basis.

Duplicate coverage. Most general health insurance policies already cover cancer treatments. Doubling your coverage by buying a cancer policy won't necessarily double the money you receive, since many general health policies refuse to pay for treatments covered by other insurance. Read your regular health insurance policy carefully before buying a cancer policy.

Payment caps. Some policies pay out a lump sum while others pay a set amount per service — $100 for each day in the hospital, $1,000 for radiation, or $1,500 for surgery — all far below the actual cost of these services. Don't expect a cancer policy to cover all or even half your expenses.

Related illnesses. Most won't pay for treating cancer-related illnesses and complications, such as infection, diabetes, or pneumonia.

Vitamin offers new hope for cancer

Thirty years ago, two-time Nobel prize winner Linus Pauling reported that high doses of vitamin C could cure cancer. Mayo Clinic studies found no such benefit, and doctors stopped pursuing it. Now, new evidence suggests he could have been right.

In Pauling's studies, people with cancer took vitamin C by mouth as well as intravenously (IV). However, in the Mayo Clinic studies that followed, people only took it by mouth. Experts now think IV treatments hold the key.

American Cancer Society screening guidelines

Age	For	Suggested tests
40s	Women	Annual mammogram.
	Women	Yearly clinical breast exam as part of regular checkup.
	Women	Regular Pap test yearly, or new liquid Pap test every two years. After three normal Pap tests in a row, women may get Pap every two to three years.
	Men	At age 45, black men and others at high risk for prostate cancer begin annual PSA screening.
50s	Men	All other men begin yearly PSA screening for prostate cancer.
	Both	FOBT or FIT annually plus sigmoidoscopy every five years; or colonoscopy every 10 years for colon cancer.
60s	Both	Continue screenings begun in 40s and 50s.
70s	Women	After three normal Paps in a row with no abnormal results in last 10 years, women may stop cervical cancer screening.
	Both	Continue all other screenings begun in 40s and 50s.
80s	Men	Men expected to live fewer than 10 more years may stop PSA screening for prostate cancer.

Getting it through an IV raises blood levels of vitamin C 25 times higher than taking the same dose by mouth. Concentrated C is toxic to cancer cells but not to normal, healthy tissue. Once it reaches the tumor, this super-dose of vitamin C reacts with other fluids to create hydrogen peroxide, which seems to kill cancerous cells. Scientists say it's impossible to get enough vitamin C by mouth to raise blood levels high enough to produce hydrogen peroxide.

Three recent case studies in a prominent medical journal make a strong case for this old treatment. Three people each with different types of cancer got high doses of vitamin C by IV weekly and monthly for up to four years. Each person saw their tumors shrink and the cancer enter remission.

All three people took other nutritional supplements in addition to the vitamin C, and two of the three underwent traditional therapy, such as surgery and radiation. Researchers say this could account for these miraculous "cures," but they still believe vitamin C played a strong role. Experts say it's too soon to tell cancer sufferers to seek IV vitamin-C treatments, but they believe enough evidence exists to warrant real clinical trials in people.

Even if it proves effective, this therapy probably will not work for all types of cancer, and not everyone is a candidate for high doses of vitamin C. Experts say people with renal failure, iron overload, a history of oxalate kidney stones, or on dialysis should not try this treatment.

Dollars&Sense
Secret to saving up to 50 percent on drugs

Your prescription drug could be one of the few health items that qualifies for a two-for-one deal. The secret is pill splitting. You can buy twice the dosage you need for a few cents more, then split the pill in half for two cheaper doses. But be careful. Some people have experienced dangerous effects and overdoses from splitting the wrong pill or splitting improperly. It's important to know how to do it safely.

First of all, never use a knife. Research suggests you could swallow up to 20 percent more or less medicine than you need if a pill does not break perfectly in half. Low-cost drugstore pill splitters are your best option, but even they cannot split odd-shaped pills accurately. You can invest in a $25 pill splitter customized for your drug to help you split safely. Call 800-925-6738 or visit *www.precisionpillsplitters.com* to learn more.

Avoid the possible problems and side effects of splitting pills by remembering these don'ts.

▸ Don't split capsules, extended-release tablets, enteric-coated pills, or pills containing more than one drug.

▸ Don't split pills without a score mark — the line on the pill that helps it break.

▸ Don't split a tablet if taking precisely the right dose is critical — as with warfarin.

▸ Don't split pills if you have poor vision, arthritis, or another problem that prevents precise splitting. Ask your pharmacist or someone else for help.

Studies suggest the following pills are safe to split and can save you up to 50 percent in prescription costs: atorvastatin (Lipitor), citalopram (Celexa), clonazepam (Klonopin), doxazosin (Cardura), lisinopril (Zestril), nefazodone (Serzone), olanzapine (Zyprexa), paroxetine (Paxil), pravastatin (Pravachol), sertraline (Zoloft), and sildenafil (Viagra). Ask your doctor and pharmacist about others.

Cataracts

Hold on to your sight — and your savings

Cataracts are responsible for 40 percent of all cases of blindness in the world. And more than half of all Americans develop this vision problem by age 80. In fact, Medicare spends $3.5 billion on cataract surgeries every year — around $33 of taxpayer money for each household in the United States.

Cataracts occur when the lens in your eye starts clouding over, often turning your vision dimmer or blurrier. Cataract surgery can usually restore vision, but your best — and cheapest — bet is to prevent cataracts altogether. Experts suspect cataract surgeries might drop by half if people could slow their cataract development by just 10 years. This chapter shows you ways to prevent cataracts and tips to save money while doing it.

Watch out for top cataract-causing drugs

Keep your eye on this disturbing list of drugs that can lead to sight-stealing cataracts. The ones with an asterisk are the most likely troublemakers.

▶ *corticosteroids like prednisone

▶ *tamoxifen but not raloxifene

▶ *psoralens

- *glaucoma medicines including demecarium, isoflurophate, and echothiophate

- *antipsychotic medicines like chlorpromazine

- quetiapine

- tetracycline antibiotics

- thyroid hormone

- potassium-sparing diuretics

- allopurinol

- amiodarone

- tricyclic antidepressants

In addition, Zocor and Pravachol can make cataracts worse if you already have them.

Talk to your doctor if you take any of the medicines above. You may be able to switch to a drug that doesn't raise cataract risk — or possibly take other precautions.

Uncover the drug danger no one talks about

Your eyes are already in danger from the damaging ultraviolet (UV) rays that boost your cataract odds. Even worse, some medicines make your eyes more sensitive to these rays, so you must stay out of the sun while taking them. Examples include sulfacetamide, adalimumab, anakinra, pain-relieving eye drops including those used after cataract surgery, amiodarone, risperidone, antibiotics like gatifloxacin or moxifloxacin — including the eye drop version taken after surgery — and herbs like St. John's wort.

4 ways to fight cataracts every day

You can lower your chances of developing cataracts by taking steps to avoid certain risk factors.

Go unleaded. Surprising new research shows that lead exposure can raise cataract odds. If the water pipes in your home are dull gray and can be scratched with a key, they may be tainting your water with lead. Either use a water filter that promises to remove lead, or get your water tested.

Think lean. Control your weight, and you'll help control your risk for cataracts. You may have even more to gain by losing pounds if you have diabetes, high blood pressure, glaucoma, or other eye diseases. All these conditions raise your cataract risk, too.

> To absorb the most eye-saving lutein and zeaxanthin, add foods that have some fat. In a small study, people absorbed seven times as much lutein from a salad with avocado compared to a salad that was fat-free.

Quit and win. Research shows that heavy smokers and people who drink alcohol frequently have a higher chance of cataracts. Find ways to quit.

Say N-O to UV. Exposure to UV light from sunlight raises your risk of cataracts, but that doesn't mean you have to spend big bucks on designer sunglasses. In fact, testing shows that sunglasses under $10 can give you enough protection. The trick is to find the right ones.

▸ Look for labels that say "UV absorption up to 400nm," labels that promise to block 99 percent of UV, or shades with the Skin Cancer Foundation's Seal of Recommendation.

▸ Choose wraparound frames and lenses that are large enough to cover your eyes well.

▶ Don't assume that mirrored or polarized glasses block enough UV light. These features only block glare. A darker lens also doesn't affect the amount of UV light blocked.

Don't wait to buy sunglasses if yours don't offer adequate protection. But to get the best deal on a spare pair or a replacement, shop in August when bargains are more likely.

Save your sight with smart food choices

Eat six to 10 servings of fruits and vegetables every day, and you could cut your cataract risk by as much as 15 percent, according to a recent study. Emphasize foods like spinach, collards, tomato juice, and kale. They're high in the eye-saving carotenoids lutein and zeaxanthin. Although eye damage from sunlight may help cause cataracts, these super nutrients may slash that damage by up to 60 percent.

Stick with whole foods. You can try lutein-zeaxanthin supplements, but most people get 2 milligrams (mg) per day from their diet already. It's not too difficult to eat the 6 mg daily associated with a reduced risk of cataracts. Just a half cup of cooked kale or spinach will supply that amount. Celery and broccoli are also good, convenient choices.

Some medicines — like cholesterol reducers — may blunt your ability to absorb lutein and zeaxanthin. Ask your doctor or pharmacist whether medicines you take affect absorption, and get his advice on what to do about it.

Choose fats wisely. A new research study suggests that women who eat the most omega-3 fish oils may have up to 12 percent less risk of cataracts than women who eat the least. But additional research found that those more prone to cataracts were the women who ate the most omega-6 fats from foods like mayonnaise, sunflower oil, safflower oil, and soybean oil.

Trim your carbs. U.S. Department of Agriculture research has found that you're more likely to get cataracts if you eat high amounts of carbohydrates — 200 grams or more — per day. Limit your carbohydrates by getting rid of junk foods like sweets and potato chips.

Other foods that may help fight cataracts include green and black tea, turmeric, and glutathione-rich foods like asparagus, avocado, and orange juice as well as quercetin-rich foods like onions.

Secrets to picking eye-saving supplements

Vitamins and herbs may be touted for their eye-helping abilities, but check them out thoroughly before spending your hard-earned money on supplements.

Be smart about vitamins. Although research initially suggested high doses of vitamin C might help prevent cataracts, a recent large study found that neither vitamin E nor vitamin C had any effect. However, newer research shows that vitamin E supplements and B vitamins like riboflavin and thiamin may help slow the progress of cataracts if taken for years. But before taking supplements, make sure you get enough vitamins from your diet, and ask your doctor or pharmacist whether vitamin supplements interfere with medicines you take.

Try a "berry" good idea. Your eyes may benefit from a secret of World War II fighter pilots. They ate bilberry jam regularly to perfect their vision for air missions. Scientists think this European blueberry may help prevent cataracts, especially if you also take other steps to lower your risk. Researchers also suspect bilberry supplements may improve diabetic retinopathy. Just keep in mind that bilberry supplements may have side effects like lowering blood pressure or blood sugar, so talk to your doctor before trying them.

Say no to eyebright. Consider this before you spend money on the herbal supplement eyebright. Professionals say no research supports the use of eyebright for cataracts, and using eyebright as an eye wash puts you at high risk for eye infection. Increases in eye pressure and problems with vision are also possible.

Get eye exams and more for free

Free eye care could be just a phone call away. Discover the programs that slash your eye care costs — often right down to nothing.

Name/contact info	Benefits and details
National Eye Care Project (NECP) 800-222-3937	Get free eye care — even with cataracts — including one eye exam and treatment for any condition diagnosed. No out-of-pocket costs even if you have Medicare. Call for other eligibility requirements.
Vision USA 243 North Lindbergh Blvd. St. Louis, MO 63141 800-766-4466	Your entire household may qualify for free eye exams, but eligibility requirements vary by state. Call or write for requirements. Must go through application process.
Medicare glaucoma benefit 800-633-4227 or www.medicare.gov	Must have one or more risk factors for glaucoma, such as diabetes. Medicare will pay most of the cost of an annual eye exam to check for glaucoma.
Celebrate Sight 800-391-EYES	Offers free exams and glaucoma treatment to those with no medical insurance.
Lions Club International 300 22nd Street Oak Brook, IL 60523-8842	Many Lions Clubs help you get vision care at little or no cost. Find local chapters under Fraternal Organizations in your phone directory. Eligibility requirements vary by locale.

Play the waiting game like a pro

Not everyone needs cataract surgery right away. If you do, your doctor will spot the signs and let you know. Otherwise, you probably don't need it until cataracts interfere with your vision, your ability to drive, or your daily living.

Your doctor may recommend stronger glasses or contact lenses instead of immediate surgery. If that happens, get the most out of your fading vision with these tips.

▸ Use more task lighting, such as lamps that can be placed close to your activity.

▸ Cover shiny tables and other shiny surfaces to reduce glare.

▸ Sit closer to the television.

▸ Assign distinct storage for items that are hard to distinguish. "Containerize" the item in its own box, jar, or tray if needed.

▸ Use different-colored containers for shampoo and conditioner, and use a soap color that shows up clearly against the soap dish.

▸ Put dark-colored drinks and foods in light-colored cups or dishes. Put light-colored edibles in dark dishes.

▸ Ask your pharmacist for prescription labels and drug information sheets in large print.

Get great bargains when surgery can wait

If your vision is fading, use these tricks to get the most quality of life for the least amount of money.

▸ Take advantage of large print books and audio books at your local library.

▸ Get used audio books at half price from Blackstone Audiobooks. Call 800-729-2665, or write P.O. Box 969, Ashland, OR 97520 to find out how.

▸ Take advantage of bargain large print books available from *www.amazon.com*. Go to the book section, and look for a link to the large-print bargain closeout page full of slashed prices.

▸ Help yourself even more with reasonably priced products for low vision. Find page magnifiers, magnifying glasses, large print cookbooks, and much more at Independent Living Aids. Call 800-537-2118 or write to 200 Robbins Lane, Jericho, NY 11753 to request a free catalog.

Make surgery more affordable

You may be eligible for free or cheap cataract surgery especially if you can't afford it. If you're uninsured and don't have Medicare or Medicaid, call Mission Cataract USA toll-free at 800-343-7265. Leave a message with your name, address, and phone number.

The Knight's Templar Eye Foundation is another source of help for cataract surgery — particularly when government agencies won't fully cover your surgery costs. Check the phone book under Fraternal Organizations, visit *www.knightstemplar.org/ktef*, or write them at 5097 North Elston Ave, Ste 100, Chicago, IL, 60630-2460.

Avoid eye surgery dangers

When you agree to cataract surgery, tell your doctor if you've ever taken tamsulosin, other alpha-blocker drugs, or medicines for a urinary tract problem like benign prostatic hyperplasia (BPH.) These medications can cause cataract surgery problems even if you haven't used them lately. Also warn your doctor if you take these medicines:

▸ blood-thinners like warfarin

▸ drugs that affect platelets

▶ latanoprost

▶ steroid eye drops

These drugs can make your surgery more risky, interact with the eye drops you need after surgery, or make your eyes more sensitive to sunlight. Ask your doctor how to avoid these problems, and be sure he knows about any other medicines, herbs, or supplements you take. And don't forget to tell your doctor if you use other eye drops, eye ointments, or eye washes. Taking all your eye products at the same time could be hazardous.

Weigh the pros and cons of multifocal lenses

Cataract surgery usually means new replacement lens implants for your eyes. Standard lens implants can help correct nearsightedness or far-sightedness — but never both. So you'll probably need new reading glasses, regular glasses, or contact lenses after surgery. But if you opt for the newer multifocal lens implants, you may no longer need glasses.

The problem is that Medicare will only reimburse you for the cost of standard lens implants and surgery, so you must pay the cost of the multifocal lenses — usually at least $2,000 out-of-pocket. What's more, these lenses may cause side effects like glare and halos. Talk to your surgeon about the risks, benefits, and prices of these lenses before you decide which ones are right for you.

Search out eyewear discounts

You don't have to pay full price for new glasses or contact lenses after cataract surgery — or at any other time.

Use your AARP card. Buy your next pair of eyeglasses through AARP Eye Health Services, and you can slash up to 55 percent off frames and lenses, including those with special options. Just show your AARP card at a participating optical store in Sears, Target, JC Penney, or Pearle Vision. Or find a participating independent optometrist by either visiting AARP's Health Care Options Web site at *www.aarphealthcare.com* or calling toll-free 888-352-3924.

Take advantage of AAA. American Automobile Association members who participate in the "Show your Card & Save" discount program are eligible for up to 30 percent off eye exams and eyeglasses and up to 10 percent off contact lenses. Visit *http://www.aaa.com/save* or call 800-222-1134 for more information.

Consider online or mail-order sellers. If you don't need your contacts or eyeglasses quickly, you may find discounts here that you can't get locally. Before you buy from any online or mail order vendor, ask about return policies, and check out dealers you haven't used with the Better Business Bureau (BBB). Call your local BBB or visit online at *www.bbbonline.org*.

Plan to send a copy of your prescription as well as eyeglass frame measurements to the vendor you choose. Get the prescription from your eye doctor, who is legally bound to give it to you. For your glasses measurements, check the inside of your current glasses frames, or ask your eye doctor. To help you choose eyeglass frames, vendors like FramesDirect.com and 39DollarGlasses.com even offer "try-on technology," but you will have to judge for yourself how helpful it is.

Apply to a special program. Ask your local United Way agency, senior center, Lions club, church, or other community organization how to get free glasses from the Gift of Sight program. They can provide a voucher or referral and send you to a participating optometrist. Or call a nearby LensCrafters store, ask for the Gift of Sight store captain, and ask him which organizations he works with. Then contact those groups about getting glasses through the program. Each group has its own financial eligibility requirements you must meet.

Colds

Simple, cheap remedies are still the best

Americans suffer a billion colds each year and spend untold time and money trying to cure them. The unpleasant reality is that colds are incurable viral infections. Drugs may ease your symptoms, but the main reason you get better is because your cold has run its course.

Adults average two to four colds a year, usually marked by a stuffy nose, sore throat, and cough. The best treatment is still the time-honored formula of bed rest and fluids. You can search forever for the right medicine — even demand a prescription from the doctor — but in the long run, it will be the simplest and cheapest remedies that do the most good.

No. 1 way to prevent a cold

You don't need special medicines or pills to keep from catching a cold. The best prevention is as simple as washing your hands.

Any one of more than 200 different viruses can give you a cold. You may breathe in airborne germs from coughs or sneezes, but contamination mainly comes from touching something that has a cold virus on it and then touching your eyes, mouth, or nose. When you keep your hands clean, the germs can't get from place to place.

Ordinary soap is all you need. Use warm water, lather up for 15 to 20 seconds, and rinse well. Teach your children and grandchildren to do the same. It's one of the most effective ways to keep from catching or spreading colds and flu.

Waterless, alcohol-based hand cleaners work well when you're not near a sink, but antibacterial soaps offer little protection against viruses. One study suggested that ordinary dishwashing liquid is up to 100 times more effective at killing a virus that causes pneumonia.

Easy way to choose the right remedy

You can spend a lot of time and money at the drugstore and still not get the relief you're looking for. To make it easier, start by checking your symptoms. The exact medicine you need depends on what is bothering you.

For example, if you only have a stuffy nose, just a decongestant will do. For aches and fever, you need a painkiller. Antihistamines relieve itching and sneezing from allergies but don't do much for colds. Cough medicines may include expectorants that thin out mucus when you're congested or suppressants that stop you from coughing.

You can buy each of these ingredients separately and take them according to your symptoms. Or you can buy combination remedies that tackle an assortment of complaints at the same time. The advantage of combinations is they usually cost less overall and they're simpler to take. But make sure you have each of the conditions the ingredients treat so you're not risking side effects for no reason.

Use the chart on the next page to determine which drugs treat the symptoms you have.

When your symptoms last more than two weeks, you may have an allergy, not a cold. Itching, sneezing, and a clear nasal discharge also come from allergies.

Then read the labels before you buy a cold remedy to make sure it contains the drugs you need without unneeded extras. Remember that generic and store brands are less expensive and just as effective as name brands with the same ingredients.

Symptom	Medicine needed	Drug name
stuffy nose	decongestant	pseudoephedrine (Sudafed)
		phenylephrine (Sudafed PE, Neo-synephrine)
coughing	decongestant	See above
	old-style antihistamine	diphenhydramine (Benadryl)
		chlorpheniramine (ChlorTrimeton)
	expectorant	guaifenesin (Robitussin, Mucinex)
	antitussen	dextromethorphan (found in combination remedies)
aches, pain, fever	pain reliever	acetaminophen (Tylenol)

Cut your cold short with natural cures

Time is the only sure cure for a cold. Drugstore medicines can make you more comfortable while you suffer, but a healthy diet, bed rest, and fluids cost less and help just as much. Here are some other natural cures that may help relieve your symptoms.

Boost immunity with echinacea. Consumers spend more than $300 million a year on echinacea to treat or prevent colds. Echinacea supporters say it beefs up your immune system, which fights colds and other infections. Although scientific proof is lacking, it may not hurt to try it — unless you have allergies. Since the echinacea plant is related to daisies and ragweed, it may cause a similar allergic reaction.

Dissolve a zinc lozenge. Take zinc within 24 hours of the sign of a cold and then every two or three waking hours until it goes away, say zinc supporters. It comes as lozenges or a gel and is supposed to strengthen your immunity and shorten the duration of your cold. When buying lozenges, look for zinc gluconate glycine, which is easily released when you suck on the lozenge. Too much zinc can be dangerous though, so don't use it more than three to five days without medical supervision.

Drinking lots of water can break up thick phlegm just as well as cough medicines with mucus-thinners and expectorant drugs.

Reap the benefits of salt. Home remedies like ordinary table salt are often better than over-the-counter drugs. You can gargle with salt water or use it to wash out your stuffy nose. To soothe your sore throat, gargle several times a day with a quarter to half teaspoon salt in a cup of warm water. The salt relieves the swelling of inflamed throat tissues.

Use a teaspoon of salt in two cups of water to clean out your stuffy nose. Repeat this easy, no-frills method several times a day:

▸ Lean your head over the sink, and pour some of your home-made solution into the palm of your hand.

▸ Inhale the salt-water solution through your nose, one nostril at a time.

▸ Spit out the excess solution, and gently blow your nose.

Sip chicken soup. This folk remedy really works. The warm liquid not only gives you an emotional lift, it soothes your throat and helps clear out your nose. One study concluded chicken soup may contain a number of substances that ease your symptoms. It seems the antioxidants in the vegetables and other ingredients team up to give your body a super anti-inflammatory boost.

A new nasal spray called Vicks First Defense claims to cure colds by forming a gel layer at the back of your nose to trap, disarm, and help flush out the cold virus.

Soothe a sore throat with honey. Combine warm liquids and honey to help a sore throat without expensive drugs. Honey eases pain by coating your throat, and its golden goodness is full of compounds that stop bacteria, reduce inflammation, and promote tissue growth. Just the warmth alone from tea, soup, or broth can calm your sore throat and improve circulation.

Foil infections with 2 simple foods

Garlic and yogurt are two foods that act as excellent natural antibiotics and can help you overcome most infections without drugs. Although colds are viral — not bacterial — infections, these foods also boost your overall immune system, which protects you against cold germs along with other infectious invaders.

Garlic has long been a folk remedy for a variety of ills. It is a natural antibiotic that conquers bacteria even some prescription antibiotics can't handle. Plus, it's a flavorful and easy addition to your recipes. A British study found that people taking a daily supplement of allicin — the primary active ingredient in garlic — caught fewer colds and got over them faster than those who took a placebo.

Yogurt made from live bacterial cultures is a probiotic. This type of nutrient encourages growth of beneficial bacteria while it strengthens your immune system. A study in Finland found children given milk fortified with live cultures had fewer colds, and workers in Sweden were 55 percent less likely to take sick leave when they took a daily probiotic.

Beef up your system with a balanced diet

Vitamins — particularly vitamin C — may help prevent and cut short colds under certain circumstances. But you don't need to overload on pills to get the C you need to stop your sniffles. Too many vitamin supplements can throw your system out of balance, not to mention run up your costs.

The bottom line on decongestants

You may remember the big scare about phenylpropanolamine (PPA). It was withdrawn from the market because a study found it might contribute to stroke. Now authorities are concerned about pseudoephedrine because it can be used to make illegal methamphetamine drugs. Some 200 types of cold or allergy products containing pseudoephedrine will be reduced to only 25 or 30, and they will be harder to get.

So what else can you take for your stuffy nose? The new decongestant of choice is phenylephrine. If you find this one does not work as well, you still have the option of buying a pseudoephedrine product. But you'll have to get it from your pharmacist, not off the shelf.

Most experts recommend foods rich in vitamins A and C, rather than artificial supplements, for help with respiratory infections. It's better to get your vitamins each day from a balanced diet full of fruits and vegetables, light on saturated fats, and free of processed and junk foods. A daily multivitamin may be all the supplement you need.

Experts aren't sure massive doses of vitamin C will stop a cold anyway. You only need 75 mg a day — 90 mg for men — for normal antioxidant protection, and the maximum recommended is 2,000 mg a day. Some advocates suggest taking up to 4,000 mg for a cold, but too much vitamin C can lead to side effects like bloating and diarrhea. It may also make you absorb too much iron, lead to kidney stones, or erode the enamel on your teeth. Plus, vitamin C is water soluble, and if you take in more than you need, your body will simply flush it away.

A little extra vitamin E may be helpful, though. A Tufts University study found elderly nursing home residents who took 200 IU of vitamin E a day had fewer colds. The usual recommended daily intake is 22 IU.

Save money — and your immune system, too

Antibiotics kill bacteria, but they have no effect on the viruses that cause colds and flu. You need an antibiotic only if you suffer complications like strep throat, severe sinusitis, or pneumonia. Don't be one of those people who pressure their doctors into prescribing an antibiotic when an over-the-counter remedy will do. If you get one when you don't need it, you'll not only waste your money, you'll give bacteria a chance to build up an immunity to the drug. Then, when you do need an antibiotic, it may not work.

Dollars&Sense
Free or low-cost Rx drugs at any age

Believe it or not, you could qualify for free medication even if you're under age 65. In fact, some people with insurance or Medicare Part D still get help with their drug costs. Discover the variety of options that could ease the hardship of paying for your prescription drugs.

Get wise to Patient Assistance Programs. Drug companies offer Patient Assistance Programs (PAPs) to help people living on low incomes get free medication. You're most likely to qualify if you are ineligible for other assistance programs and earn less than $19,600 a year as a single person or $26,400 as a couple. But keep in mind income eligibility requirements can be higher or lower.

Plan to apply separately for each medication you take and be ready to provide proof-of-income documents. Your doctor or another health professional must also fill out forms on your behalf, so be prepared. And don't hesitate to fill prescriptions you'll use soon. It could take several weeks to find out if you qualify.

You may have heard you won't qualify for assistance if you enroll in Medicare Part D. But some programs have recently declared Part D participants eligible again, like the one sponsored by Nexium-maker AstraZeneca. Regardless of whether you're enrolled in Part D or not, contact these organizations to find programs you might qualify for.

▸ **Partnership for Prescription Assistance (PPA).** Call toll-free 888-477-2669 or visit *www.pparx.org*. You'll find more than 180 drug company PAPs and dozens of other programs for free or low-cost drugs. You can even get help with enrollment forms.

▸ **RxAssist.org.** Call 401-729-3284 or visit *www.rxassist.org*. The Web site includes application forms for some programs, but you must register for a free account to use the site.

▸ **NeedyMeds.com.** Visit *www.needymeds.com* or call 215-625-9609. You'll find drug company PAPs plus government programs, discount drug cards, and generic drug assistance.

▸ **BenefitsCheckUp.** Visit *www.benefitscheckup.org* if you're 55 or older. Learn which programs you qualify for if you don't have Medicare Part D, or if you have Part D, check whether you're eligible for additional savings from the "Extra Help" program.

▸ **Together Rx Access.** Apply for the Together Rx Access drug discount card for up to 40 percent off medications from 10 big-name drug companies. To qualify you must meet income requirements, be ineligible for Medicare, and have no prescription drug coverage. Call 800-444-4106 or visit *www.togetherrxaccess.com*.

▸ **The Medicine Program.** If your medication costs are a financial hardship and you lack drug coverage, you could qualify for assistance regardless of age even if you earn $60,000 a year. Visit *www.themedicineprogram.com* or call 573-996-7300. Although you must pay a $5 processing fee, the money is refundable if you do not receive drug payment help.

Don't confuse The Medicine Program with My Free Medicine. My Free Medicine is a fraudulent program that charges $200 every six months for patient assistance application forms. You can get these forms free from Partnership for Prescription Assistance and other sources.

Slash insurance copays. If you have insurance, help is available for steep copayments that cause financial hardship.

▸ **Patient Services, Inc.** Get up to two years of copay assistance for selected illnesses and conditions. Call 800-366-7741 or visit *www.uneedpsi.org* for more information.

▸ **Patient Advocate Foundation Co-Pay Relief.** Call 866-512-3861 or visit *www.copays.org* to find out the medical and financial requirements for this program. You can qualify even if you have Medicare Part D.

Constipation

Ease the discomfort for less

"Around $200 million" may sound like the budget for a blockbuster movie, but that's how much Americans spend on over-the-counter laxatives every year. What's more, several million people say they feel constipated most of the time.

Constipation happens when the muscles in your colon, or large intestine, move waste along too slowly. As a result, your colon withdraws too much water from the waste, leaving you with dry, hard stool and constipation.

If your constipation doesn't improve after a week, see your doctor. Constipation can be a symptom of many serious conditions. But if your doctor says disease isn't the cause of your problem, there are simple, inexpensive ways to find relief.

Surprising cause of irregularity

Lack of fiber contributes to constipation, but it isn't the only cause. Over-the-counter cold, flu, or allergy medicines could also be making you constipated, warns drug watchdog, worstpills.org. Check the labels on your drugs. Limit or avoid the ones that contain chlorpheniramine (Chlor-trimeton), clemastine (Tavist), or brompheniramine (Dimetane.) What's more, some antacids can lead to constipation, too. Bypass the ones that contain aluminum hydroxide, magnesium hydroxide, or calcium carbonate. Iron and calcium supplements are also culprits. Ask your doctor or pharmacist to suggest good substitutes.

And don't forget to check your prescription medicines. Drugs like these can also cause constipation or make it worse.

▸ sedatives and antidepressants

▸ diuretics

▸ cough syrups with codeine

▸ painkillers that contain narcotics

▸ Mevacor (lovastatin)

Talk to your doctor or pharmacist. Ask whether medicines you take might make you constipated and what you should do about it. You might be able to switch to another medicine or take a lower dose. Getting back to normal could be just that easy. Just remember — never stop taking a drug your doctor prescribed without his approval.

New drug fights chronic constipation

A new prescription drug may finally help older adults with "chronic idiopathic constipation," the stubborn kind that isn't caused by disease. Until now, tegaserod (Zelnorm) was the sole drug approved for this condition, but doctors only recommended it for people under age 65. Unfortunately, it carries a risk of severe diarrhea and life-threatening intestinal problems.

But now lubiprostone (Amitiza) is FDA-approved for adults of all ages. The capsules stimulate fluid secretion in your

> Drink more water and other liquids as you boost the fiber in your diet. Increasing your fiber intake without adding extra fluids can make your constipation worse.

Get tough with fiber

Fiber comes in two varieties — insoluble and soluble. Each has its own set of benefits, but both can help keep your digestive tract healthy.

▸ Insoluble fiber adds bulk and speeds food through your digestive system. It also softens stool so it's easy to pass. Foods high in insoluble fiber include whole grains, wheat bran, fruits, veggies, legumes, brown rice, and popcorn.

▸ Soluble fiber dissolves easily in water. It makes food gummy or gel-like, helping it move along faster. It also helps soak up extra cholesterol and keep your blood sugar under control. You can get it from fruits, veggies, seeds, rye, oats, barley, rice bran, peas, and beans.

intestines so you can get back to normal. Some people may experience side effects like nausea, headache, diarrhea, abdominal pain, or flatulence, but the makers of the drug say these dwindle over time. Cutting back to one dose a day also reduces side effects, but this may make the drug less effective.

Although the FDA has approved Amitiza for long-term use, no studies have determined if this is safe. In addition, no cheaper generic version of the drug is available at this time. Ask your doctor if natural, drug-free remedies might help you avoid spending money on this drug.

Hidden hazards of popular laxatives

A fiber supplement containing 7 grams of fiber taken twice a day works just as well as laxatives, according to a study at New York Methodist Hospital in Brooklyn. That's good news because many

Laxative class	Consumer concerns
Stimulants: cascara, senna (Senekot, Fletcher's Castoria), castor oil, bisacodyl (Dulcolax, Ex-lax), ennosides (Correctol)	▶ Doctors have deemed long-term use of bisacodyl as risky for older adults ▶ Can cause abdominal cramps, nausea, or vomiting ▶ Laxative abuse can lead to serious health problems. See your doctor if you need them for more than a week.
Osmotics: magnesium hydroxide (Milk of Magnesia), sodium phosphates (Fleet Enema), magnesium citrate (Citroma), lactulose	▶ Can interfere with your ability to absorb drugs taken by mouth ▶ Possible link between phosphate laxatives and kidney damage. Avoid magnesium laxatives if you have kidney problems ▶ May cause abdominal cramps, nausea, or diarrhea
Lubricants: mineral oil	▶ Can keep you from absorbing vitamins and calcium ▶ May interfere with blood thinner drugs
Stool softeners: docusate calcium (Surfak), docusate sodium (Colace)	▶ Better for hemorrhoid sufferers and people recovering from surgery ▶ May interact with mineral oil causing toxicity and a kind of pneumonia ▶ Stop taking and call a doctor if severe cramping occurs

laxatives have dangerous side effects, which are more likely and more severe in adults age 60 and older. See the table above for the latest information.

A fifth class of laxatives, bulking agents, work more like your own body. These include psyllium (Metamucil), methylcellulose (Citrucel), calcium polycarbophil (Fibercon), bran, flaxseed, and glucomann. Bulk laxatives are a safer way to make the stool softer and easier to move. Side effects include gas and bloating, but you might avoid these if you start with small amounts and gradually increase your dosage. Best of all, these laxatives may be as effective as harsher laxatives — but cost less. Just be sure to keep these precautions in mind.

▶ Drink plenty of fluids with bulk laxatives so they won't get stuck in your esophagus.

▶ Check with your doctor if you take any prescription drugs. Bulk laxatives may prevent your body from absorbing some medications, such as tetracycline antibiotics.

▶ Look for a sugar-free brand if you are diabetic, and then ask your doctor if it's safe for you.

Thrifty ways to get more fiber

Fiber doesn't have to carry a big price tag, and these tips can help you prove it.

▶ Wash fruits and veggies and eat the skin, along with the delicious interior. It won't cost you one penny extra.

▶ Add canned or dry beans to soups and stews. Beans and other legumes are inexpensive and a great source of fiber. To avoid gas,

Watch out for whole grain imposters

When you read the ingredient list for a product, don't be fooled by terms like "100% wheat," "enriched flour," "multigrain," "wheat flour," "degerminated cornmeal," or "stone ground." These don't guarantee that a product is "whole grain." Instead, check for terms like whole oats, whole wheat, oatmeal, whole rye, cracked wheat, whole grain corn, pearl barley, brown rice, or graham flour.

start with small amounts and gradually add more — or soak dried beans, discard the water, and rinse the beans before cooking.

▶ Compare cereal prices. Cereals with dried fruit already added may cost more than tossing your own sliced or dried fruit into plain cereal.

▶ Trade low-fiber foods, like candies, puddings, cakes, and pastries, for fresh fruits, like apples and figs, and crisp, raw veggies. Don't be surprised if the produce costs less. Store-bought goodies can be pricey.

Eating whole grains, fruits, vegetables, and legumes is the best — and cheapest — way to increase your fiber intake. These foods offer vital nutrients and delicious taste that laxatives don't have, and you'll avoid dangerous side effects, too.

New products offer benefits at a cost

Today's newest constipation-fighting products promise more features than ever before. Use this information to help separate the good values from the hype.

Fibersure. This clear-mixing powder from the makers of Metamucil provides 5 grams of fiber per heaping teaspoon. It dissolves quickly in liquids, and you can add it to your favorite recipes. Yet, Fibersure's main claim to fame is that it delivers more fiber than any other fiber supplement on the market. While that may be true, consider how much you'll pay for that fiber. Fibersure costs around 6 cents per gram of fiber, but generic versions of Metamucil provide a gram of fiber for about 3 cents.

Add more fiber, juiciness, and taste appeal to your sandwiches. Spruce them up with sliced green or red sweet peppers, lettuce, sliced carrots, spinach leaves, cucumbers, or tomato.

Activia. This new, low-fat yogurt from Dannon contains a trademarked probiotic called *Bifidus regularis*. Probiotics are beneficial bacteria that help keep your intestines healthy. Activia claims this unique probiotic is the only one that can survive stomach acid and move waste out of your body more quickly. Studies done by the maker of Activia seem to confirm that it speeds waste through your colon. However, the studies also suggest you'll have to wait at least 10 days for results. Moreover, you must eat two or three containers of Activia on every one of those days. That's a minimum of 20 containers, and Activia isn't cheap.

Adding too much fiber too fast can lead to gas and other uncomfortable symptoms that often make people avoid fiber altogether. Build up your intake slowly for long-term success.

Consumer Reports pitted the probiotics in Activia against the less-expensive Dannon Natural Flavors yogurt in a test to see how many could survive passage through the acid in an average stomach. A small percentage of Activia's 3 billion *Bifidus regularis* bacteria did survive, but so did a few other probiotics from both yogurts.

4 ways to beat constipation — for free

If you've relied on laxatives in the past, now is the time to try natural ways to keep your digestive tract on a regular schedule.

▸ Take a walk every day. A mild workout like this stimulates your bowels naturally.

▸ Schedule a visit to the bathroom at the same time every day, perhaps after a meal or upon waking. Pick an idle part of the day so you won't try to rush or strain. But if you need to go at another time, don't wait.

▶ Massage your abdominal area in a clockwise motion. Some natural healers believe this helps relieve constipation.

▶ Try sitting quietly for 15 to 20 minutes each day, focusing on deep, even breathing. Other simple relaxation techniques may work well, too.

Get more fiber for your money

Item	Grams of fiber per serving	Cost per gram of fiber
Kellogg's All-Bran Original (1/2 cup)	9	7 cents
Bush's Black Beans (1/2 cup)	7	3 cents
Pace's Refried Beans (1/2 cup)	5	5 cents
Metamucil powder (1 rounded tablespoon)	3	3 cents
Citrucel (2 capsules)	1	30 cents

Depression

Self-help strategies and money-saving tips

Feeling a little down in the dumps is one thing. Depression is quite another. When you suffer from depression, you may feel overwhelming sadness, lose interest in things you once enjoyed, have trouble sleeping, or experience changes in appetite or weight. You might also have trouble concentrating or making decisions; feel guilty, worthless, or hopeless; and often think of death or suicide.

The cause of depression remains unknown, but chemical imbalances in the brain, genetic factors, B-vitamin deficiencies, certain medications, and illness are all possible causes.

Depression is a serious medical condition. You can't just "snap out of it." You need professional help. The most common treatment options include medication, therapy, or a combination of the two. But you can also take some steps to help yourself. Read on to discover these self-help strategies, money-saving tips, and alternatives to prescription pills, as well as drug warnings.

Low-cost way to brighten your mood

You may need a handbag, but you don't need a Louis Vuitton when a cheaper one works just as well. Similarly, you may need medication to treat your depression, but you don't need an expensive brand name prescription drug.

Generic versions of popular antidepressants have already hit the market. With the same active ingredients as their brand name counterparts, generics may be a good way to save money while getting the treatment you need.

According to *Consumer Reports Best Buy Drugs*, which took into account effectiveness, safety, side effects, and cost, here are the best buys for generic antidepressants. Ask your doctor if one of these drugs may be right for you.

▶ Generic fluoxetine (Prozac) capsules or tablets, 10 milligrams (mg) or 20 mg taken once a day, cost about $35 a month.

▶ Generic citalopram (Celexa) tablets, 20 mg or 40 mg taken once a day, cost about $51 a month.

▶ Generic bupropion (Wellbutrin) tablets, 75 mg or 100 mg taken three times a day, cost about $66 a month.

Risks of common antidepressants

Generic (brand)	Side effects
bupropion (Wellbutrin)	seizures, headache, insomnia, nausea, vomiting, agitation, dizziness
citalopram (Celexa)	drowsiness, insomnia, nausea, increased sweating, dry mouth
fluoxetine (Prozac)	nervousness, headache, drowsiness, dizziness, insomnia, nausea
mirtazapine (Remeron)	increased appetite, weight gain, constipation, dry mouth, drowsiness
paroxetine (Paxil)	sexual dysfunction, excessive sweating, dizziness, nervousness, constipation
sertraline (Zoloft)	headache, dizziness, insomnia, nausea, diarrhea, dry mouth, indigestion
venlafaxine (Effexor)	nervousness, headache, dizziness, insomnia, nausea, constipation, dry mouth

Sidestep little-known drug dangers

Depression often strikes seniors — but not all antidepressants help them. In fact, some can be downright dangerous. Two drugs you should watch out for are the tricyclic antidepressants amitriptyline (Elavil) and doxepin (Sinequan). Both drugs can lead to an irregular heart rate or a drop in blood pressure resulting in lightheadedness when standing up.

A recent study found that even though these drugs are not recommended for people older than age 65, doctors often prescribe them to seniors anyway. Seniors are also more likely to experience side effects from other antidepressants. Your doctor may prescribe smaller doses for that reason.

Of course, it's not just seniors who need to be careful when it comes to antidepressants. For instance, duloxetine (Cymbalta), which is also used to treat pain from diabetic neuropathy, may lead to liver damage.

One surprising side effect of antidepressants is the possible blunting of your emotions. You may find it harder to cry, worry, get angry, or care about the feelings of others. This can take a toll on your marriage or other relationships. If you experience marital problems while taking an antidepressant, ask your doctor if a change in drugs might help.

Mixing antidepressants with certain drugs, including other antidepressants, can lead to dangerous drug interactions. Make sure to tell your doctor about all the medications, including dietary supplements, you're taking, so you can avoid any complications.

Herbal remedy blasts the blahs

Mild depression should not put a major dent in your wallet. Instead of costly prescription drugs, try a proven natural remedy. Studies show that St. John's wort, an over-the-counter herbal supplement, works as well as standard antidepressants with fewer side effects — at a fraction of the cost.

A one-month supply of St. John's wort costs around $10. The standard dosage is 900 milligrams a day. You can take two 450-mg doses or three 300-mg doses. Look for standardized formulations. Otherwise, you're not sure what you're getting.

> One way to cheer up is to make frowning literally impossible. A recent study found that Botox injections relieved depression in some women. Then again, many experts say the study was flawed.

Remember, St. John's wort should only be used as a short-term treatment for mild depression. Major depression usually requires prescription drugs.

Do not take St. John's wort if you're already taking a prescription antidepressant. A dangerous reaction called serotonin syndrome could result. St. John's wort may also interact with other drugs, so it's important to let your doctor know you are taking it.

Easy alternative to popping pills

Did you take your pills today? Sometimes it's hard to remember, especially when you need to take them at specific times. Now there's an easier way to take your medicine — with a skin patch. This new form of the monoamine oxidase (MAO) inhibitor selegiline, called Emsam, recently hit the market.

Selegiline, which is also available in an oral form called Eldepryl for Parkinson's disease, has been shown to help older people with depression who do not respond to other medications or treatments.

Instead of trying to remember the right dosage or time for your pills, you just stick a new Emsam patch to your upper torso, upper thigh, or upper arm each day. Patches come in 6-, 9-, or 12-milligram doses. The medicine is released gradually throughout the day.

The low-dose version comes with an added bonus — it does away with the usual dietary restrictions that come with MAO inhibitors. But, if you need the higher doses, you still need to avoid foods containing tyramine, such as beer, aged cheeses, aged or smoked meats, soy sauce, sauerkraut, and very ripe bananas.

Emsam is not cheap. Each patch costs $12.85, and a monthly supply comes to $385.50. But, if it means freedom from pills and dietary drawbacks, it may be worth it.

Lighten your load with light therapy

Just as there is a baseball season or hurricane season, some people experience a depression season. For people with seasonal affective disorder (SAD), the winter months and their lack of sunlight can bring on depression. Researchers think changes in the levels of certain brain chemicals might be responsible.

Because darkness seems to trigger SAD, it makes sense that light could help cure it. Although not much solid research exists, the few well-designed studies do support this theory. In fact, light therapy seems to help people with regular depression as well as those with SAD. Light therapy may even work as well as some antidepressants.

If neither drugs nor therapy relieve your depression, consider an implanted pace-maker-like device that sends electrical pulses to your brain. The technique, called vagus nerve stimulation, may have long-lasting effects.

The key is the bright artificial light, measured in units called lux and delivered through a special light box. Typical therapy is at 10,000 lux and involves sessions lasting from 30 minutes to two hours a day. Just sitting near the light box does the trick. You could read, listen to music, or watch TV. Usually, early morning is the best time for light therapy.

You can buy 10,000-lux light boxes on the Internet or in some drugstores or hardware stores. Prices range from $200 to $500. Some health insurance companies will cover the cost.

Light therapy comes with some safety concerns. Possible side effects include headache, eyestrain, nausea, and agitation. What's more, some products are unsafe or ineffective. Make sure you talk to your doctor before trying light therapy on your own.

High-tech way to lower therapy bills

A recent University of Louisville study found that computer-assisted cognitive therapy worked just as well as standard cognitive therapy. In the 45-person study, 15 people received standard cognitive therapy in nine 50-minute sessions. Another 15 had therapy sessions only half as long, but they also spent 20 to 30 minutes using a multimedia computer software program that included self-help exercises. The remaining 15 were put on a waiting list.

Despite spending roughly half as much time with a therapist, the computer-assisted group responded just as well to treatment as the standard therapy group.

You can buy a self-help version of the software used in the study, *Good Days Ahead: The Interactive Program for Depression and Anxiety*, for $99.95 through the Web site *www.mindstreet.com*.

Top tips for beating the blues

Not every remedy for depression comes from the drugstore. When you're feeling blue, you can perk yourself up with these simple strategies.

Exercise your cares away. Many studies have found that moderate to strenuous exercise can help brighten your mood while it strengthens your body. A recent study found exercise to be as effective as medication or therapy for mild to moderate depression. People in the study, who exercised on a treadmill or on a stationary bicycle three to five times a week, reduced their depression symptoms by nearly 50 percent after 12 weeks. The key is to exercise at a moderate intensity at least 30 minutes a day most days of the week. Choose an activity you particularly enjoy so you'll be more likely to stick with it.

More women than men experience depression. In fact, depression strikes up to 25 percent of women at some point in their lives.

Surround yourself with music. You always knew it was true, and now science proves it. Music can cheer you up. Just by listening to music, people suffering from chronic pain reduced their depression up to 25 percent. Music works to calm your nerves whether you listen to classical or jazz or take part in making it. Researchers in the field of music therapy say that playing a specially designed music-making computer program, playing an instrument, or just singing along with others reduces stress.

Pamper yourself with massage. Don't think of a massage as overindulgence — think of it as an investment in your good health. Research has shown that various forms of massage, from the relaxing Swedish massage to the invigorating aromatherapy massage, can help lower blood pressure as well as your heart rate. On top of that, certain essential oils used in aromatherapy massage may help relieve depression. Find a qualified massage therapist through the locator service of the American Massage Therapy Association by calling toll free 877–905–2700 or going online at *www.amtamassage.org*.

Amazing way to relieve depression

Try an easy, five-minute, four-step method that lowers blood pressure, relieves depression, and improves the immune system of cancer patients — without drugs or pills of any kind. It's called progressive muscle relaxation, and here's how to do it.

▸ Find a quiet, comfortable place to sit.

▸ Start by taking a few slow, deep breaths.

▸ Close your eyes and gradually relax the muscles of your body, one group at a time. Begin by clenching the muscles of your toes while you count to 10, then relax them for a count of 10.

▸ Tense and relax your leg muscles, then move on through the other muscle groups in your entire body. By the time you get to your head, you should feel more calm.

---

4 foods to improve your state of mind

When you feel depressed, maybe you turn to food. Sweets, like ice cream, cookies, and chocolate, may seem like just what the doctor ordered, but they'll actually leave you feeling worse a short time later. Try these foods to help lift your spirits.

▸ **Fish.** Low fish consumption has been linked to depression. A recent Finnish study found that women who rarely ate fish were more than twice as likely to develop depression as those who regularly ate fish. The omega-3 fatty acids found in fish work wonders for your brain. Eating more cold-water fish, like salmon, sardines, and herring, or taking fish oil capsules can give you the omega-3 you need.

▶ **Fortified breads and cereals.** Low levels of folate, a B vitamin, have also been linked to depression. Besides fortified breads and cereals, you can find folate in legumes, seeds, and dark green leafy vegetables. Folic acid supplements are also available.

▶ **Green tea.** Sip a cup of this soothing beverage. Theanine, an amino acid in green tea, helps calm your brain.

▶ **Saffron.** A small Iranian study found this staple of traditional Persian medicine to be effective in treating mild depression. The study used saffron capsules, but you can try adding some of this popular Middle Eastern spice to your dishes. It's expensive, however. An ounce of saffron costs about $35.

You might also consider magnesium and chromium picolinate supplements, which may help mood-stabilizing drugs work better.

Dollars&Sense
Watch out for Medicare Rx scams

Every year you get a golden opportunity to enroll in a Medicare prescription drug plan that saves you money. But make sure you don't end up losing money by giving your business to an illegal provider. Here's what you need to know.

Medicare has teamed up with private companies to offer Part D prescription drug coverage to everyone eligible for Medicare. Although the plans conform to Medicare's standards, their features, list of drugs covered, and their costs can vary widely. So you need information from the plans to make the best choice.

That's where the scam artists come in. They pose as government officials or representatives for Part D plans. They may call, e-mail, or even visit your home to sell fake plans or a new Medicare card. They may say they need payment for an enrollment fee or some other cost, but they really want your bank account number, credit card number, or other personal information.

Avoid the scams. If someone contacts you about a Medicare prescription plan, remember these points.

▶ You can only sign up for a Part D plan during the November 15 to December 31 enrollment period. Be suspicious of anyone who contacts you at other times of the year.

▶ Legitimate Medicare providers should not ask for your bank account number or for payment over the phone or Internet. They should bill you or mail you an offer for automatic withdrawal.

▶ Part D plans have no enrollment fee.

▶ Medicare plan providers cannot use unsolicited e-mails or uninvited door-to-door sales calls.

▸ Providers should be willing to mail you information about their plan — and wait for you to review it — before you enroll in a plan.

▸ Don't enroll in a plan during the first phone call. Instead, ask for the company's name and phone number. Then call 800-633-4227 to check whether the caller's company is a legitimate Medicare plan provider.

Ask money-saving questions. Even if the caller turns out to be legitimate, don't enroll in any plan until you get answers to questions like these.

▸ Would this plan cover my current medications? If it doesn't, it's not much use to you. At the very least, you need one that covers your most expensive drugs.

▸ Can I use my regular pharmacy? Others may not charge the same prices.

▸ What will my medications cost per month? What co-pays, deductibles, and premiums can I expect?

▸ When will the plan stop paying for my drugs? Part D plans have a point at which they will no longer cover your drug costs until you pay an additional amount. Find out whether the plan will provide any benefits within this coverage gap.

These questions are a good start, but you need more information to make a money-saving decision. For example, some people who have prescription drug coverage will save money by sticking with it instead of enrolling in Part D. Yet others should enroll in Part D to avoid financial penalties.

Medicare personnel can help you figure out what to do. They can also provide publications to help you pick a plan. Call 800-633-4227 or visit *www.medicare.gov* for more information.

Diabetes

Manage blood sugar and minimize cost

It's no secret people are getting fatter. The rate of obesity among American adults rose from 15 percent in 1980 to 32 percent in 2004. For many people, being overweight leads to serious health problems, including type 2 diabetes.

Almost 21 million Americans have diabetes, and many don't know it. While the death rates from heart disease and cancer have been dropping, the death rate for diabetes has been going up — by about 45 percent from 1970 to 2002.

Although diabetes can be deadly, there are plenty of things you can do to keep it under control. Some are simple, like getting more exercise and watching what you eat. Others involve checking your blood sugar and asking your doctor about new diabetes drugs. Either way, dealing with diabetes requires lifestyle changes to help you avoid severe complications, like heart disease, kidney failure, blindness, and amputations.

'Miracle cure' in your medicine cabinet

New research has uncovered some amazing possibilities for aspirin. In fact, the American Diabetes Association suggests that people with diabetes take an aspirin a day to cut their risk of heart disease. Aspirin in small, regular doses helps prevent blood clots from forming, which reduces your risk of heart attack and stroke. For people with diabetes, aspirin also helps by warding off diabetic retinopathy, which can result in blindness.

But the benefits of aspirin don't end there. Recent studies on overweight mice showed that aspirin in extremely high doses reversed some signs of type 2 diabetes and reduced low-grade inflammation, which is linked to insulin resistance.

Insulin is a hormone that turns blood sugar into energy. When your body resists insulin, sugar builds up in your blood. Dangerously high levels of blood sugar can damage your heart, blood vessels, kidneys, and eyes.

About 40 to 50 percent of people with diabetes don't take their medicine correctly. Follow instructions on the package carefully. If there's anything you don't understand, call your doctor or pharmacist.

The high doses of aspirin used in the study effectively reversed diabetes in the mice. Researchers are now investigating how this high-dose aspirin therapy might work on people. Unfortunately, aspirin in high doses can cause intestinal bleeding and harm your liver and kidneys.

For now, ask your doctor if you should try daily, low-dose aspirin therapy to reduce your risk of heart attack and stroke. Even though researchers have known for a long time about the benefits of aspirin therapy for diabetics, only about 12 percent of people with diabetes take aspirin regularly.

New drugs melt away extra pounds

When watching your diet and exercising more aren't enough to control type 2 diabetes, doctors often turn to drugs. Unfortunately, some drugs, including insulin and thiazolidinediones — Actos and

Avandia — can cause significant weight gain. Excess weight tends to make diabetes worse. But now, several new drugs to control blood sugar have the added bonus of helping you lose weight.

Exenatide (Byetta) is a new injectable drug that helps control blood sugar for people with type 2 diabetes. Although it is inject- ed twice a day using a pre-filled pen, people seem to prefer it to other diabetes drugs. Why? This new drug, approved by the Food and Drug Administration (FDA) in 2005, promotes diges- tion and insulin production. People taking Byetta say it also works like an appetite suppressant. They eat less, which makes them shed pounds.

How much weight do people lose on this new drug? In one study, people taking Byetta lost an average of 5 pounds in six months, while another study found people lost 12 pounds in two years. What's more, the longer people take Byetta, the more weight they lose. Byetta is expensive, about $170 a month, but most health insurance companies cover it. Some people experi- ence side effects like nausea, rashes, and fever, but they often diminish over time.

Drug companies are working on more options to control blood sugar and aid in weight loss. Sitagliptin (Januvia) was recently approved and vildagliptin (Galvus) is being tested. So far, both new drugs control blood sugar better than some of the tra- ditional drugs, and they are helping many people with diabetes lose weight. These new drugs seem to work even better in people who are elderly or obese.

Ancient herb controls sugar, boosts energy

Feeling tired all the time? The herb ginseng, used in traditional Chinese medicine, not only lowers blood sugar in type 2 diabetics, it also raises energy levels.

Sometimes known as the "king herb," ginseng has long been trusted as a treatment for diabetes and other ailments. Ancient Chinese healers have used the plant for 2,000 years. For decades, its main active ingredients, ginsenosides, have been isolated from the ginseng root to treat the high blood sugar of diabetes. Ginsenosides from both the American ginseng and the Asian ginseng plant can help balance blood sugar levels and increase the amount of insulin in the blood. Repeated, high-quality research has tested the effects in numerous studies.

But what about the rest of the ginseng plant? Now scientists are using ginseng berries, which contain more of the compound ginsenoside Re — one type of ginsenoside — to see how diabetic symptoms can be reduced. Researchers at the University of Chicago tested ginseng berry extract on overweight mice with type 2 diabetes to see how blood sugar and weight were affected.

Mice who received the extract every day showed improved blood sugar levels. They also had better scores on a glucose-tolerance test, which shows how fast the mice removed excess blood sugar from their blood. In addition, the mice lost weight — about 10 percent of their body weight in 12 days — because they ate less and were more active. When the ginseng berry injections stopped, the mice regained the weight. A control group of nondiabetic, normal-weight mice didn't show any of these changes.

> Australian researchers found drinking at least 8 ounces of clarified, or filtered, tomato juice a day lowered the risk for atherosclerosis, heart attack, and stroke in type 2 diabetics.

Other studies have shown similar effects from ginseng berry extract, making it a great candidate to treat diabetes. The leaf of the ginseng plant, which contains even more ginsenosides of different types than the root or berry, has also shown promise for controlling blood sugar. More research needs to be done, however, to prove the success of ginseng leaf for people with diabetes.

Action plan for low blood sugar

If you take insulin for diabetes, you may be plagued by episodes of hypoglycemia, or low blood sugar. Doctors say to treat these incidents by eating about 15 grams of a fast-acting carbohydrate, like glucose. Special tablets and gels contain pure glucose, but candy with sucrose, or table sugar, also works — just not as fast. Candy bars and other treats with chocolate contain lots of fat, which slows digestion and the absorption of sugar. They should be your last choice.

Product	Glucose (grams/serving)	Calories	Price
Dex 4 glucose tablets	16 g (in four tablets)	60	$.55
BD glucose tablets	15 g (in three tablets)	60	$.85
Glutose 15 glucose gel	15 g (single tube)	60	$4.23
Glutose 45 glucose gel	15 g (one-third of tube)	60	$4.15
Insta-Glucose glucose gel	24 g (single tube)	96	$4.49
LifeSavers hard candy	16 g (in eight pieces — slower-acting sucrose)	80	$.36
Gu nutrition gel	12 g (in three packs — slower-acting fructose and maltodextrin)	300	$2.97

You should not eat diabetic snack bars or meal bars, like Extend Bar or Nite Bite, if you have an episode of low blood sugar. These bars are made to prevent low blood sugar, and they act too slowly.

New tools take the pain out of diabetes

Needles, syringes, lancets, finger pricks — if you have diabetes, you understand the pain that goes along with checking your blood sugar level and taking an insulin injection.

Fortunately, new types of blood glucose monitors can test smaller samples of blood accurately. Some monitors, like the Sidekick or the FreeStyle Freedom, are made to test blood taken from someplace other than your fingertip, where so many nerve endings make it painful.

But what about injecting insulin? Why hasn't someone invented an insulin pill? The problem is, insulin is broken down during digestion and can't make it into the bloodstream to do its job. Researchers are working on various coatings and carriers so insulin could be taken by mouth. Also, patch forms of insulin may work if a method can be found to get the large insulin molecule to penetrate the skin. For now, however, there are a couple of new, pain-free ways to take insulin.

Jet injectors. These needle-free devices work by using pressure to force a small stream of insulin through the skin. Jet injectors sometimes cause a bruise. You'll want to have your doctor monitor your glucose levels carefully while you get used to using a jet injector.

Insulin inhalers. The most exciting new development for diabetics is the insulin inhaler, approved by the Food and Drug Administration (FDA) in 2006. Exubera works like an asthma inhaler, releasing a measured dose of insulin powder that is inhaled through the mouth into the lungs and bloodstream. This form of insulin can replace the fast-acting insulin injection that some people must take before eating a meal, but it can't replace daily injections. Exubera costs about $5 a day compared to $1.50 for injectable insulin.

Smart advice for buying a glucose monitor

People with diabetes must keep a close eye on their blood sugar levels. You may have to check your glucose a dozen or more times each day. Using an up-to-date glucose monitor that's made for home use can really help keep your blood sugar under control. Dozens of styles are available for a wide range of prices. Here are some features to consider before you buy.

Cost. Before you make a purchase, check with your insurance company to see what products are covered. Machines can range from less than $100 to more than $700 if you have to foot the bill. Also, remember that the cost of test strips, which you need each time you test and are specific to each monitor, will probably be higher than the cost of the machine over time. You'll want to factor that difference into your choice.

Women with diabetes are at higher risk for hip fractures. A long-term study shows the risk is doubled for women with type 2 diabetes and six times higher with type 1 diabetes.

Features you need. Some monitors made for sight-impaired people give verbal directions for each step in the testing process and an audio output of the results. Sounds handy, but these monitors are the most expensive.

Ease of use. All of the new monitors are small, light, and portable, with some weighing just a few ounces. Try to "test drive" a few models to see how comfortable they feel in your hand and whether the screen is easy to read. Other features to consider include how much blood is needed and how long you must wait for results.

Accuracy. All meters on the market are quite accurate if you use them correctly. Be sure to check the readings at least once a month to calibrate your monitor. Some monitors calibrate themselves, while others require extra steps.

Record-keeping. Many monitors store test results for days or weeks at a time, but you may want even more information. Data-management systems can help you keep track of information such as glucose reading, date, time, food eaten, exercise levels — everything you and your doctor need to know to keep your blood sugar under control.

Alternate testing sites. Some monitors let you test blood that is drawn from sites other than your fingertips, making for less-painful testing. Ask your doctor if it's right for you.

Once you've bought a glucose monitor, read the directions and use it carefully. The Food and Drug Administration (FDA) has had reports of people accidentally changing the units of measurement on their monitors, which can cause the reading to appear to be 18 times higher or lower than it really is. So be careful when you change the time or date on your monitor, and check the settings if you accidentally drop it.

Hit the road with fewer hassles

Living with diabetes can be hard enough, but traveling can really complicate things. Don't stay home for fear of being without your medicine or not finding the right food when you need it. People with diabetes can travel for fun or commute to a job — as long as they plan ahead and follow these simple steps.

Carry plenty of supplies. Some people carry at least five days' worth of extra supplies for blood sugar testing or insulin injections — no matter where they go. You can usually purchase supplies for the lowest price when you use your insurance benefits at certain drugstores. If you don't plan ahead and have to buy emergency supplies, you could pay a lot more.

Don't skip exercise. If you drive a long way to work or spend lots of time in airports or on trains, you may have trouble fitting exercise into your schedule. Make time on your lunch hour for walking, or take some laps around the airport terminal while you wait for your flight.

Seek out the best food options. Eating in a restaurant can be tricky, but many offer low-fat or other healthy meal options.

5 easy ways to combat diabetes

The American Diabetes Association offers new eating advice for people with diabetes. Follow these rules to maintain a healthy weight, control your blood sugar, and avoid dangerous complications.

▸ Eat more healthy carbohydrates, like fruits, vegetables, legumes, low-fat milk, and whole grains.

▸ Limit saturated fats to less than 7 percent of your total calories. You'll find them in meat, egg yolks, whole milk, butter, cream, and cheese.

▸ Avoid trans fats. Check package labels to find where trans fats lurk.

▸ Cut cholesterol to less than 200 milligrams a day.

▸ Eat fish at least twice a week. Make it baked, broiled, or blackened, but not fried.

Some chain restaurants carry nutritional information on their Web sites, so you can see your options before you arrive. Carry extra rations, like Glucerna Meal Bars or DiabetX Snack Bars, in case there's nothing on the menu that will work. In a pinch, stop by a grocery store for whole-grain bread and peanut butter or cheese.

Keep snacks in your car. Dangers of hypoglycemia, or low blood sugar, increase if you have to drive. Low blood sugar can make you feel weak and fatigued, and it also impairs your thinking and eyesight. Know your own warning signs, and carry plenty of glucose tablets or snacks with you. Don't assume you'll be able to find a snack when you travel.

Pack supplies in your carry-on bag. Although airport security has become more strict, you can take your insulin, syringes, glucose-testing supplies — even lancets and needles — on an airplane. Prescription medication must have a professionally printed label identifying the medication and manufacturer's name or a pharmaceutical label. The prescription medicine must match the name on the passenger's ticket. The Transportation Security Administration (TSA) also allows people with diabetes and similar medical conditions to carry glucose gel packets, tablets, or other sugar sources to use in case of low blood sugar.

Protect your drugs. Don't leave insulin, other drugs, and testing strips in a hot car, and don't pack them in a suitcase to be checked on an airplane. Too much heat or cold can damage drugs, especially liquids. It can also harm testing strips. Carry your fragile supplies in an insulated bag, and never leave it in a hot car.

9 ways to keep your feet healthy

Each year almost 80,000 people have a toe or foot amputated because of problems related to diabetes. In fact, aside from accidents, diabetes is the main cause of foot amputations.

About a third of all people with diabetes suffer from neuropathy, or nerve damage. Neuropathy can make your feet unable to feel heat, cold, or pain. You could step on a tack and not even feel it. High blood sugar can damage your blood vessels, causing circulation problems. If this happens, cuts, scrapes, or blisters can take a long time to heal and become infected. Eventually, the infection can spread to your bones.

Treating the bone infection, called osteomyelitis, requires a week's stay in the hospital and costs about $19,000. About 8 percent of people with osteomyelitis have a foot or leg amputated, 23 percent a toe.

The best way to avoid problems is to pay attention to your feet. Follow these suggestions from the American Diabetes Association to keep your feet healthy.

▸ Inspect your feet daily for cuts, blisters, sores, or swelling. Get someone to help you or use a mirror if you can't see the bottoms of your feet.

▸ Have your feet checked by your doctor at least once a year — more often if you have had foot problems.

▸ Call your doctor if you have an ingrown toenail, numbness, or pain, or if you see a change in skin color.

▸ Wash and dry your feet carefully every day. To prevent dry skin, use a lotion on the tops and bottoms of your feet.

▸ Cut your toenails straight across, but file down sharp corners that might cut the next toe.

▸ Never go barefoot, even in your house. Keep slippers by your bed to avoid bumping into things at night.

▸ Wear shoes that fit well and don't rub. Check the insides of your shoes for bumps, tears, or other places that could cause trouble.

▸ Wear socks that are soft and thick enough for extra protection. Choose material that will draw moisture away from your skin, like acrylic.

Where to find free eye care

Poor control of your blood sugar can damage the small blood vessels in your retina and lead to blurred vision and blindness. This complication of diabetes, called diabetic retinopathy, is the most common cause of blindness in adults, making people with diabetes 25 times more likely to become blind than other people. An eye doctor can see the problem by dilating your eye and looking at your retina.

The Diabetes EyeCare Program offers free exams and one year of care for people with diabetes. You must be at least 65 years old and a U.S. citizen or legal resident. Also, you can't be receiving health care through an HMO or the Veterans Administration. For more information, call 800-272-EYES (3937).

▶ Get in the habit of wiggling your toes and flexing your ankles while you sit to improve circulation. Don't cross your legs when you sit. This keeps blood from flowing freely to your legs and feet.

If you have diabetes and a history of foot ulcers or amputation, you may be eligible for help. Medicare will pay 80 percent of the cost of specially prescribed shoes and inserts under its Part B coverage.

Flu

Low-cost prevention is your best option

If you think the flu is just an overblown cold, think again. More than 200,000 people are hospitalized and about 36,000 die every year from influenza and related complications. Although it begins like a cold, the flu quickly knocks you off your feet. Suddenly your head hurts, your body aches, you have a fever, and you're so tired you can barely move. The virus can spread quickly, too, especially when people are in close contact.

Your annual flu shot goes a long way toward keeping you well, but it's not a guarantee. People over the age of 65 have the highest risk and are more likely to fall victim to pneumonia and other bacterial infections. Complications like these may develop when you're weak from the flu, and chronic illnesses like heart disease, asthma, and diabetes can get worse.

It doesn't cost much to keep yourself safe. As the old adage says, "an ounce of prevention is worth a pound of cure."

Beat the flu with smart protection

An annual flu vaccine is the best thing you can do to prevent the flu. You build up immunity to the virus when your body reacts to killed viruses in the vaccine. It's important to get one every year because flu viruses constantly change, and fresh vaccines meet the challenge of new and different bugs.

But flu protection does not have to cost you a fortune. For starters, your employer or local health department may offer free flu vaccinations. Medicare Part B and some other insurance plans also will pay for it. You can get a flu shot from your doctor, the health department, or other health care provider. Private health-care companies also set up clinics in grocery stores, drugstores, and other locations. Look on the American Lung Association's Web site *http://flucliniclocator.org* for a list of places that offer flu shots.

If you can't get a free shot, check the cost before you roll up your sleeve. Prices during the 2005-06 flu season ranged from $18 to more than $40 per shot, about a 25-percent increase from the year before. Some places, like Costco pharmacies, provided shots at break-even prices, while doctor's offices tended to charge more.

Flu shots are safe for anyone older than six months unless they have a severe allergy to chicken eggs, are running a fever, or

Second shot knocks out pneumonia

While you're getting your flu shot, roll up the sleeve on your other arm and get a pneumonia shot, too. The pneumococcal polysaccharide vaccine (PPV) protects you against 23 kinds of pneumococcal bacteria, including some that lead to pneumonia, a serious complication of the flu.

Pneumococcal diseases are now more resistant to penicillin and other drugs that used to control them, so it's important to prevent them through vaccination. Everyone over age 65, as well as younger people with health problems, should have a PPV shot.

experienced a previous reaction to the vaccine. Groups especially encouraged to get a flu shot every year include:

▶ people over 50 years old and those with certain chronic medical conditions.

▶ people living in nursing homes or similar facilities.

▶ children under 5 years old.

▶ caregivers for people with high influenza risk, including those listed above and children less than six months old.

October and November are the best times to get your flu shot, but you can still get vaccinated later since the flu season sometimes lasts until May. It takes about two weeks for the protective antibodies to kick in, and protection peaks in four to six weeks. The vaccine will work faster if you've previously had a flu shot or the flu itself.

Don't be too quick to bring fever down. It's your body's natural defense against flu viruses, which die off when body temperatures rise above normal.

You can't get influenza from a flu shot, but it may cause aches, a low-grade fever, or a sore arm. These side effects go away in a day or two.

Recent research has shown the flu vaccine may not be as effective for older people as once thought. But it still offers significant protection, so don't be tempted to skip it. If you get the flu in spite of the shot, it won't be as bad and you'll likely avoid serious complications like pneumonia, hospitalization, and death.

6 secrets to staying healthy

A healthy lifestyle is important if you want to avoid the flu. By keeping your body in top shape, you have a better chance of fighting off illness. The same formula you follow to head off a cold works wonders for the flu, too.

- Wash your hands often. You can pick up viruses from any contaminated object, including doorknobs and telephones.

- Stay away from crowds and people who appear sick. The flu virus spreads in tiny droplets tossed into the air from coughing and sneezing.

- Eat a healthy diet. Include yogurt with immune-boosting live cultures and whole-grain cereals full of selenium.

- Drink lots of fluids. They keep your throat lining moist and supple so it won't crack and let viruses in.

- Get plenty of rest. It builds up your resistance to illness and helps your whole system stay in balance.

- Quit smoking, if you need to. It raises your risk for respiratory infections. Avoid air pollution and second-hand smoke, too.

A little stress may boost your flu shot. Women in a British study who exercised physically or mentally just before getting the shot produced more flu antibodies.

Cut short symptoms with antiviral drug

You normally fight the flu the same as you do a cold — with rest, fluids, and over-the-counter remedies that make you feel better while the illness runs its course. But if you are over 65 or have a chronic health condition, you are at high risk for complications. That means your doctor may want to prescribe an antiviral medicine to cut short or even prevent the flu. It won't give you immunity, though, so you still need your annual flu shot.

Tamiflu (oseltamiver) is the most effective antiviral drug. It's the one governments are stockpiling in case of a "bird" flu pandemic.

But it is expensive — about $10 per pill — and it takes two pills a day for five days to treat the flu. You need just one pill a day for prevention, but you're only protected while you're taking the medicine.

Flu vaccine also comes in a nasal spray instead of a shot, but it is only approved for healthy people between 5 and 49 years old who are not pregnant.

Tamiflu will only work you if you take it within 48 hours of your first flu symptoms. So this is one time where you should consult your doctor as soon as you start feeling sick. Unfortunately, antiviral drugs are similar to antibiotics in that overuse can lead to resistant viruses. This has happened with two other antiviral medicines — Flumadine (rimantadine) and Symmetrel (amantadine) — which are not currently recommended. So you don't want to use Tamiflu as a routine treatment. Leave it to your doctor to decide if it's your best course of action.

If you don't feel better after four or five days, you may have complications like bronchitis or pneumonia, which Tamiflu won't help. Then your doctor will need to prescribe a bacteria-fighting antibiotic.

Feel better with 3 natural flu fighters

Many people prefer natural remedies to fight the flu. If you would rather rely on non-drug solutions, here are three you should consider. They're not guaranteed to work, but they won't hurt you and there is strong support for each of them.

Elderberry. The flowers and berries of this ancient bush have been used for centuries as folk cures. Scientific research suggests the extract may be an effective remedy for the flu. In a study of 60 Norwegians, flu symptoms went away an average of four days quicker for those who took Sambucol, an elderberry syrup product. The

Easy clues to the flu

Symptom	Flu	Cold
extreme exhaustion	usual, early, often severe	never
fever	usual, high (102-104 degrees F), lasts 3-4 days	rare
general aches, pains	usual, often severe	slight, maybe not at all
fatigue, weakness	usual, can last 2-3 weeks	possible, but mild
headache	almost always	rare
chest discomfort, cough	common, can be severe	mild to moderate, hacking cough
sneezing	sometimes	usual
stuffy nose	sometimes	common
sore throat	sometimes	common

Source: National Institute of Allergy and Infectious Diseases

leaves and stems of the elder tree are toxic, so look for commercially prepared elderberry extracts in liquid, capsule, or tablet form.

Astragalus. This Chinese medicine staple strengthens your immune system, say its supporters. It particularly increases resistance to viruses and is a great source of the powerful antioxidant selenium. It comes in many forms, but herbalists prefer to use it as a tincture. Take astragalus long-term for prevention of colds and flu rather than waiting until you are sick.

Sauerkraut. Korean scientists say *lactobacilli* bacteria, which give fermented cabbage its tangy sourness, have antiviral powers. In a recent study, they cured chickens infected with bird flu by feeding them kimchi, Korea's national cabbage dish. And no reports of bird flu in humans have surfaced in Korea or Japan, where kimchi is also popular. Sauerkraut, another fermented cabbage product, has the same protective power, say the scientists.

> What many people call the "stomach flu" is not influenza but gastroenteritis, caused by other viruses, bacteria, or toxins.

Simple ways to guard against bird flu

The entire world has been on edge because of the threat of bird flu — officially avian influenza A ($H5N1$) — which so far is only transmitted among birds. The first human case of $H5N1$ was reported in 1997, and since then only a few hundred people have caught it. Unfortunately, more than half of them died. It has spread to poultry and wild birds in more than 50 Asian and European countries, and epidemiologists expect the birds' flight patterns will eventually carry it throughout the world.

Direct contact with birds has been the only way people have caught this virus, but experts fear $H5N1$ will mix with other viruses and pick up the ability to spread from human to human. If this happens, it could spread rapidly and cause many deaths. Unfortunately, scientists can't develop a bird-flu vaccine until a human-transmitted virus exists.

Americans are not threatened as long as bird flu is limited to birds on other continents. So it's not worth panicking and trying to stock up on antiviral drugs, which may not work anyway. Here are some simple things you can do to protect yourself.

▶ **Guard against regular flu.** Get a flu shot, wash your hands, and do everything you can to keep normal viruses in check. Bird flu becomes a problem when H5N1 mixes with human-transmitted viruses.

▶ **Beware the birds.** Stay away from blood, feathers, and droppings of all birds. Make sure chicken and other poultry is well cooked before you eat it, and don't eat raw or undercooked eggs. Commercial mayonnaise is safe because it is pasteurized.

▶ **Keep up with the news.** The World Health Organization and other agencies monitor the bird-flu virus closely, so watch for reports on the status of the threat as it builds or goes away. Be prepared to follow suggestions from local and national health authorities.

Dollars&Sense
Get free drugs the easy way

You could save hundreds of dollars with free prescription drugs including virtually every brand name available. You might even nab extra savings from free over-the-counter drugs. You just need to know where to look.

Claim your prescription freebies. Drug companies constantly shower doctors with free samples of prescription drugs to hand out to patients like you. So don't hesitate to ask your doctor for free drug samples anytime she writes a prescription. Samples can save you money in ways you might not expect.

For example, you'll have time to comparison shop for the best prices until your samples run out. Finding the cheapest source for your medicine could lead to years of savings. Moreover, prescription drug samples are a golden opportunity to road test a drug that is new to you. You won't lose a dime if the drug causes unbearable side effects or turns out to be ineffective.

Try over-the-counter drugs for free. You could also nab free samples of over-the-counter medications, like Metamucil, Motrin IB, Tylenol P.M., Alka-Seltzer, and more. Check with your doctor first, especially if she recommends the medicine. Drug companies are not limited to giving out prescription samples, so your doctor may have nonprescription freebies, too.

If your doctor does not have free samples, consider these options.

▶ Visit the product's Web site. For example, you can sign up for a package of free product samples just by filling out a questionnaire at *www.Metamucil.com*. Although some sites may not currently offer free giveaways, you could still find money-saving coupons.

▶ Visit *www.all-free-samples.com*. Click the "Health" link to see current offerings of free drug samples.

Gallstones

Sound strategies for a healthy gallbladder

About 700,000 people have their gallbladders removed every year, but you don't have to be one of them. Here's how you can keep your gallbladder healthy and prevent troublesome gallstones.

Gallstones start with bile, a fluid made in your liver that helps digest fat. Bile is a valuable mix of water, cholesterol, fat, salt, bilirubin, and protein, and it's stored in your gallbladder. Stones can form if too much cholesterol, bile salts, or bilirubin builds up in your bile and stagnates in your gallbladder. Many stones can develop, or just one. They can be as small as a grain of sand or as large as an egg. But even a small stone can cause trouble.

When bile is needed to help digest a meal, your gallbladder squeezes it into your intestines through tiny tubes called ducts. If a stone creates a blockage in a duct, it can cause inflammation, infection, and pain. People who have frequent problems may decide to have surgery to remove the gallbladder.

Slash risk with one easy trick

Here's a cheap and easy way to reduce your risk of gallstones — take a walk. Women who did the least walking had a 59-percent greater risk of gallstone disease than women who walked the most, a recent

University of Pittsburgh study reports. Not surprisingly, exercise doesn't just work for women. Men can gain protection, too.

But walking isn't your only option. You can choose a different activity, like swimming, biking, or dancing. As long as you get moving, you're on the right track. And if you burn up some calories and fat, you might lower your gallstone risk even more.

Aim for two to three hours of exercise every week. Some chores count as exercise, too. According to the Calorie Control Council, the following chart shows how many calories a 150-pound person would burn by doing a particular activity for just 30 minutes.

Slash gallstone risk with household chores

Activities	Calories burned
Scrubbing floors	189
Raking	171
Gardening	162
Mowing the lawn	162
Washing a car	153
Walking a dog	149
Grocery shopping	122
Vacuuming	85

The danger of crash diets

Being overweight significantly raises your gallstone risk, especially if you carry extra weight around your middle. In fact, research shows that women with bigger waists are more likely to have gallbladder removal surgery.

Fortunately, weight around your middle is the easiest kind to lose. Getting rid of it may lower your risk for heart disease and diabetes, as well as gallstones. Here's how it works.

Scientists have discovered that deep abdominal fat, the kind that wraps around your liver and other organs, can trigger gallstones and other health problems. Moreover, extra pounds make your liver churn out extra cholesterol, raising your odds of developing gallstones even more.

You'll lower your risk by losing inches around your waist, often before you lose pounds. If you don't have much fat around your waist, you can still cut your chances of developing gallstones by reaching and maintaining a healthy weight.

Here's something else to remember — forget starvation diets when you are trying to lose weight. Scientists say rapid weight loss, crash diets, or repeatedly losing and regaining weight will make your liver produce extra cholesterol. Gallstones develop in a surprising number of people who lose weight quickly. Instead, talk with your doctor about a sensible weight loss plan. If she recommends rapid weight loss for health reasons, she can prescribe medication to help dissolve any small gallstones that form.

Some herbs can be dangerous to use if you have gallstones. Talk to your doctor before using artichoke leaf, turmeric, dandelion, and ginger.

Otherwise, stick to a healthy diet and exercise regularly to lose one or two pounds a week. It's far cheaper than stone-dissolving treatments, and you may discover new dishes and activities you'll wish you'd uncovered years ago.

Simple ways to stop stones cold

The next time you're at the grocery store, spend more time in the produce aisle. Foods that grew up in a sunny field or orchard can help you fight gallstones. Try these super suggestions, too.

Eat more fiber. Fruits and vegetables, hearty whole-grain breads and cereals, and delicious seeds and nuts are all fierce gallstone fighters thanks to their fiber. When you don't get enough fiber, your body reabsorbs too much cholesterol. That excess cholesterol can form gallstones if it gets into bile.

However, soluble fiber absorbs cholesterol-loaded bile in your intestines and sweeps it out of your body. Enjoy oranges, oats, barley, beans, and asparagus to get more soluble fiber.

Insoluble fiber helps cut bile production and keep digestive products moving. It also reduces other risk factors for gallstones. Rich sources of insoluble fiber include brown rice, whole grains, wheat bran, seeds, beans, and popcorn. Most fruits and veggies contain both kinds of fiber.

Boost vitamin C intake. Researchers found less gallbladder disease in women who had high blood levels of vitamin C. They've also linked deficiency in this vitamin to a higher risk of gallstones. Scientists think vitamin C may help break down the cholesterol in bile. So add more pineapple, papaya, and oranges and other citrus fruits and juices to your diet. Or try tasty foods like sweet peppers, strawberries, kiwi, frozen peaches, and broccoli.

Watch the carbs. A recent study shows that people who eat lots of carbohydrates, including bread, cereal, sugar, and starchy vegetables like potatoes, have a higher risk for gallstones. A high-carbohydrate diet increases insulin production, which can boost your cholesterol. The researchers recommend avoiding high-carbohydrate, low-fat diets. If you eat too little fat, the gallbladder won't contract and empty its bile. You need a meal with about 10 grams of fat for the gallbladder to contract normally.

Choose fantastic fats. Eat the same healthy fats as the Greeks, and you might avoid your own personal Stone Age. Research suggests that the unsaturated fats found in the Mediterranean diet may fight gallstones.

▸ Enjoy peanuts, walnuts, almonds, and even peanut butter. Harvard researchers discovered that women who ate the most nuts had 25-percent less risk of gallbladder removal surgery than women who avoided nuts or rarely ate them.

▸ Choose olive oil, canola oil, flaxseed, and the omega-3 fatty acids in fish to lower your gallstone risk. If you are worried about mercury and other toxins in fish, choose these varieties — salmon, herring, sardines, mackerel, and flounder. And only eat fish twice a week.

▸ Limit or avoid meats, butter, whole milk, cheese, fried foods, stick margarine, and packaged foods that contain trans fatty acids or saturated fat. New research shows trans fatty acids can raise gallstone risk in men. What's more, too much saturated fat slows digestion and raises cholesterol, the main ingredient in most gallstones.

> In a study of 800 women, those who ate meat were twice as likely to develop gallstones as the vegetarians.

Take a coffee break. Caffeine might help. One study found that men who drank two or three cups of coffee a day were less likely to develop painful stones than men who didn't drink it regularly. More recently, the Nurses Health Study found that you have to drink four cups of coffee a day for the protective effect.

Uncover a secret cause of gallstones

The latest research suggests some prescription drugs can raise your risk of developing gallstones. Talk to your doctor if you take drugs like these.

▶ hormone replacement therapy or birth control pills

▶ ceftriaxone (Rocephin)

▶ clofibrate (Atromid-S)

▶ octreotide (Sandostatin)

▶ cholesterol-busters, like gemfibrozil (Lopid), fenofibrate (Tricor), and bezafibrate (Bezalip) — but not statins, like lovastatin (Mevacor), pravastatin (Pravachol), simvastatin (Zocor), or atorvastatin (Lipitor)

Never stop taking prescribed medication without your doctor's approval. Instead, ask her if a drug you take could increase your gallstone risk. She might be able to prescribe a different drug. For example, if you take estrogen replacement therapy, you may be able to switch from estrogen only to a combination pill. The combo carries less risk.

4 tips for successful treatment

If recurring gallstone attacks lead you to consider gallbladder removal surgery or its alternatives, use these tips to make more cost effective — and health protective — decisions.

Know your no-surgery options. These medical treatments are not effective for everyone. Doctors can use ultrasonic shock waves to break up and dissolve stones in a procedure called lithotripsy. But only 15 percent of the people with gallstones have the kind of stones lithotripsy can tackle. Besides, many medical experts say this procedure is not very effective.

About 30 percent of gallstone sufferers have the right size and type of stones to try ursodiol (Actigall.) This drug may dissolve all your stones, but it could take years of treatment costing thousands of dollars a year.

In a third option, a specially trained doctor injects a powerful chemical into the gallbladder to dissolve the stones. Although the treatment works quickly, complications and serious side effects are possible.

The problem with all three of these options is that half the people who try them usually develop more stones within a few years. Work with your doctor to find a treatment that's right for you.

Pick the right surgeon. When choosing a surgeon, ask how many gallbladder removal surgeries he has performed. Accidental injury to the bile ducts is less likely after a surgeon has performed 50 of these surgeries.

Ask about results. If you're considering gallstone surgery, ask your doctor these questions.

▶ How much improvement can I expect in my symptoms after surgery?

▶ Could other digestive conditions be causing my symptoms? If so, which ones?

▶ What are the risks and benefits of testing for those conditions?

Here's why these questions are important. Out of 145 women who had gallbladder removal surgery, more than 40 percent claimed their pain was no better than before surgery, according to researchers. Yet, delaying surgery has risks, too. You'll need both sides of the story to make the best decision.

Sidestep complications. Accidental injury to the bile ducts is a rare, but serious, problem that can happen during gallbladder removal surgery. If it happens to you, you'll get the best possible

After gallbladder surgery, keeping tabs on your cholesterol may be more important than it was before. Get your cholesterol checked regularly.

outcome if your surgeon discovers the damage during surgery or very soon after. Unfortunately, 60 percent of bile duct damage isn't detected during surgery.

Doctors say they're more likely to discover the problem if they use a procedure called cholangiography. During this procedure, dye is injected into the bile ducts, and X-rays are taken, which can show damage to the ducts. Ask your surgeon about this procedure.

GERD

Low-cost and no-cost solutions for heartburn

Americans spend more than $6 billion a year on prescription drugs to fight gastroesophageal reflux disease (GERD). If you're one of the 60 million people who get heartburn, you might have GERD, too.

When you eat, food passes through your esophagus to your stomach, where hydrochloric acid and other juices break down the food. To keep this powerful acid out of your esophagus, a valve at the top of your stomach closes. This valve is called the lower esophageal sphincter (LES), and it only relaxes to let food into your stomach. But if the LES relaxes when it shouldn't, stomach acid splashes up into your esophagus. This is called reflux.

Frequent reflux can irritate the lining of your esophagus leading to serious damage. Up to 12 percent of GERD cases turn into Barrett's esophagus, a condition linked to esophageal cancer. Most people diagnosed with this cancer die within a year.

10 tricks to tame heartburn

Even if you've never been overweight, moderate weight gain could make your GERD symptoms worse, a recent study suggests. Researchers found that women at a healthy weight who gained a modest amount of weight also gained an extra risk of nagging symptoms.

On top of that, your odds for GERD and esophageal cancer can double when you're overweight. Extra pounds put pressure on your stomach area, which can loosen the LES and send digestive juices into your esophagus. Lose weight and you might lose your GERD symptoms, too.

> Oklahoma researchers found that antacid tablets gave greater, longer-lasting relief than liquid antacids, even within the same brand.

In fact, why take Nexium when there are easy, no-cost solutions for acid reflux. Try these inexpensive tips and tricks before you take your chances with dangerous medicine.

End nightly heartburn. Sleep on your left side for relief that really works. Your esophagus angles slightly to the left where it connects to your stomach. So when you rest on your left side, acid faces a tough uphill climb to reach your esophagus. A sleeping wedge behind your back may keep you facing left.

Take advantage of acid's "low tide." Give stomach acid time to dwindle. Don't eat for at least two hours before bedtime and don't lie down for at least two hours after eating.

Delay after-dinner activity. Wait 90 minutes after eating before starting any strenuous exercise.

Avoid straining. Heavy lifting and straining makes your abdominal muscles contract and squeeze stomach acid into your esophagus.

Ease the pressure. Wear clothes and belts that fit comfortably around your stomach. Give away anything that's too tight.

Sit up straight when you eat. Never stand, lie down, or bend over after eating. This drives food and stomach acid back up into your esophagus.

When to call for help

Signs that your chest pain is something more serious than heartburn include nausea, sweating, weakness, breathlessness, fainting, or shooting pain from your jaw to your arm. If you experience one or more of these symptoms, you might be having a heart attack. Call 911 or ask someone to drive you to the hospital.

Get help from gravity. Let gravity pull the contents of your stomach away from your esophagus so you can sleep. Place blocks under your bedposts to raise the head of your bed about 6 inches, or tuck a sleeping wedge under your mattress.

Tame tablet trouble. Make pills go down and stay down. Take medications with plenty of water, and don't lie down after swallowing a pill.

Stop carrying a torch. Nicotine boosts acid production and relaxes the LES, allowing stomach acid to creep into your esophagus. Although saliva washes the acid back out of your esophagus, smoking decreases saliva, too. Find a way to quit to ease your symptoms.

Get both sides of the alcohol story. Large amounts of alcohol can irritate the lining of your esophagus. Combine that with smoking and you may raise your risk of deadly esophageal cancer. However, a recent study suggests that a small amount of alcohol may protect the esophageal lining. Just don't forget that drinking alcoholic beverages still increases stomach acid and relaxes the LES.

Fight fire with food

Guess what may be back on the menu if you have GERD — chocolate, spicy foods, orange juice, and coffee. Eliminating these foods may not help heartburn or other GERD symptoms, according to a new study.

But the study's researchers say this might not apply to everyone. In fact, another study showed that 44 percent of people with GERD symptoms saw improvement after changing their diets. So here's your best bet. Keep a detailed diary of the foods you eat, when you eat them, when your heartburn occurs and when it doesn't. Pay special attention to these heartburn triggers.

▸ citrus fruits and juices — orange, lemon, lime, and grapefruit

▸ foods and drinks containing peppermint or spearmint

▸ chocolate

▸ tomato products, including ketchup

▸ mustard, pepper, onions, garlic, and vinegar

▸ high-fat foods, especially foods high in saturated fat

▸ greasy or spicy foods

▸ beverages that contain caffeine

▸ carbonated beverages

Soon you'll know which foods trigger trouble and which ones don't. You can also unleash more weapons against GERD and cancer with these dietary secrets.

Strike back with fiber. The more fiber you get, the lower your risk of GERD symptoms. So enjoy more whole grains and low-acid fruits and vegetables. Not only can whole grains help soak up extra stomach acid, but selenium-rich whole grain products may help defend against dangerous cell changes in Barrett's esophagus.

Treat yourself to green tea. You may have less chance of getting esophageal cancer if you drink green tea often, studies suggest. Polyphenols, antioxidants found in tea, may be the reason why. Green tea has the most polyphenols, followed closely by black and oolong teas.

Uncover the cause of your heartburn

Antacids and over-the-counter versions of prescription drugs may suppress symptoms while GERD stealthily wreaks more damage. If heartburn bothers you twice a week or more, see your doctor. He can check your esophagus for damage and uncover what's causing your symptoms.

Make water your ally. Water rinses acid out of your esophagus and dilutes the acid in your stomach. Aim for six to eight 8-ounce glasses daily. In fact, try drinking small amounts of water throughout the day. Drinking too much at once could distend your stomach and rev up your heartburn. And don't drink liquids with meals or you might not get enough stomach acid to digest your food. Stop drinking an hour before and resume an hour after eating.

Pass on processed meats. The nitrates and chemicals in these meats may raise the risk of esophageal cancer in people with GERD.

Encourage easier swallowing. If you have trouble swallowing, avoid tough meats, vegetables with skins, and pasta.

Stop overeating. Large meals raise acid production, and a full stomach is more likely to spill over into your esophagus.

Beware of heartburn-free GERD

Even if you don't have heartburn, you might still have GERD. Constantly clearing your throat is a symptom of GERD. So are these.

▸ trouble swallowing
▸ sore throat

▸ chest pain

▸ abdominal pain

▸ the feeling that something is stuck in your throat

Other surprising signs that you may have GERD — with or without heartburn — include a hoarse voice, chronic cough, erosion of your tooth enamel, breathing difficulty in people who have asthma, and lung disease. If you have these symptoms, see your doctor.

Smart way to lower your risk

Some medicines can raise your risk of GERD or make your symptoms worse. Consider these examples of known offenders.

▸ over-the-counter ibuprofen (Motrin, Advil) and naproxen (Aleve), aspirin (Bufferin, Ecotrin), and other nonsteroidal anti-inflammatory drugs (NSAIDs), including prescription-strength

▸ bisphosphonates, like Fosamax, Boniva, and Actonel, for osteoporosis

▸ benzodiazepines, like diazepam (Valium) and alprazolam (Xanax), used to treat anxiety

▸ calcium channel blockers for angina and high blood pressure

▸ tricyclic antidepressants, including amitriptyline (Elavil) and imipramine (Tofranil)

Ask your doctor if any of your medications can bring on GERD. You may be able to try a lower dose or another drug. Just remember — never stop taking any medication your doctor prescribed without his approval.

Get more for your health care dollar

You might save big bucks if your doctor has prescribed Nexium, Prevacid, Protonix, Aciphex or Prilosec — the drugs called proton pump inhibitors (PPIs). According to *Consumer Reports Best Buy Drugs,* Prilosec OTC, the kind you can get without a prescription, is just as effective. If you must pay the full cost of your prescription drugs, ask your doctor whether you can safely try Prilosec OTC instead of your prescription PPI. The nonprescription drug costs so much less you might save up to $200 a month.

On the other hand, if health insurance pays for your prescription drugs, *Consumer Reports Best Buy Drugs* suggests you ask whether your health plan offers a discount coupon for Prilosec OTC. If not, work with your doctor and insurance company to figure out which GERD medicine you can get for the lowest out-of-pocket cost. Research shows that all of these drugs are equally effective at their starting doses.

> Maalox and Mylanta Classic can calm diarrhea and intestinal gas, while easing heartburn. But Rolaids and Mylanta Supreme don't contain potentially harmful aluminum salts, which can weaken bones.

And here's a bonus tip. If you already take a PPI twice a day and still get overnight heartburn, don't waste your money on a nightly round of H2 blockers, like Tagamet, Pepcid, Zantac, or Axid. Although these drugs reduce stomach acid production, research shows adding them probably won't help.

4 essential questions to ask your doctor

Doctors are concerned about the unexpected effects of drugs that keep your stomach from making or secreting acid. This

Dodge high prices and dangerous interactions

Drug class	Brand names	Average cost of 30 pills		Possible interactions
		Brand	**Generic**	
H2 blockers (reduce the amount of acid the stomach makes)	Tagamet Pepcid Zantac Axid	$75.41	$17.28	antacids (take one hour before or after), aspirin, blood thinners like warfarin (may increase effects), iron supplements, guarana or caffeine (may increase effects), yerba mate (toxic substances may accumulate in the body)
Proton pump inhibitors (block the secretion of stomach acid)	Nexium Prevacid Protonix Aciphex Prilosec	$125.27	$41.11	heart medicines, warfarin, St. John's Wort (increases sunburn risk)

doesn't include antacids because they just neutralize the acid that's already there.

But right next to those antacids on your drugstore shelf, you'll find over-the-counter drugs like Pepcid, Tagamet, Zantac, and Axid. This family of drugs called H2 blockers lower the amount of stomach acid produced. Even more powerful are the prescription and nonprescription proton pump inhibitors, or PPIs. They block the cells that pump acid into your stomach.

According to the *Wall Street Journal*, some scientists think these drugs allow bile, which is alkaline and can also cause damage, to flow into your esophagus, increasing your risk of esophageal cancer.

Until researchers reach a conclusion, doctors say you shouldn't stop taking acid-suppressing drugs. Acid reflux still causes serious damage. But you should ask your doctor these questions.

▶ How high is my risk for Barrett's esophagus and esophageal cancer?

▶ Should I be screened regularly for these conditions? If so, what are the risks and benefits?

▶ Is there discomfort during and after the procedure?

▶ How much does the screening cost?

Recent research also suggests that acid-suppressing drugs may raise your risk of infections, including pneumonia and at least one kind of diarrheal infection. Stomach acid helps kill some infection-causing microbes, but acid-suppressing drugs may weaken that protection. If you take these drugs, ask your doctor if you need a pneumonia vaccine and yearly flu shots.

Tired of waiting for your H2 blocker to take effect? Ask your doctor about Pepcid Complete. This over-the-counter drug combines a quick-acting antacid with the lasting effects of an H2 blocker.

Drugs or surgery: Which one is right for you?

Surgery is a relatively new option for GERD, so researchers are still debating whether it's better than existing drug treatments. One recent study reported that people who had surgery for GERD saw more symptom improvement than people who took PPIs.

Yet, a new review by the Agency for Healthcare Research and Quality (AHRQ) discovered that surgery doesn't improve symptoms any better than drugs. The report also found no evidence that surgery prevents Barrett's esophagus or esophageal cancer more effectively than medication.

Your best bet is to discuss the benefits and risks of surgery with your doctor. Here's what you should know before you do.

▶ **Fundoplication.** This surgical procedure, the most common one for GERD, helps strengthen the LES. The surgeon lifts up part of the stomach, wraps it around the lower esophagus, and sews it in place. When done using a laparoscope, this means small incisions and less time in the hospital.

▶ **Endoscopic gastroplication.** In this newer — and cheaper — procedure, the surgeon stitches a "pleat" to narrow the opening between your stomach and esophagus. This won't require incisions, general anesthesia, or a hospital stay.

Other endoscopic procedures make scar tissue or use injections to strengthen the LES. These methods can have serious side effects and are still being studied.

Surgery can cause uncomfortable aftereffects, like bloating, diarrhea, excessive gas, and difficulty swallowing. It also carries the risk of serious, even fatal, complications. What's more, the AHRQ reports that between 10 and 65 percent of the people who have surgery still need medication. And since surgery and endoscopic procedures are new, their long-term effectiveness is still being determined.

Dollars&Sense
Order up amazing drug bargains

Slash the high cost of prescriptions, and discover where to get the best deals, legally, safely, and best of all, cheaply.

Order meds by mail. If you're an AARP member, call AARP Pharmacy Services toll-free at 800-289-8849 for a price quote on your medication and instructions for ordering by mail.

Cut drug prices. Save money and get your prescriptions delivered right to your door by shopping online. Internet pharmacies have fewer costs than drugstores, so they often offer better prescription discounts.

You can also compare prices at your computer instead of driving store-to-store or calling around. Try this little-known site that helps get the lowest price for your meds. Visit *www.medicarerights.org* and click the Search link. Type "compare drug prices" in the Search box. For a list of sites that compare drug prices, click the results link that features "Prescription Drug Price Comparison Websites" in its description.

Avoid online dangers. You can use your computer to get the very best price on your prescriptions, but you must also know which pharmacies you should never get a prescription from. After all, some sites sell medications that are contaminated, expired, too weak, too potent, or even counterfeit. Sites also may not warn you when a new medication could interact dangerously with drugs you already take. To protect yourself, never buy from a pharmacy that:

- does not require a prescription for prescription drugs.
- "prescribes" medicine based on an online form you fill out.
- does not offer a licensed pharmacist to answer your questions.

▸ does not provide a United States address and phone number to contact if problems occur.

▸ does not have the VIPPS (Verified Internet Pharmacy Practice Sites) seal on its Web site.

The VIPPS seal means the pharmacy is licensed by the states where it operates and has passed the National Association of Boards of Pharmacy (NABP) requirements for quality and security. For an updated list of VIPPS certified Internet pharmacies, visit the NABP Web site at *www.nabp.net,* or call 847-391-4406.

Check the fine print. For safety and savings, follow these tips before you order.

▸ Read the privacy policy. Make sure your financial and personal information won't be sold to others.

▸ Read the refund policy.

▸ Figure out how much your taxes and fees will cost. Sometimes they're more than your savings.

▸ Check whether the site promises that its security software encrypts and protects your information from hackers.

Reap big savings. Keep practicing online safety so you can take advantage of opportunities like these to save up to 65 percent on prescription drugs from now on.

▸ Use the "prescription price checker" at *www.drugstore.com* to save up to 65 percent on medicines like the generic version of prescription-strength Pepcid.

▸ If you have no other drug coverage or discounts, sign up for a discount card at *www.omnichoicerx.com*. You could save far more than the $7.95 monthly fee. In fact, if you take prescription-strength generic Zantac, you could put at least 783 prescription dollars back in your pocket in just seven months.

▸ Visit *www.themedicineprogram.com* for a free drug discount card that promises savings of up to 65 percent.

Gingivitis

Take the bite out of gum disease

Here's good news for your teeth. Unlike previous generations, the majority of baby boomers are expected to keep their own teeth for their whole lives, thanks to widespread water fluoridation, fluoride toothpastes, and improved dental care.

But not all is rosy in those tooth-filled mouths. More than 90 percent of the population has gingivitis, or inflammation of the gums, which causes redness, swelling, pain, and bleeding when you brush your teeth. Gingivitis can lead to more serious gum disease called periodontitis. This could mean loss of connective tissue and bone that supports your teeth. Gum disease can also contribute to serious illnesses, like heart disease, stroke, diabetes, and pneumonia.

With a few inexpensive tools, attention to diet, and regular professional care, you can reverse the course of gum disease and avoid costly health problems.

3 simple ways to reduce your risk

Some people might be naturally prone to excess bacteria and plaque buildup on their gums, which leads to gum disease. Yet, certain things can make it worse — like diabetes, rheumatoid arthritis, and obesity; smoking or chewing tobacco; certain medications; poorly fitting bridgework or dentures; and menopause.

Not surprisingly, the greatest cause of gingivitis is not taking care of your teeth and gums. Follow these recommendations from the American Dental Association (ADA) to keep plaque-causing bacteria at bay.

▸ **Brush your teeth at least twice each day.** Do this carefully and thoroughly for at least two minutes using a soft-bristled brush that fits your mouth. Gently brush your tongue, too. Bacteria like to lurk there. Use toothpaste with fluoride that has the ADA seal of acceptance on the label.

▸ **Floss every day.** Yes, floss. Although only about 24 percent of American households actually use floss on a regular basis, dentists say it is the best — and simplest — way to remove plaque and food in tight spaces between teeth. You may have heard using mouthwash is as good as flossing. Many professionals say it can help in the fight against plaque, but so far, there's not enough evidence to prove it's a substitute for flossing.

▸ **Visit your dentist twice a year.** It's important to catch trouble quickly. Because early gingivitis may have few symptoms, you might not even know you have a problem until your dentist tells you.

By testing your saliva for certain bacteria, doctors can tell if you have mouth cancer even before you have symptoms. Saliva tests are also being developed to check for periodontitis and other conditions.

Don't think you are off the hook when it comes to oral care if you wear partial or full dentures. Brush your dentures twice a day with a soft brush and a nonabrasive denture cleaner. Remove your dentures at night to soak, and clean your gums with a soft, wet cloth or soft toothbrush. Finally, visit your dentist regularly so he can check for signs of gum disease and mouth cancer.

Action plan for healthy gums

Likely your mother told you to stay away from sugar so your teeth wouldn't rot, but that's only part of the story. A study at Case Western Reserve University found that those who followed the 2005 USDA Food Pyramid recommendations lowered their risk of gum disease by 40 percent. USDA guidelines are different for each person based on age, weight, sex, and activity level, but in general they include:

▸ Lots of fruits, vegetables, whole grains, and low-fat dairy products. New research finds that eating three servings of whole grains every day can reduce your risk of gum disease.

▸ Plenty of lean meats, fish, poultry, eggs, beans, and nuts.

▸ Very little salt, sugar, trans fatty acids, and saturated fats. Trans fatty acids are found in hydrogenated oils, like margarine and vegetable shortening. Cheese, whole milk, fatty meat, and butter are high in saturated fats.

Besides this basic plan for good gum health, certain nutrients and foods can help protect you from gum disease.

Vitamin C. This famous vitamin is in charge of making collagen, which helps hold together your body's cells and tissues. It

Save money on dental care

You can save money on professional dental care without cutting back on visits. Dental schools offer low-cost treatment done by dental students who are closely supervised by licensed dentists. Or you can look for a clinical trial that needs people to test a new treatment. You might gain free or reduced-price care and even be paid for participating. Find a list of dental schools at the American Dental Association's Web site *www.ADA.org*.

Energy or sports drinks, non-cola soft drinks, and commercial lemonade can cause your tooth enamel to erode, even more than colas. If you drink these beverages, rinse out your mouth with water when finished.

also supports your bones and teeth. Citrus fruits and juice, strawberries, sweet red peppers, and broccoli are good sources.

Vitamin D. Recent studies found its anti-inflammatory abilities might help gums heal faster and bleed less during dental exams. You can get vitamin D from fortified milk and fatty fish, like salmon and mackerel. When you're exposed to sunlight, your body makes vitamin D. Go outside and soak up some sunshine for about 15 minutes every day.

Polyphenols. These potent antioxidants, found in foods like cranberries, red grapes, blueberries, grape juice, and strawberries, seem to work by cleaning up the waste products of the body's immune system. That allows your immune system cells to attack more of the bacteria that cause gum disease.

Raisins. If you've always believed nature's candy is bad for your teeth, think again. Scientists have found that certain compounds in raisins, especially oleanolic acid, actually help kill the bacteria that cause gum disease and cavities. It also prevents bacteria from sticking to your teeth and forming plaque.

Garlic. An extract of this potent herb kills the bacteria that cause gingivitis. In laboratory studies, the effect began almost immediately. More research is needed to determine if the extract has the same effect in people.

Your dentist can save your life

The best reason to take care of your teeth is to keep your beautiful white smile, right? Not quite. A recent survey found that nearly all doctors and dentists see a link between gum disease and other serious diseases. Taking good care of your teeth and gums might help ward off these life-threatening conditions:

▸ **Heart disease.** In one study, 91 percent of people with heart disease also suffered from serious gum disease. One theory is the same disease-causing bacteria that camp out in your mouth move through your bloodstream, eventually forming plaques in your arteries. Yet another idea is that inflammation caused by serious gum disease damages your blood vessel walls.

▸ **Stroke.** Severe gum disease can raise your risk of stroke by causing plaques to form in your carotid arteries, which supply blood to your brain. Reduced blood flow to the brain caused by a blockage can lead to a stroke.

▸ **Diabetes.** What comes first — diabetes or gum disease? Both these conditions can make the other worse. People with diabetes often experience dry mouth, which allows bacteria to build up and worsen gingivitis. Wounds, including small mouth infections, are also slower to heal for people with diabetes. On the other hand, some mouth infections can make it difficult to control blood sugar.

Sweet solution for unruly plaque

Xylitol, a natural sugar from fruits and other plants, has been shown in more than 300 studies to prevent tooth decay. This amazing sweetener works by blocking plaque-forming bacteria from sticking to the surface of teeth and gums. No plaque — no decay. It's now available in chewing gum, candy, and even toothpaste. Look for products containing xylitol as the only sweetener. Trident regular gum, Trident Splash, and Trident fusion flavors are sweetened with xylitol.

▶ **Runaway infections.** While it's not pleasant to imagine, an untreated infection in your mouth can spread to your bones, muscles, skin, heart — and even your brain. The result can be agonizing pain, severe inflammation, and even death in rare cases. So much for toughing out a toothache.

Broadband light, used to whiten teeth in your dentist's office, may soon be used to control gum disease. Research shows these lights quickly kill the most harmful strains of gingivitis-causing bacteria.

Not horrified yet? Gum disease may also be connected to pneumonia and mouth cancer. And don't forget the basic purpose of teeth — to help you eat a wide variety of foods. Studies have shown that people who keep more of their own teeth throughout life enjoy better nutrition as they age. Poor oral health can be very costly.

Give high-tech claims the brush-off

Just because it's newer doesn't mean it's better. That's important to remember when shopping for oral-care products. You may be tempted to spend more money on fancy toothbrushes, gadgets that sterilize, and toothpastes and mouthwashes that make big promises. Some features of these new products might be nice to have, but few are necessary to give you a cleaner mouth.

Pick the perfect toothbrush. You can pay as much as $140 for a rechargeable electric toothbrush. Those with timers can let you know when to stop brushing, and some with lights can alert you if you are pressing too hard on your gums. But as far as cleaning goes, in the right hands, the good old $2 variety does as good a job as any. The only exception might be brushes with circular movement in both directions, called rotation oscillation action, which do a better job of removing plaque from tight spaces.

Stay away from sterilizers. You like things clean, especially things you put in your mouth. That's why marketers have been successful with new devices made to sterilize your toothbrush. These gadgets, selling for as much as $80, use heated water or ultraviolet light to kills germs.

Remember, your mouth is already full of germs — around 350 kinds of bacteria — most of which are harmless. Only certain types can lead to gingivitis when they remain in large numbers on your gums.

To keep your toothbrush clean, rinse it after use and let it air dry. If you have a lowered immune system or are getting over an infection, buy a new toothbrush more frequently than the usual recommendation of every three months.

Stop wasting money on toothpaste

If you are willing to plunk down two to three times the price of a regular tube of toothpaste for one that's labeled "organic" or "all-natural," you better beware. Many of these high-price toothpastes don't contain the most important ingredient — fluoride. Check the label and be sure it includes the ADA's seal of acceptance.

Product	Contains fluoride	Price
Colgate regular toothpaste	Yes	$0.38/ounce
Crest regular toothpaste	Yes	$0.40/ounce
Tom's of Maine Natural Activity toothpaste	Yes	$0.73/ounce
Kiss My Face AloeDyne natural toothpaste	No	$1.76/ounce
Jason Powersmile natural toothpaste	No	$0.95/ounce

Gout

Don't pay royally to treat the "disease of kings"

Gouch! If you are among the more than 2 million Americans who suffer from this form of arthritis, you understand how painful an attack can be. Uric acid crystals build up in the joints, often in the toes or fingers, causing sudden and severe pain, inflammation, and even fever.

Although you may think of gout as a men's disease, women suffer, too. It's true that men are struck with gout during mid-life twice as often as women, but that changes with age. After menopause, women's uric acid levels increase, putting them at greater risk for symptoms. Gout is equally common among men and women age 60 and older. Unlike men, who tend to have pain in a single toe, older women most often suffer from gout in several finger joints, which can become swollen and deformed.

Gout is twice as common as it was 40 years ago, but there are some changes you can make to live with this "disease of kings" without paying royally.

Eat right and spend less on medicine

If you suffer from gout, you know it's caused by too much uric acid in the blood, sometimes brought on by eating foods rich in purines. While it's nearly impossible to avoid all purines in food, you should steer clear of these troublemakers:

- red meats, including beef, pork, and lamb

- organ meats, like beef or pork liver

- some seafoods, such as anchovies, sardines, and herring

- chocolate, which can raise blood uric acid levels

- alcohol, especially beer and liquor — but not wine, according to a 2004 study

Some vegetables, like spinach and pinto beans, also contain lots of purines, but these don't seem to cause problems for people with gout. What's more, research has shown that some dietary choices can help you avoid a bout of gout.

- Dairy products, especially low-fat choices like skim milk and low-fat yogurt, seem to keep the amount of uric acid circulating in your blood under control.

- Coffee helped lower uric acid levels in a recent study of 1,955 people ages 18 to 65.

Surprising causes of gout

Gout is not all about what you eat. Family history can determine whether your love of bacon will bring on a bout of pain, since some 18 percent of people with gout have a family history of the disease. Gout can also be brought on by some common medical treatments.

- thiazide diuretics, which are water pills taken to lower high blood pressure

- large doses of niacin, also called vitamin B3, sometimes prescribed for high cholesterol

- kidney, heart, or liver transplant

▶ Cherries have long been known to lessen joint pain and the inflammation of gout and other types of arthritis. Although in a recent study, researchers had women eat a bowl of 45 cherries to test the effect, you can opt for dried cherries or cherry juice for relief.

▶ Water — your mother's good ol' standby advice actually works. Drinking lots of water can help flush out the extra uric acid that might be lurking, waiting to cause you more pain.

Ditch low-carb diet to cut your risk

It's no coincidence that the rate of obesity is rising at the same time as the number of gout cases. Boston researcher Dr. Hyon K. Choi found that men whose weight increased by more than 30 pounds after age 21 doubled their chances of getting gout.

You better beware of low-carbohydrate diets, too. They might be all the rage, but they are not a good idea for people with gout. Because such plans have you eating lots of meat and other purine-rich food, while avoiding dairy products, they tend to raise uric acid levels. Stick to a healthy weight-loss plan involving moderate exercise and low-fat food choices. Don't go overboard — fasting can bring on a gout flare-up.

> Stay in bed during a gout flare-up and for at least 24 hours after, doctors advise, since movement can cause inflammation and yet another attack.

Tools easy on your joints and wallet

You can continue to enjoy your favorite hobbies even if gout has attacked your hands. Shop around for some of the many adaptive tools and aids designed for people who need a little help. The

Arthritis Foundation picks some of the best to receive the Ease-of-Use commendation.

If your favorite hobby involves gardening or needlework, you can make smart choices and modify some of the tools you already have to keep your condition from draining your wallet.

Get a grip on gardening. If you like spending time in the dirt, try these tricks to work around your gout.

▶ Make time in the garden count. Decide which tasks are needed, and which you enjoy most, and delegate or skip the rest.

▶ Wear large, well-padded gloves to save your hands.

▶ Tape tool handles for less stress on your hands. Use electrical tape, foam padding, or Bubble Wrap for a better grip and extra cushioning.

▶ Try seed tape. Laying out a line of tape is easier than digging individual holes for seeds.

> Vitamin C reduces uric acid levels in your blood. A daily intake of 500 milligrams (mg) of vitamin C is recommended by health experts to get its full effect.

Keep your knack for needlework. Modifying or purchasing certain tools can help you continue to enjoy sewing and needlework.

▶ Use layers of tape or foam hair curlers (dig out your old pink ones) to create a better grip on knitting needles or crochet hooks.

▶ Many styles of needle threaders, from the simple to the spectacular, can save both your eyesight and your fingers.

▶ Switch from hand sewing to using your sewing machine whenever possible and you can save your fingers for those important projects where your beautiful stitches will be noticed.

▶ Fusible webbing, iron-on shapes, and fabric glue can help you avoid tedious and painful hand sewing. And the effect can be fantastic.

▸ The right scissors or rotary cutter can make a big difference in reducing hand stress. Try one of the new styles of spring-action or electric scissors, which keep your fingers from having to squeeze too hard.

Know your treatment options

Relieving pain and swelling is likely your top priority during a gout attack. Doctors have a few choices when it comes to prescribing drugs, depending on whether your body produces too much uric acid or simply can't get rid of it all. These drugs work, but some people suffer from serious side effects.

Steroid injections to the joint can help, too. The relief may last for only a few months, but steroids can be a good option if you can't take other pain medicines.

Pain relievers like naproxen (Aleve) and indomethacin (Indocin) can get you through a serious attack. These and other types of non-steroidal anti-inflammatory drugs (NSAIDS) work well in people with no liver or kidney problems. But don't take aspirin for gout. In low doses, like the 81-milligram baby aspirin you take for your heart, it can actually bring on a gout attack.

New hope for gout victims

A new drug, febuxostat, seems to work better than allopurinol at lowering uric acid levels. Now awaiting FDA approval, this drug could be the first advance in gout treatment in more than 35 years. This would be great news for the roughly 20 percent of gout sufferers who can't tolerate the traditional medicines.

The following table explains why your doctor might prescribe a drug for you and the possible side effects.

Drug name Generic (Brand) Class	Why take it	Common side effects
allopurinol (Zyloprim) xanthine oxidase inhibitor	Lowers the amount of uric acid produced by the body to prevent a gout flare-up	Skin sores or rash, hives, itching, nausea, vomiting
probenecid (Benemid, Probalan) uricosuric drug	Flushes uric acid from the body to prevent a gout flare-up	Joint pain, headache, loss of appetite, nausea, vomiting
colchicine — generic only antigout drug	Relieves or prevents joint inflammation	Stomach pain, nausea, diarrhea, vomiting, hinders the absorption of vitamin B12
probenecid and colchicine (ColBenemid, Proben-C) combination drug	Flushes uric acid from the body and relieves or prevents joint inflammation	Diarrhea, loss of appetite, nausea, vomiting, headache

Hair loss

Attack the problem at its roots

"Hair" today, gone tomorrow, right? For too many people, this phrase becomes more and more true as they age.

Roughly 50 percent of all men face the prospect of thinning or disappearing hair. Surprisingly, 75 percent of women older than 65 also experience some hair loss. Hair loss, or alopecia, is an age-old problem, and maybe that's why people stake their hopes — and their dollars — on outlandish claims and "magic" potions. Modern science has made progress, so you don't need to rely on empty promises.

If your head has been looking less like Rapunzel's and more like Kojak's, you can take steps now to slow or even reverse your hair loss. Some products and treatments are expensive, but in many cases you get what you pay for. Shop around and compare to find the best treatment for you.

Get top results with proven treatments

You finally admit you have a hair-loss problem, and now you want a solution. You can choose from all sorts of miraculous cures and "guaranteed" products, most with impressive test statistics and a convincing celebrity spokesperson. But if all these amazing cures work so well, why doesn't everyone enjoy a full head of hair?

The answer, of course, is that not all these promises are true. Researchers have tested a variety of products that claim to regrow hair or stop its loss, and a few have proven effective. Don't waste your money on the others.

Minoxidil (Rogaine) is a solution applied to the scalp. It's approved by the Food and Drug Administration (FDA) to treat pattern baldness, with a 5-percent solution available for men and a weaker 2-percent solution for women. Scientists are not sure how minoxidil works, but it seems to stimulate inactive hair follicles to regrow hair and keep hair from falling out. If you stop using minoxidil, hair loss will continue. Side effects can include scalp irritation and some unwanted hair growth for women.

Finasteride (Propecia) is a pill approved by the FDA for men only. It works by blocking the conversion of testosterone to a byproduct (DHT) that damages hair follicles, so men may have some sexual side effects. Finasteride is not approved for women because of the chance for birth defects. This treatment can slow hair loss and regrow hair, but these symptoms will come back if you stop taking it.

Hair transplantation is a permanent way to put hair back once it's gone. Available since 1952, hair transplants have greatly improved as they have become more common, with more than 80,000 Americans undergoing the treatment in one year. Unfortunately, the process won't work if you're completely bald because you must have areas of growing hair the surgeon can retrieve as donor follicles.

Certain drugs, like chemotherapy for cancer treatment, colchicine for gout, beta blockers, or anticoagulants, can cause hair thinning or complete loss.

Help your hair from the inside out

A healthy crop of hair can be a sign of health and good nutrition. The reverse may also be true. Thinning hair may be related to what is missing from your diet. Long before drugs were developed to treat hair loss, people found natural remedies to help save their locks. But before you buy, consider the pros and cons of these supplements touted for hair loss.

Iron. For some cases of hair loss, low iron in the blood could make the problem worse. Even if your iron level is not low enough to signal anemia, it could be low enough to keep you from growing a thick crop of hair.

Not everyone agrees. But researchers at the Cleveland Clinic who study people with thinning hair check blood levels of ferritin — a protein that helps the body store iron — to see who's at risk. They have found that even when ferritin levels are in a range considered normal, many people still suffer from hair loss. The researchers think this is because growing hair follicles need more iron than other cells in the body. When they add iron supplements to other treatments, it seems to improve people's ability to grow hair.

But don't take iron supplements on your own. Talk to your doctor first, and ask him to check your ferritin level. Getting too much iron can be dangerous since your body can't easily get rid of the extra. Also, iron pills can cause constipation and stomach upset. Your best bet is to get more iron from your diet by eating foods such as spinach, beans, tofu, raisins, and lean beef.

Speedy weight loss brings on hair loss. If your diet doesn't include enough protein, iron, vitamin D, and other nutrients, your hair may get thinner along with your waistline.

Saw palmetto. This ancient remedy for hair loss might actually do the trick. It's an herb that works like the drug finasteride. It keeps testosterone from changing to a byproduct (DHT) that damages hair follicles. In fact, one study found that 60 percent of the men who tried it saw improved hair growth. However, this study was small, and the men were also taking another supplement, so saw palmetto might not be entirely responsible for the benefits. More research still needs to be done.

It's normal to lose about 100–150 hairs each day as your locks progress through the normal cycle of growing, resting, shedding, and regrowth.

Fenugreek. Long used as a spice, this legume has been studied to see if it can lower blood sugar in people with diabetes, fight stomach ulcers, and battle colon cancer. Some people believe it may also slow hair loss and help with regrowth, but little scientific evidence has shown this effect.

A Danish product called Folligro is a fenugreek combination packaged especially for people who battle hair loss. You may want to think twice about herbal remedies with fenugreek until more research is done. And avoid fenugreek completely if you regularly take nonsteroidal anti-inflammatory drugs (NSAIDs) because the combination can cause bleeding.

4 ways to make the most of what you have

You can spend a lot of money and effort trying to make your thinning hair grow back. Or you can look for other solutions. Here are four options to think about.

Consider a cut. If you wear your hair long and pulled into a ponytail or bun, you may show more exposed scalp than you need to. A shorter cut that allows bangs or layers of hair to cover any thinning spots can help make the most of your remaining hair.

Hair cloning: hope for the future

It may seem farfetched, but researchers are working on ways of multiplying, or "cloning," a person's hair follicle cells. If this method of regrowing hair works, you would have a few follicle cells removed, let them multiply in a lab dish, then have them "planted" where you need them. Because hair cells appear to adapt to changes in location and will even grow on different people, this kind of regrowth is likely to be possible in a few years.

Extend your look. Hair extensions are human or synthetic hair that is woven in, sewn on, or glued to your own hair. It can be a natural-looking way to improve your appearance. Styles and prices vary widely, but you can expect to spend upwards of $200–$2,500 for well-applied extensions of good-quality human hair. Extensions require maintenance every two to 12 weeks depending on whether they are glued or sewn in, adding to the cost. To save money, you can get do-it-yourself clip-in extensions for under $100, but you must remove them every night.

Pump up the volume. You've probably seen ads for shampoos, conditioners, and styling products designed to add volume to hair. These can help make your thinning mane appear thicker. In addition, certain products help camouflage thinning hair.

▸ Masking lotions are applied to the scalp and base of the hair to reduce the contrast between the two. They stay in place during swimming and styling but wash out with shampoo. Pick a lotion to match your hair color. Couvré and Millefolium offer masking lotions.

▸ Powders matched to your hair color can coat remaining hairs, allowing them to spread out for better scalp coverage. These last through exercise and the swimming pool, but they come out when you wash your hair. Try powders from DermMatch or MagiHair.

▶ Products containing microfibers of keratin, the same protein that makes up hair and nails, are shaken over the thinning area to bond with the hair. Manufacturers promise their products will last through bad weather but not a dip in the swimming pool. You might try Toppik or The Great Cover-Up brands.

Cover up the problem. Wigs have come a long way in the past few years. Nowadays they are realistic-looking and comfortable

Compare cost of hair-loss treatments

Treatment	Cost	Men or women	Effectiveness
Rogaine (minoxidil)	$24.66/month $19.99/month (generic)	men (5% solution)	effective as long as treatment continues
	$24.99/month $15.66/month (generic)	women (2% solution)	
Propecia (finasteride)	$62.95/month	men only	66% effective as long as treatment continues
Folligro (fenugreek)	$49.95/month	both	little evidence
Saw palmetto	$3/month	both	some evidence
Hair transplants	$7,000–$15,000	both	highly effective, permanent
Laser light therapy	$2,800–$3,500 for 6 months of treatment	both	still experimental, requires maintenance treatment

and won't fall off if you put them on correctly. A wig stylist can help you select one to match your hairstyle and color if you show her an old photograph of yourself. Prices vary widely, from around $195 for synthetic hair to $1,500 for human hair. If that's more than you want to spend, make a fashion statement instead. Tie a scarf around your head, or wear a hat.

Calm your nerves to save your locks

It's a vicious cycle. Stressful events or lifestyles can lead to loss of hair, and hair loss can trigger extra stress. Many people — both men and women — seem overly bothered by the idea their hair is thinning.

But hair has symbolic value far beyond the protection and warmth it provides for the head. It can be a symbol of beauty for women and a sign of youth for men. Losing it can be traumatic, and studies have found that people experiencing hair loss can feel depressed, ashamed, angry, and embarrassed. Unfortunately, certain hair-loss conditions are made even worse by these stressful attitudes.

Poor choice of hairstyles — excess use of hot combs or tightly pulled braids, pony-tails, or topknots — can lead to temporary or even permanent loss of hair.

To stop this vicious cycle, doctors recommend a variety of stress-reduction techniques, such as exercise, music, massage, and relaxation. Use these tricks to help yourself feel better while your hair is thinning. You'll find details in the *Depression* chapter in *Top tips for beating the blues*.

Dollars&Sense
Foreign drugs: are they worth the risks?

Americans spend more money buying drugs than do people in other countries — an average of $728 per person in 2003 compared to $507 in Canada and $261 in Ireland. One reason is many brand-name drugs cost more in the United States because the government does not regulate prices.

You've probably heard of people buying drugs in other countries, either by traveling to Canada, Mexico, or overseas — or by ordering them online. Saving money may be tempting, but there are a few things you should consider.

Know the law. For a while, authorities looked the other way when people brought a 90-day supply of their prescriptions across the border from Canada, even though it's illegal. But things have changed. Starting in 2005, the Food and Drug Administration (FDA) and U.S. Customs began confiscating prescriptions sent from foreign pharmacies to U.S. addresses. Instead of getting their drugs, many buyers got warning letters from the government. Then the policy was reversed. To check the current law, see the Web site of U.S. Customs and Border Protection at *www.cbp.gov*.

Consider the source. If you order from a foreign pharmacy, you don't really know what you're getting and where it comes from. The FDA does not control drugs shipped from other countries, so they can have serious problems, such as wrong labeling, old ingredients, unapproved versions, lack of refrigeration, watered-down liquids, or just plain fakes. Even online pharmacies that appear to be based in Canada may actually be located in a Third-World country, where regulations may be slack and conditions poor.

Understand what you're buying. Don't assume your prescription carries the same name in another country as it does at home. The Institute for Safe Medication Practices issued a safety alert in 2005 about drugs sold in other countries that have different ingredients as U.S. drugs with the same names. You may pop into a drugstore while on vacation in Europe or South America to buy Flomax only to get a different drug with different effects.

Check your cost savings. You may not even save money by buying in a foreign country. Studies have found that many commonly used U.S. generic drugs are cheaper than the same drugs bought in other countries — either generic or brand name. Besides that, the new Medicare Part D drug plans have made buying many drugs at home less expensive and more secure than going to Canada, Mexico, or overseas. And if you buy from a foreign pharmacy, you can't deduct the cost from your income taxes.

If you've compared prices and still think buying drugs from a foreign pharmacy is your ticket to savings, take these precautions to stay safe and avoid scams.

▶ Go in person. If you can travel to a brick-and-mortar drugstore, you can be more certain of getting the drug you think you're getting. You can also talk to the pharmacist about your drugs, side effects, and possible interactions.

▶ Choose an Internet or mail-order pharmacy carefully. Be sure it has a working toll-free phone number answered by live operators, is located at a physical street address, and requires a prescription for your drug.

▶ Get information at *www.pharmacychecker.com*. You can compare prices and get ratings on online pharmacies.

▶ Sign up at *www.safemedicines.org* for warnings through the SafeMeds Alert System. Government alerts about counterfeit and bad drugs will be sent to your e-mail address. It's a free service.

Heart disease

Bypass high costs of standard treatments

Heart disease is the world's No. 1 killer — so preventing heart disease should be your No. 1 priority. When you have heart disease, your coronary arteries, the blood vessels around your heart, become clogged or blocked. This can lead to serious problems, including heart attack, angina or chest pain, heart failure, and an irregular heartbeat called arrhythmia.

Lifestyle changes, such as a healthy diet and regular exercise, can help prevent heart disease. But you may also need medication. New drugs promise greater protection than ever, but at what cost?

Find out what steps you can take to guard against heart disease, which drugs to watch out for, and how you can help your heart without hurting your pocketbook.

Little pill has big benefits — and hazards

Popping a daily aspirin is an easy, cheap, and effective way to ward off a heart attack or stroke. It works as a blood thinner so it gives your body its own natural, clot-busting protection. But aspirin works differently for men and women. And it's not recommended for everyone.

Recent studies show that daily aspirin therapy helps men prevent heart attacks and women prevent strokes, but not vice versa.

Another large study found that aspirin might help prevent heart attacks in women over age 65. Younger women, perhaps because of the protection of estrogen, did not benefit from aspirin.

Your doctor may recommend aspirin if you're at risk for heart disease or if you've already had a heart attack. In fact, researchers recently discovered that taking aspirin before and after bypass surgery could save 8,000 lives a year in the United States.

Air pollution, loud noise, and high humidity can harm your heart. If you can get away, head for the mountains and take an uphill walk. It's good for your heart.

But if you're perfectly healthy, you may be doing more harm than good. Because aspirin works as a blood thinner to keep your blood from clumping and clotting, it boosts your risk for major bleeding and even hemorrhagic stroke. Other possible problems include ulcers and kidney failure.

Remember, aspirin can interact with other drugs. Let your doctor know which medications, including vitamins, supplements, and herbs, you are taking. If your doctor recommends aspirin therapy, follow his instructions carefully.

The lowdown on 2 risky drugs

When it comes to heart medication, there's good news and bad news. Some heart drugs, such as statins and the new angina drug Ranexa, show outstanding promise — but not all drugs are safe.

Trasylol, a drug often used to reduce blood loss during heart bypass surgery, boosts your risk for kidney failure, heart attack, and stroke. Researchers studying this drug also discovered that cheaper alternatives were just as effective, and they didn't cause dangerous side effects.

Another way to save money is to pass on Plavix, or clopidogrel. Taking this "super-aspirin" along with regular aspirin does not double your protection. Rather, it has no effect on preventing death from heart attack or stroke. But it does increase your risk of internal bleeding. And costs more than 100 times as much as aspirin.

Heart medication should not be your only concern. Often, drugs that help other conditions may pose a risk to your heart. These include:

▶ painkillers called nonsteroidal anti-inflammatory drugs (NSAIDs), such as ibuprofen and naproxen

▶ painkillers called COX-2 inhibitors (Celebrex)

▶ diabetes drug rosiglitazone (RSG)

▶ breast cancer drug raloxifene

▶ prostate drug doxazosin

▶ attention deficit hyperactivity disorder drugs, like Ritalin

Tell your doctor about all your medications — not just those related to heart disease — so you can avoid dangerous interactions. And never stop taking a drug your doctor prescribed without his approval.

'Shocking' way to save your life

You don't always have time to call "911" when you experience signs of a heart attack. Some heart attacks, called sudden cardiac arrest, stop your heart right away.

For cases like that, consider buying a home defibrillator. These devices use an electric shock to restart a heart attack victim's heart. They come with instructions and are easy to use, but it's a good idea to get some training. You can never be too prepared for an emergency.

There's just one problem — you can't use a defibrillator on yourself. So if you live alone, it doesn't make much sense to buy one. But if you live with family or your family spends a lot of time at your house, a home defibrillator can be a lifesaver.

In 2004, the FDA cleared the Philips HeartStart Home Defibrillator for use. It costs around $1,500. You can find it at some Sam's Clubs, or you can order online from drugstore.com, Walgreens.com, or Target.com.

The 10 best hospitals for heart surgery

Heart surgery, no matter how minor the procedure, is scary enough. But it's even scarier when you don't know where to have the surgery done. How do you know you're getting the best care?

You could choose one of the top 10 hospitals for heart surgery, according to *U.S. News and World Report*. If you're at very high risk, likely to spend time in an intensive care unit, or need treatment requiring the latest technology, the big-name facilities listed in the chart on the next page may be your best bet.

But, often, your local community hospital can be just as good and cost much less. It all comes down to experience — the more, the better. Ideally, you want a hospital that performs at least 450 bypass surgeries a year. The surgeon you choose should do 125 or more each year.

Feel free to ask your surgeon questions about his experience, including number of operations, death rates, and rates of other complications. You may even be able to find such information online at the Web site *healthcarechoices.org*. A little research can go a long way toward finding the best care — and much-needed peace of mind.

Top 10 heart hospitals

Hospital	City
Cleveland Clinic	Cleveland
Mayo Clinic	Rochester, Minn.
Johns Hopkins Hospital	Baltimore
Massachusetts General Hospital	Boston
Brigham and Women's Hospital	Boston
St. Luke's Episcopal Hospital — Texas Heart Institute	Houston
Duke University Medical Center	Durham, N.C.
New York — Presbyterian Hospital	New York
UCLA Medical Center	Los Angeles
Barnes-Jewish Hospital — Washington University	St. Louis

5 ways to keep your heart healthy

You can't control all of your risk factors for heart disease. For instance, you can't change your age, gender, or family history. But you can do something about the others. Is it possible to lower blood pressure, cholesterol, and blood sugar without expensive drugs? The experts say yes.

In a 12-week study at the Center for Heart Disease Prevention in Savannah, Ga., people with risk factors such as high cholesterol or high blood pressure managed to lower these levels significantly by sticking to an individually tailored exercise plan, meal plan, and other lifestyle changes.

Making these changes takes some work, but it's cheaper than drugs — without any side effects. Eating a healthy diet, exercising regularly, losing weight if you're overweight, and quitting smoking will put you on the path to a healthy heart, but there are other steps you can take.

Cut your chances of a heart attack by 74 percent — without drugs, surgery, diet, or exercise. The secret? Learn how to handle mental stress, which can trigger a heart attack. People with heart disease drastically lowered their risk for heart attack with four months of stress management training.

Hostility, intense arguments, and road rage have all been linked to heart attacks. Finding a healthier, more productive way to deal with stress can mean the difference between life and death. Along with stress management, try these helpful tips for better heart health.

▶ **Laugh more.** Laughter relaxes blood vessels and increases blood flow. Rent a funny movie or spend time with humorous friends or relatives.

▶ **Skip the siesta.** Daily afternoon naps can boost your risk of a heart attack, according to a Costa Rican study.

▶ **See the glass as half full.** Optimism helps ward off heart disease. A Dutch study found that optimistic men were half as likely to die from cardiovascular disease, including heart attack, stroke, and coronary heart disease, as their less optimistic counterparts.

▶ **Listen to music.** Italian researchers found that music may have a beneficial relaxing effect on your heart.

▶ **Get a pet.** Studies have linked pet ownership to a reduced risk of heart disease.

And that's not all — alcohol may have a protective effect on your heart if you are a postmenopausal woman or man over age 50. Just remember — if you drink alcohol, drink in moderation. That means no more than two drinks a day for a man and one for a woman. Before you toast your good health, remember that alcohol can have harmful effects on your health, too, including alcohol dependency.

Reap 'fin-tastic' protection from fish

Ever wish for an easy way to fight heart disease? Well, stop wishing and start fishing. Eating fish does wonders for your heart. That's because it's rich in omega-3 fatty acids. Researchers who recently examined several studies determined that eating fish lowers heart disease risk by roughly 10 percent and fatal heart disease risk by nearly 20 percent.

A recent Greek study found that eating fish reduces the risk for heart attacks or chest pain by 38 percent. Oddly, the benefits stopped at 5 ounces of fish a week. More fish did not mean increased benefits.

Fish oil helps heart attack survivors live longer, fights inflammation, lowers elevated heart rates, and even counteracts the damage that air pollution can do to your heart.

> Brushing and flossing can save your heart, as well as your teeth. That's because the inflammation that comes with gum disease also boosts your risk for heart disease.

So why don't more people eat fish? Maybe because they're worried about pollutants. Recent reports of excessive mercury and contaminants called PCBs have called into question the safety of farm-raised fish, the kind most often available in supermarkets.

Don't let the fear of mercury and other toxins turn you into a landlubber. The proven heart benefits of eating fish far outweigh the slight risk of developing cancer from any contaminants. In fact, the American Heart Association still recommends you eat fatty fish twice a week.

But, just to be safe, you can take the following measures to limit mercury and PCB exposure.

▶ Avoid tilefish, shark, swordfish, and king mackerel.

▶ Choose fish lower in mercury. These include salmon, herring, sardines, shad, trout, mackerel, and whitefish.

▶ Pay attention to state advisories about the safety of fish caught in local lakes, rivers, and coastal areas.

▶ When cooking farm-raised salmon, grill or broil it to let the juices drip out, cook the fish until the internal temperature reaches 175 degrees Fahrenheit, and remove the skin before eating.

Some experts even recommend taking fish oil supplements rather than eating fish in order to avoid toxins. But supplements come with their own concerns. A recent study found that fish oil supplements might cause arrhythmia in some people.

Help your heart with a cup of coffee

Wake up and smell the coffee. Better yet, pour yourself a cup. A recent study found that drinking one to three cups of coffee a day might help protect you from heart disease. That's because coffee, rich in antioxidants, fights inflammation, which plays a major role in the development of heart disease. This stands in contrast to a previous study, which found that lifelong caffeine consumption might contribute to heart disease.

The type of coffee you drink may make a difference. Drinking filtered coffee does not appear to boost your risk of heart disease, even if you drink six cups or more a day. However, unfiltered or boiled coffee, such as the kind you make with a French press, may be harmful because it contains substances that raise cholesterol levels.

Coffee may also be dangerous if your body metabolizes it slowly. Because of an inherited trait, some people metabolize coffee slower than others. Unfortunately, this puts you at much greater risk for a heart attack. If coffee makes you feel weak or lightheaded, quickens your pulse, or causes pain in your chest, don't drink it.

Drinking coffee right before exercising may cause problems because it narrows your blood vessels, which decreases blood flow through the arteries supplying oxygen to your heart. If you start your day with a cup of coffee, wait at least an hour before exercising.

If coffee isn't your thing, drink tea instead. It's also chock-full of antioxidants and other health benefits.

High blood pressure
Smart ways to stop silent killer

High blood pressure can sneak up on you — and kill you. This serious condition, also known as hypertension, often has no symptoms. You may not know you have it until you get it checked at your doctor's office.

Blood pressure, which refers to the force of your blood as it moves through your blood vessels, is measured in millimeters of mercury, or mm Hg. It includes both systolic pressure, when your heart contracts, and diastolic pressure, when your heart relaxes between contractions. Systolic pressure comes first in a blood pressure reading. A reading of 140/90 or higher indicates high blood pressure. You want to keep your blood pressure below 120/80. Anything higher falls under the label "prehypertension," a risky condition recently recognized by health experts. Consider prehypertension a warning sign.

If left untreated, high blood pressure can lead to several serious health problems, including stroke, heart disease, heart failure, kidney disease, and blindness. Luckily, high blood pressure can be controlled with medication, as well as changes in diet and lifestyle.

10 terrific tips for reducing blood pressure

You can fight high blood pressure without risky drugs. Just follow these steps to lower blood pressure the natural way.

- ▶ Reduce salt. This means not only salt from your saltshaker but also the sodium in processed foods.

- ▶ Cut back on fat, red meat, and sweets — including sweetened drinks.

- ▶ Eat more fruits, vegetables, and whole grains.

- ▶ Maximize your minerals. Potassium, magnesium, and calcium play key roles in controlling your blood pressure, so make sure your diet provides them. It's as easy as reaching for beans and bananas. Beans are a good source of magnesium, while bananas are packed with potassium. To boost your calcium intake, try nonfat and low-fat dairy products.

- ▶ Limit alcohol. This means no more than two drinks a day for a man and one for a woman.

- ▶ Exercise regularly. Recent studies show that a 30-minute brisk walk each day can dramatically lower your blood pressure.

- ▶ Lose weight. As your weight decreases, so will your blood pressure.

- ▶ Quit smoking. It stiffens your arteries.

- ▶ Get enough sleep. Sleeping five hours or less a night may boost your risk of high blood pressure.

- ▶ Relax. Listen to music, get a massage, spend time with loved ones, or find other ways to reduce stress.

Sticking to these simple lifestyle and dietary changes can dramatically lower your blood pressure and help you avoid blood pressure medication entirely. That's what researchers discovered in the recent PREMIER study — 98 percent of those with high blood pressure became completely free of their medicine — with their doctor's approval — when they followed this simple advice.

The people in the study lost weight, exercised, reduced salt and alcohol intake, and followed the National Heart, Lung, and Blood Institute's Dietary Approaches to Stop Hypertension (DASH) diet — which stresses many of the dietary tips listed earlier. For more information about the DASH diet, you can order a copy of *Your Guide to Lowering Blood Pressure with DASH* by calling the NHLBI Health Information Center at 301-592-8573. The cost is $3.50 for a single copy. Be sure to have your credit card handy. To view this publication online for free, go to *www.nhlbi.nih.gov/health/public/heart/hbp/dash*.

Drink up to drive blood pressure down

Pour yourself a glass of skim milk and you might skim your risk of developing high blood pressure in half. In a recent two-year study of nearly 6,000 people, those who had more than two or three daily servings of skim milk and other nonfat dairy products were half as likely to develop high blood pressure as people who rarely or never consumed these foods.

You can sip your way to lower blood pressure with the following beverages as well.

▶ **Grape juice.** In a Korean study, men drinking Concord grape juice significantly lowered both their systolic and diastolic blood pressure. Natural compounds called flavonoids found in grape juice likely deserve the credit.

▶ **Cocoa.** Drinking a special flavonol-rich cocoa beverage improved blood vessel function in healthy men and women in one small study. Look for this special flavonol-rich cocoa in Dove dark chocolate and CocoaVia products. For more information, visit *www.cocoapro.com*.

▶ **Fermented milk.** A Finnish study found that this popular Scandinavian beverage, made by adding the good bacteria *Lactobacillus* to milk, lowered blood pressure by about three points after 10 weeks. Fermented milk works in the same manner as ACE inhibitors, by blocking angiotensin-converting enzyme, a chemical that raises blood pressure.

If you need a cup of coffee to get going in the morning, here's some good news. Coffee boosts blood pressure in the short run, but regular coffee drinking does not seem to have an effect on developing high blood pressure. Yet, if you already have high blood pressure, you may want to limit your coffee consumption. Other beverages that may raise your blood pressure include beer, wine, and colas — including diet colas.

> Religion is not only good for your soul, it's good for your heart. Regular religious activity, such as attending church and praying, has been linked to lower blood pressure.

One beverage you should never drink if you're taking high blood pressure medicine is grapefruit juice. This fruit juice will drive your blood pressure to toxic levels. That's because when you take calcium-channel blockers with grapefruit juice, you end up with a much higher — and dangerous — amount of the drugs in your body. Recently discovered chemicals in grapefruit juice called furanocoumarins are responsible for this dangerous interaction.

4 tasty ways to defeat the silent killer

What you eat has a big impact on your blood pressure. Perhaps the best approach is to follow the DASH diet, which stresses eating more fruits, vegetables, whole grains, and low-fat dairy products while limiting salt, fat, alcohol, and sweets. But also make room for the following foods, which just might give you an edge in the battle against high blood pressure.

Celery. Long a staple of Chinese medicine, this crunchy vegetable contains compounds called pthalides, which relax the muscles lining your blood vessels. This allows them to dilate, or widen, so blood can get through more easily. Four stalks of celery should do the trick.

Potatoes. Scientists recently discovered that potatoes contain kukoamines, chemicals that lower blood pressure. Kukoamines were previously only known to occur in an exotic plant used in Chinese medicine. You'll preserve the health benefits of kukoamines by boiling rather than frying your potatoes.

Fish. Several studies show that eating fish or taking fish oil supplements lowers blood pressure. The omega-3 fatty acids in fish help relax the cells lining your arteries, which improves circulation. Besides fatty fish like salmon, mackerel, or tuna, you can get omega-3 from flaxseed, canola oil, walnuts, wheat germ, and some green leafy vegetables, like collard and turnip greens.

Chocolate. A Dutch study found that older men who ate about a third of a bar of chocolate a day had lower blood pressure. Cocoa beans contain flavonols — natural compounds that can help keep your blood vessels working as they should. Visit *www.cocoapro.com* to learn about the health benefits of specially processed cocoa.

Uncover hidden sources of salt

Salt, also known as sodium chloride, is an important mineral that is 40 percent sodium and 60 percent chloride. Unfortunately, sodium can wreak havoc with your blood pressure. Health experts recommend getting no more than 2,300 milligrams a day, but that's tough to do — especially when you don't know how much salt lurks in foods you eat every day.

To help people eat less salt, the American Medical Association (AMA) recently recommended that restaurant meals, fast food products, and processed foods cut their sodium content in half over the next decade.

In the meantime, the best approach is to cut back on restaurant meals and limit how many processed foods you eat. When you prepare your own food, using fresh fruits, vegetables, and meat, you can control how much salt you are getting.

Salt can also pop up in some surprising places, like your medication. Among over-the-counter drugs, antacids, laxatives, anti-inflammatory drugs, and cold medicines may contain large amounts of sodium. To find out how much sodium is hiding in the medication you take, read the labels on over-the-counter drugs. And ask your pharmacist to check the package inserts that come with prescription drugs.

The following chart shows the sodium content of some common foods.

Food	Sodium (milligrams)
apple	0
cheese pizza (1 slice)	282
raisin bran (1 cup)	362
American cheese (1 slice)	422
apple pie (1 slice)	444
creamed corn (1 cup)	572
hot dog	638
small cheeseburger	725
macaroni and cheese (1 cup)	1,061
breakfast biscuit	1,470

Walk your way to healthier blood pressure

Get off the couch and start moving if you want to lower your blood pressure. Aim for at least 30 minutes of moderate exercise, such as walking, cycling, or swimming, most days of the week. Studies show regular exercise can shave three or four points off your blood pressure reading.

If you already have high blood pressure, you may be reluctant to exercise because of the temporary rise in blood pressure that comes with activity. But a recent study found that it is safe for older people with mild high blood pressure to work out. Just check with your doctor before beginning any exercise program.

Sure, it's safe, you might say, but who has time to exercise? You do, as long as you can spare 10 minutes now and then. A recent Indiana University study found that four 10-minute sessions on a treadmill lowered blood pressure just as much as one continuous 40-minute session — and the effects lasted longer. So if you don't have time for a long walk, try squeezing in three or four short ones during your day.

Every little movement helps. You don't need to come up with an elaborate exercise routine or pay big bucks to join a gym. Just performing everyday activities, like gardening or walking up and down stairs, can help. A seven-year Japanese study of middle-age men found that those who were the most active in everyday life were much less likely to develop high blood pressure.

Blood pressure tends to shoot up in cold weather and go down in hot weather. However, a recent Italian study found that in people over age 65 nighttime blood pressure actually increased in hot weather.

To see how many calories you can burn just by doing

household chores or running errands, check out the chart on page 142 in the *Gallstones* chapter.

Short-circuit dangerous drug interactions

Even if you eat right and exercise, sometimes you need medication to keep your blood pressure under control. But many blood pressure drugs come with important warnings. Here are a few to watch out for.

Nix nifedipine. Lowering your blood pressure with short-acting nifedipine, a calcium channel blocker, can cause a heart attack. High doses of this common medicine used to treat high blood pressure are especially dangerous. Your doctor may not think to tell you about this, so make sure to ask about safer alternatives.

Pay attention to potassium. ACE inhibitors can boost the level of potassium in your blood. Potassium can be good for your heart, but too much in your blood can be fatal — and this high blood pressure medicine can make it skyrocket. Use caution when taking ACE inhibitors, especially if you're also taking potassium supplements or potassium-sparing diuretics (water pills).

Pass on painkillers. Pain pills and some blood pressure drugs do not mix. Nonsteroidal anti-inflammatory drugs (NSAIDs), such as ibuprofen, may blunt the effectiveness of ACE inhibitors. They may also raise your blood pressure. Play it safe and choose acetaminophen instead.

Dodge diabetes. While some drugs help control your blood pressure, they may increase your risk for other conditions — like diabetes. Common prescription drugs that may actually cause type 2 diabetes include diuretics and beta blockers. What's more, they might also boost your stroke risk. Are you unknowingly taking them? Ask your doctor if other options would be safer. Keep in

Important information about common BP drugs

Class	Side effects/warnings
ACE inhibitors Examples: benazepril (Lotensin), captopril (Capoten), enalapril (Vasotec), lisinopril (Prinivil, Zestril), perindopril (Aceon), quinapril (Accupril), ramipril (Altace)	Can increase potassium in your blood to a toxic level. Most common side effect is persistent dry cough. Less common side effects include excessively low blood pressure and headache.
Beta blockers Examples: acebutolol (Sectral), atenolol (Tenormin), betaxolol (Kerlone), carvedilol (Coreg), metoprolol (Lopressor, Toprol XL), nadolol (Corgard), penbutolol (Levatol), pindolol (Visken), propranolol (Inderal), timolol (Blocadren)	May boost risk of diabetes. Avoid if you have asthma, emphysema, or chronic bronchitis. Side effects include fatigue, depression, slow heartbeat, and reduced sex drive.
Calcium channel blockers Examples: amlodipine (Norvasc), diltiazem (Cardizem, Dilacor, Tiazac), felodipine (Plendil), isradipine (DynaCirc), nicardipine (Cardene), nifedipine (Adalat, Procardia), nisoldipine (Sular), verapamil (Calan, Isoptin, Covera, Verelan)	May cause gum problems. Do not take if you have heart failure. Interacts with beta blockers and other heart drugs. Do not take with grapefruit juice.
Diuretics Thiazide: chlorothiazide (Diuril), chlorthalidone (Thalitone), hydrochlorothiazide (HydroDiuril, Microzide), indapamide (Lozol) Loop: bumetanide (Bumex), furosemide (Lasix) Potassium-sparing: amiloride (Midamor), spironolactone (Aldactone), triamterene (Dyrenium)	May boost risk of diabetes. May trigger gout, raise cholesterol, and increase risk of gastrointestinal bleeding. Thiazide and loop diuretics reduce potassium levels, which can lead to an irregular heartbeat.

mind that the benefits of these drugs may outweigh the risks. Never stop taking a drug your doctor prescribed without his approval.

Check your BP like a pro

For many people, the intimidating atmosphere of a doctor's office results in higher blood pressure readings. This phenomenon is called "white coat hypertension."

To make sure your doctor's presence is not affecting your blood pressure reading, consider buying a home monitor. Do-it-yourself monitoring may be more convenient, less costly, and even more accurate than standard approaches. It also makes you more likely to keep your blood pressure under control.

A Finnish study found that using a home device works just as well as ambulatory monitoring, which involves wearing a monitor that automatically records your blood pressure over a 24-hour period.

You can buy an aneroid monitor, which comes with a cuff, bulb, dial gauge, and stethoscope, for about $25. If you have hearing or vision problems or arthritis, this manually operated monitor may be difficult for you to use.

More than half of those with sleep apnea also have high blood pressure. Luckily, a technique called continuous positive airway pressure (CPAP), which delivers air through a mask while you sleep, helps both conditions.

Electronic monitors, which range from $35 to $125, come with a cuff that automatically inflates or deflates and a digital screen, making them easier to use. Choose an arm monitor rather than a wrist or fingertip model for a more accurate reading.

No matter which device you use, follow these tips for accurately measuring your blood pressure at home.

▶ Do not smoke or have any caffeine in the 30 minutes before you take your blood pressure.

▶ Sit and rest for 5 minutes before you begin.

▶ Average the results of two or more readings, taken at least a minute apart, to determine your blood pressure.

Remember to get your blood pressure checked by a doctor at least once a year, even if you are monitoring it yourself at home.

High blood pressure linked to insomnia

You may not be too worried about your sleepless nights. After all, if you're tired during the day, you can take naps to catch up. But beware of sleeping too little during the night — you may see your blood pressure jump as a result.

When you sleep, your body relaxes, your heart slows down, and your blood pressure drops. But if you only sleep for short periods at a time, your blood pressure may stay elevated. A recent study showed that sleeping five hours or less a night could boost your risk for this dangerous condition.

If you suffer from insomnia, don't delay getting treatment. It's one condition that affects all aspects of your health.

High cholesterol
Win the war with simple, low-cost tactics

Your body needs cholesterol to function, but you can have too much of a good thing. When you have high cholesterol, you put yourself at risk for atherosclerosis, heart disease, heart attack, and stroke. You may even increase your risk for Alzheimer's disease.

Cholesterol comes in two main forms. LDL, also called "bad" cholesterol, carries cholesterol to your artery walls. HDL, known as "good" cholesterol, whisks cholesterol to your liver and out of your body. You want to lower your LDL levels while boosting your levels of HDL.

Everyone should strive for LDL levels below 160 mg/dL and HDL levels above 40 mg/dL. But new guidelines call for even lower LDL for those at greater risk for heart attack. People at moderate risk should aim for 130 mg/dL or lower, while those at higher risk should shoot for 100 mg/dL or lower. People at the greatest risk should set a goal of less than 70 mg/dL. Your doctor will help you determine your ideal cholesterol goals.

Save a bundle on statins

Now you can lower your cholesterol at a lower price. That's because generic versions of popular brand-name statins have recently hit the market. Two new generics — simvastatin, the generic version of Zocor, and pravastatin, the generic version of Pravachol — joined lovastatin (Mevacor) to give you three, low-cost options.

Generic statins contain the same active ingredients as the brand-name drugs — at a fraction of the cost. Expect to cut your costs by one-third to one-half by switching to generics. If your health insurance covers your medication, you should still save with lower co-payments.

Even if you're taking a statin that does not yet have a generic version, you may still be able to switch to one of the generic statins. All statins work the same way, although some are more potent than others. Statins block an enzyme called HMG-CoA reductase, which your liver uses to make cholesterol. They can lower your LDL cholesterol by 25 percent to 55 percent and boost your HDL cholesterol by 5 percent to 15 percent. Ask your doctor if a generic statin would work for you.

> Boosting your HDL cholesterol level just one point can slash your heart attack risk by as much as 3 percent.

Statins also reduce inflammation, which can play a role in the development of heart disease. They are often prescribed after a heart attack or stroke. Ask your doctor if a generic statin would work for you.

Another way to save money on statins is to split your pills. For example, instead of taking one 40-milligram pill, split an 80-milligram pill in half to get the same effect. You will need to spend about $5 to $20 on a tablet splitter, but since the pills often cost the same regardless of dose, you'll still save money. Talk to your doctor to find out if this strategy is best for you. If he agrees, he'll write a prescription for the high-dose pills.

Statins may help more than your heart. They may lower your risk for cataracts, stop the hepatitis C virus, help with erectile dysfunction, and even fight Alzheimer's disease and cancer. With all these possible benefits, sometimes statins seem like wonder drugs.

But, like all drugs, statins have side effects. These include muscle pain, liver damage, memory loss, and rhabdomyolysis, serious muscle damage that can lead to kidney problems. There have been reports of people experiencing nightmares while taking statins. They can also interact with other drugs, so make sure your doctor knows what other medication you're taking.

With higher doses come higher risks. To be safe, take only the smallest dose necessary to bring your cholesterol level down to where it should be.

Find the right statin at the right price

Statin (brand name)	Reduces LDL cholesterol by	Average monthly cost
Atorvastatin (Lipitor)	34 to 54 percent	$85 to $124
Ezetimibe/simvastatin (Vytorin)	45 to 60 percent	$95 to $98
Fluvastatin (Lescol)	22 to 35 percent	$67 to $89
Lovastatin (Mevacor)	21 to 48 percent	$33 to $148
Pravastatin (Pravachol)	18 to 37 percent	$108 to $159
Rosuvastatin (Crestor))	39 to 60 percent	$95 to $101
Simvastatin (Zocor)	26 to 50 percent	$87 to $154

4 ways to lower cholesterol without statins

Statins may be the best — and best known — of the cholesterol-lowering drugs. But they're not the only option. Some people, like those with liver disorders, cannot take statins. Others can't tolerate their side effects. And some people need more than one drug to get their cholesterol in shape. Here's a look at what else is out there.

▸ Bile acid sequestrants can reduce LDL cholesterol by 15-25 percent and can be combined with any other cholesterol-lowering drug. They include cholestyramine (Questran), colestipol (Colestid), and colesevelam (WelChol).

▸ Nicotinic acid (niacin), available as Niacor or Niaspan, is the most effective way to raise HDL levels. Skin flushing and itching may occur about 30 minutes after taking the drug. Taking an aspirin 30 minutes before taking niacin can help reduce these side effects.

▸ Fibrates, such as fenofibrate (Lofibra, Tricor) and gemfibrozil (Lopid), lower triglycerides, another fat that circulates in your blood, and boost HDL levels. But total and LDL cholesterol may go up. Long-term use may also lead to gallstones.

▸ The cholesterol absorption inhibitor ezetimibe (Zetia) lowers LDL by 18 percent. It's also available in the drug Vytorin, which combines ezetimibe with simvastatin, for more potent anti-cholesterol action.

Healthy habits hammer high cholesterol

Watch television or open a magazine, and you'll see plenty of advertisements for the latest cholesterol-lowering drugs. You might think popping pills is the only way to control your cholesterol. But eating right and making simple lifestyle changes can work just as well as drugs — and may even help you avoid them entirely.

It all starts with your diet. Some foods, like eggs, contain cholesterol, but saturated fats, the kind found in meat and dairy products, raise your cholesterol level more than anything else in your diet. You also want to limit trans fats, the kind found in foods made with hydrogenated oils, like margarine, crackers, cookies, and french fries.

Limit your total fat intake to no more than 35 percent of your daily calories. Less than 7 percent should come from saturated fat. Keep your cholesterol intake below 200 milligrams a day.

On the other hand, you want to eat more soluble fiber, the kind found in oatmeal, barley, beans, apples, and other fruits and vegetables. Aim for 10 to 25 grams of soluble fiber every day. In general, you want to eat more fruits, vegetables, and whole grains, and less meat, cheese, eggs, whole milk, processed foods, and baked goods. Besides sticking to a healthy diet, you should also take the following steps to help lower your cholesterol.

- ▶ **Lose weight.** Being overweight increases your chances of having high LDL and low HDL levels — and a whole host of health problems. To get down to a healthy weight, you must burn more calories than you take in. That means eating less and being more active.

- ▶ **Exercise regularly.** Exercise not only helps you manage your weight, it also helps boost HDL levels. Aim for at least 30 minutes of moderate activity, such as brisk walking, every day.

- ▶ **Quit smoking.** This dangerous habit lowers HDL cholesterol and plays a major role in heart disease.

- ▶ **Reduce stress.** Researchers in London recently found that stress may raise cholesterol levels. Find ways to reduce or deal with stress in your life. Stress-coping strategies include exercising on a regular basis, listening to music, and practicing progressive muscle relaxation.

Even if you successfully stick with these healthy lifestyle changes, you may still eventually need cholesterol-lowering medication. But that doesn't mean you should give up on the healthy habits you've developed. They will help your medication work even better. You may also need lower doses of less-powerful drugs, which would lessen your risk of side effects.

Eat your way to healthy arteries

You know a healthy diet has a huge impact on lowering your cholesterol levels. But when you add these tasty treats to your menu, you might cut your cholesterol even more.

Artichoke. This centuries-old folk remedy contains a compound called cynarin, an ingredient now used in modern cholesterol-lowering medicines. But you can get it from the produce aisle in your grocery store. Just watch how you eat it. Dipping

Sidestep restaurant risks

You might have trouble sticking to your cholesterol-lowering diet when you eat out. But don't despair — here are some helpful tips for avoiding high-fat traps at restaurants.

▸ Italian. Stay away from Alfredo, carbonara, parmigiana, and anything stuffed or fried. Choose entrees described as primavera, piccata, marinara, grilled, or thin crust.

▸ Chinese. Avoid crispy, crunchy, sweet and sour, and fried dishes. Look for steamed dishes and ones containing these words — jum, kow, and shu.

▸ Mexican. Rarely eat nachos, chimichangas, guacamole, and taco salad shells. Fill up on fajitas, soft corn tortillas, salsa or picante, rice, and black beans.

the artichoke leaves in a rich, buttery sauce will do your cholesterol more harm than good. Try a yogurt-based dip instead.

Fish and garlic. Fish, rich in omega-3 fatty acids, and garlic, full of sulfur compounds, team up to fight cholesterol. This dynamic food duo lowers your LDL better together than either one can do alone. A recent Indian study found that the combination of fish oil capsules and garlic supplements lowered LDL by 21 percent and boosted HDL by 5 percent. Serve up some garlicky fish for dinner. Your cholesterol — if not your breath — will improve.

Regular cholesterol screening is important. Get a complete lipid profile, which includes LDL, HDL, and triglyceride levels, every five years. If you're at risk for heart disease or diabetes, do this even more often.

Flaxseed bread. Why take Lipitor when this amazing bread works like cholesterol-lowering drugs but without the side effects? One study found that people who ate six slices of flaxseed bread every day significantly lowered their cholesterol. This remarkable bread is rich in soluble fiber and omega-3 fatty acids.

Walnuts. Full of omega-3 fatty acids, walnuts have been shown to lower cholesterol in several studies. Just don't go overboard. A handful a day should do the trick.

Grape juice. This artery-cleaning fruit juice is so powerful doctors are recommending it in lieu of drugs with none of their dangerous side effects. Both purple and red grape juice have been shown to lower cholesterol. That's probably because of quercetin, a flavonoid found in grape skins, which works like an antioxidant to prevent LDL cholesterol from building up on your artery walls.

Inside scoop on popular supplements

Many supplements promise they will lower your cholesterol, but not all of them live up to their claims. Here's a quick look at some cholesterol-lowering supplements and what you can expect from them.

Cholest-Off. This combination of plant sterols and stanols blocks cholesterol's absorption into the bloodstream, lowering LDL cholesterol but leaving HDL levels intact. Consider this supplement the 15-cent cholesterol cure — proven to work better than dangerous drugs. This pill has much fewer calories than other phytosterol-fortified products, like Benecol and other margarines. When taken as part of a healthy diet and active lifestyle, it could give your cholesterol an extra downward nudge.

> Attending religious services weekly can help extend your life almost as much as statins and exercise, according to a recent University of Pittsburgh study.

B vitamins. Niacin and B12, two vitamins found in many dairy products, could help you avoid prescription drugs by lowering cholesterol, improving circulation, and even relieving depression. Niacin in supplement form can reduce LDL levels by as much as 20 percent and raise HDL by as much as 35 percent. Some strengths of niacin are available only with a prescription. Niacin should only be taken under your doctor's supervision.

Flaxseed. Lower your bad cholesterol levels with this natural supplement. It has no dangerous side effects and costs 50 percent less than leading prescriptions. Studies have shown flaxseed can lower cholesterol by as much as 15 percent. To take advantage of flaxseed's benefits, you must grind up the seeds — or buy them already ground.

CoQ10. This supplement does not actually affect your cholesterol, but it may come in handy to counteract the side effects of statins. According to researchers at Columbia University, people who experience muscle pain while taking statins have low levels of coenzyme Q10 in their blood. More research is needed, but perhaps taking supplemental CoQ10 can help protect you from muscle pain and muscle damage.

Guggul. This herb has received mixed reviews. While some studies show it lowers cholesterol, a recent University of Pennsylvania study found it might actually raise LDL cholesterol if taken in high doses. What's more, University of Kansas researchers found that guggul interacts with cholesterol-lowering drugs, including statins, making them less effective.

Policosanol. This supplement, derived from sugar cane, seems to be a sham. A recent German study found that policosanol works no better than placebo in lowering cholesterol. Previous supportive studies for policosanol were conducted by leading sugar cane producers in Cuba.

Dollars&Sense
Get the inside scoop on the FDA

One of the main jobs of the Food and Drug Administration (FDA) is to regulate prescription and over-the-counter drugs. Drug companies can't even think of selling a new treatment until they test it extensively and prove to the FDA that it is safe and effective.

The road to FDA approval is long and expensive. Drug companies spend an average of eight and a half years testing compounds in the laboratory, then in animals, and finally in people before they can even ask for permission to sell a drug. Then, the FDA goes through a lengthy review process, looking at the evidence from studies to decide if a new drug's benefits outweigh its risks.

For every medicine the FDA approves, thousands more never make it. Only about five out of every 5,000 chemical compounds tested in the lab eventually get tested in people. Odds are, only one of those five will be safe and effective enough to get approved for sale.

The FDA's drug review process is considered the gold standard throughout the world. Still, it has problems, as recalls of high-profile drugs like Vioxx show. A drug can seem safe in studies but turn out to cause additional — and more serious — side effects once more people start taking it. Until a medicine goes on the market, experts don't always know just how safe it really is.

That's why you should stay actively involved in your health care. Question your doctor when he prescribes a new medication. Find out the facts and fine print about the latest "wonder" drug advertised on television.

You'll find more advice on sniffing out the merits of new medications in *5 questions to ask about a new drug* on page 237.

IBD

Secrets for managing distressing symptoms

Your immune system could be making you sick. Although scientists aren't certain what causes inflammatory bowel disease (IBD), they suspect a faulty immune system could trigger inflammation in your intestinal walls. That causes frequent and sometimes bloody diarrhea, abdominal pain, and other symptoms that flare-up and then fade — until the next flare-up.

The two main kinds of IBD are Crohn's disease (CD) and ulcerative colitis (UC). CD can affect your entire digestive system, whereas UC affects your large intestine, or colon.

Reaching a diagnosis can take many months and tests because IBD symptoms mimic other conditions, like appendicitis. Researchers say genetics play a role, so you're more likely to have it if someone else in your family has it. While there's no cure for IBD, there are many effective treatments and self-help strategies.

Explore natural remedies for less

Work with your doctor to find out which of these remedies could help relieve your symptoms. Then learn how to buy them for less.

Fish oil. Although steroid drugs are powerful anti-inflammatories, they can have serious side effects. Fish oil contains natural anti-inflammatories called omega-3 fatty acids. Scientists say fish oil supplements may help prevent CD relapses and reduce the amount of steroids needed to control UC symptoms.

Zinc. This important mineral fights inflammation and promotes healing. Ask your doctor whether you need zinc supplements, especially if you have Crohn's. Zinc deficiency may raise your risk of fistulas — abnormal passageways between organs caused by infection, inflammation, injury, or surgery.

Research suggests people with IBD are at higher risk for certain illnesses. Ask your doctor if you need screenings for osteoporosis, anemia, colon cancer, or other conditions connected with IBD.

Folic acid. Ask your doctor about folic acid supplements if you take methotrexate, an immune system suppressor that blocks the action of folic acid. IBD may also hamper your ability to absorb other nutrients, causing vitamin and mineral deficiencies.

Psyllium. Doctors recommend psyllium, the active ingredient in Metamucil and Fiberall, for mild or moderate diarrhea. One study even suggested psyllium might cut UC flare-up risk as effectively as the drug mesalamine.

Curcumin. This compound gives the spice turmeric its bright yellow color. According to research, it may help fight inflammation in your intestines. You'll find turmeric, the main ingredient in curry, in many Asian and Indian dishes. Supplements are available for people who can't eat spicy foods.

Sulforaphane. Some scientists think a bacterium called *Mycobacterium avium paratuberculosis* (MAP) can trigger Crohn's. MAP can infect cows, which pass the bacterium to you through their milk. Once in your digestive system, MAP might trigger CD. Although more research is needed, two scientists from Johns

Hopkins University School of Medicine think the sulforaphane in broccoli might help kill MAP. Brassica Protection Products, the company they founded, sells sulforaphane-rich products, like BroccoSprouts and Brassica teas. For more information, call toll-free 877-747-1277 or visit *www.brassica.com*.

Bromelain. Fresh pineapple contains an enzyme called bromelain. Some doctors report that bromelain supplements helped heal the colon lining of people with mild UC. Experts suggest using supplements because you might not get enough bromelain from fresh pineapple.

Talk with your doctor before trying these remedies. Some aren't safe for people who have certain health conditions or take medication.

If your doctor approves, you're ready to start looking for the best prices. The following companies may offer below-retail discounts. Call their toll-free numbers to order a free catalog or simply shop online.

▸ The Vitamin Shoppe — 800-223-1216 or *www.vitaminshoppe.com*

▸ Swanson Health Products — 800-824-4491 or *www.swanson vitamins.com*

▸ VitaCost — 800-793-2601 or *www.vitacost.com*

Just remember to play it safe. Call your local Better Business Bureau to learn more about a company before you buy from them.

Promising drug-free remedy promotes healing

People with IBD often have very few "friendly" bacteria in their gut. These bacteria help fight inflammation and harmful bacteria — but only if you have enough of them. Here's a way to get more.

Probiotic foods, like yogurt and yogurt drinks, contain live bacteria similar to the good ones living in your intestines. Experts recommend up to 10 billion probiotic bacteria daily. That's about the amount in a cup of plain yogurt, as long as the label promises live cultures.

If you can't tolerate yogurt, consider probiotic supplements. Research shows that the supplement VSL#3 may relieve Crohn's, ulcerative colitis, and even pouchitis, a surgical complication. Ask about VSL#3 at high-quality health food stores and pharmacies or visit *www.vsl3.com*.

Other probiotic supplements may help, too. In fact, one study of people with UC showed that those who got 18 billion *Lactobacillus GG* bacteria daily were no more likely to have relapses than people taking the drug mesalamine.

For the best value, remember these three tips.

▶ When buying yogurt and yogurt drinks, like DanActive, read labels and pick products that display the expected number of bacteria alive at the time of use, not the time of manufacture.

▶ Store probiotic foods in your refrigerator to extend their shelf life.

▶ Shop at discount stores, like The Vitamin Shoppe, to pay less for probiotic supplements.

Clever tactic pinpoints problem foods

Foods might not cause IBD, but some foods can ignite your symptoms or make them worse. Fortunately, you can expose these troublemakers with a food and symptom diary. Here's how.

Keep a detailed record of your symptoms, when they happen, what you ate, and when you ate it. Use that information along with the "likely suspects" list on the following page to help track down problem foods. Try weeding them out of your diet to see if your symptoms improve.

- Milk and milk products. People with IBD are often lactose intolerant.

- High-fat, greasy, or fried foods. These foods can trigger diarrhea, cramping, and gas.

- Dried fruits, caffeinated drinks, and high-sugar foods, like watermelon and grapes. They can promote inflammation.

- Alcohol, red meat, and processed meats. These foods can set off CD or UC symptoms. What's more, diets high in red meat and alcohol may triple your risk of UC relapse.

- Prunes, fresh cherries, and peaches. These fruits can act as laxatives.

- Bread and potatoes. Up to 40 percent of people with CD can't absorb these and other carbohydrates. If carbs are a problem for you, talk with your doctor.

- Wheat, oats, rye, and barley. These grains contain gluten, which can cause abdominal pain, gas, and diarrhea in some people.

- Tomatoes, eggs, and peanuts. These foods are common allergens. Corn can also cause digestive problems.

- Red pepper and other fiery spices. Spicy hot foods often ignite symptoms.

Prevent dehydration from diarrhea with this inexpensive drink. Mix 3/4 teaspoon of salt, 1 teaspoon of baking soda, and 4 tablespoons of sugar into 4 cups of water and 1 cup of orange juice.

Fiber is important for good health, but make sure you choose your fiber wisely. In his book, *The Maker's Diet*, Jordan S. Rubin, a naturopathic doctor, advises against eating the insoluble bran fiber in grains and cereals. Rubin recommends berries, celery, fruits, and vegetables with edible skins, and other low-carbohydrate foods high in fiber. Other experts warn that cruciferous vegetables, like broccoli and cauliflower, may cause trouble, especially when eaten raw.

3 easy ways to prevent flare-ups

You can make simple dietary changes to help prevent symptoms and flare-ups. Start with the ones your body will tolerate, and talk to your doctor about the rest.

Rejuvenate with fluids. Drink plenty of refreshing water to keep your body hydrated. To avoid dehydration from diarrhea, try broth, soup, and vegetable juice. They provide potassium and sodium — electrolytes your body needs. Don't rely on sports drinks, such as Gatorade, to replace lost fluids. They have relatively low amounts of electrolytes.

Replenish your proteins. When diarrhea depletes your protein supply, eat protein-rich foods like poultry, lean meat, beans, and rice. Fatty fish is also a good choice. Their omega-3 fatty acids may help prevent CD relapses and reduce the need for some UC drugs. Although some fish contain high levels of contaminants, like mercury, the Food and Drug Administration says most people can safely eat up to two servings a week of fatty fish, like salmon, sardines, and lake trout.

Hamper IBD's henchmen. Some researchers believe unstable molecules called free radicals play a role in IBD and its severity. But antioxidants like selenium, vitamin C, and vitamin E may render free radicals harmless. Eat foods rich in these powerful nutrients.

And remember this. It's not just what you eat, but how. Switch from three large meals to six smaller ones spread throughout the day. You may be surprised at the difference it makes.

Root out common cause of IBD symptoms

New research shows that people who take the prescription acne-fighter isotretinoin (Accutane) have a higher risk of developing IBD. In addition, the asthma drug, zafirlukast (Accolate) may play a role in UC. If you take either of these medications, talk to your doctor. You might be able to switch to a different drug or take other precautions.

Over-the-counter painkillers, like aspirin, naproxen sodium (Aleve or Naprosyn), and ibuprofen (Advil or Motrin), can irritate your digestive tract and trigger symptoms. Unless you take them to help prevent heart attack, stroke, or another serious condition, talk to your doctor about safer choices.

> To help fight inflammation and prevent symptoms, find ways to reduce and manage your stress. Slow, deep breathing is a good place to start.

New hope when old drugs fail

Standard treatments don't always relieve IBD, so doctors constantly seek new options. Here's a preview of exciting new uses for existing drugs and coming attractions.

▸ Remicade (infliximab) is used to treat IBD that doesn't respond to standard therapies. Unfortunately, some people develop resistance to this drug.

▸ Humira (adalimumab) is FDA-approved for rheumatoid arthritis, but it might also relieve IBD if Remicade stops working.

▸ Cimzia (certolizumab) could come to the rescue if Remicade fails. It's also more convenient to use than Remicade. Cimzia is currently awaiting FDA approval.

▸ Anti-interleukin-12 injections help prevent an immune system reaction that leads to the inflammation in Crohn's.

▸ Heparin, a blood thinner, may fight ulcerative colitis when steroids don't work, preliminary research suggests. More research is needed, so stay tuned.

▸ Antibiotics help treat infections and other complications of Crohn's disease, but preliminary studies suggest antibiotic combos might be even more powerful. In a preliminary British trial using the combination of rifabutin and clarithromycin or azithromycin, nearly 94 percent of the study participants went into remission. Two-thirds remained in remission for two years. This antibiotic treatment is still experimental.

Never stop taking your IBD medication without your doctor's approval. You could trigger a severe relapse. Instead, talk with him about trying new treatments.

The latest buzz on exciting new treatments

Over 70 percent of people with active Crohn's disease went into remission after six months of TSO therapy, researchers report. Created by a gastroenterologist, TSO is a supplement of harmless-to-humans pig whipworm eggs. For more information, ask your doctor to contact the German company Ovamed GmbH, Kiebitzhörn 33-35, 22885 Barsbüttel, Germany.

If medication isn't helping your ulcerative colitis, ask your doctor about trying an over-the-counter nicotine patch. One study suggested nicotine patch users were twice as likely to go into remission after six weeks as people taking a placebo. However, the nicotine patch is controversial. It can cause side effects, and some people shouldn't use it.

Although these experimental treatments show promise, the FDA has not approved them at this time.

Incontinence

Can't-miss tips for a leaky bladder

Over 200 million people have loss of bladder control, or urinary incontinence (UI). Many of them find the situation so embarrassing, they won't even tell their doctors. Women are more often affected than men. In fact, six out of every seven adult cases of UI occur in women. The female anatomy, as well as pregnancy, childbirth, and menopause, contribute to the problem.

There are two main types of UI — stress incontinence and urge incontinence. When you have stress incontinence, urine escapes because of weak pelvic muscles and sudden pressure on your bladder. Laughing, exercising, sneezing, and coughing can trigger it. With urge incontinence, the need to urinate comes faster than you can get to a toilet. This type is more common in the elderly.

See your doctor if you have bladder control problems. He can suggest simple behavioral strategies as a first-line defense or prescribe medication to help you.

Super strategy for better bladder control

Simple exercises called Kegels are a great way to strengthen the pelvic floor muscles that control urine flow. More than 75 percent of women participating in a pelvic muscle training study reported improvement in their urinary incontinence symptoms.

The most important part of doing Kegels is locating the correct muscles to contract. Here's how to start. Sit comfortably with your legs uncrossed and your buttocks, abdominal, and thigh muscles relaxed. Remember to breathe normally. Next, pretend you are trying to stop urinating. Keep these muscles tense for about 10 seconds, then relax. Repeat this tensing and relaxing 10 times, three times a day. To really strengthen these muscles, try three different positions — lying, sitting, and standing.

When you're doing Kegels, don't tighten your leg, stomach, or other muscles. This can put pressure on the muscles that control your bladder. If you aren't sure you're exercising the right muscles, ask your doctor or other health professional for help.

Kegels help in other ways, too. To keep stress incontinence under control, tighten your pelvic floor muscles just before lifting or doing other things that cause urine leakage, like coughing and sneezing. When urge incontinence strikes, do Kegels to help you get to the bathroom in time.

Soothe and protect your skin

When your skin comes in contact with urine for any length of time, it can become irritated or infected. Always wear undergarments that keep dampness away. If you have an "accident," clean the affected areas as soon as possible. Wash with warm — not hot — water and a cleanser designed for incontinence that allows frequent cleaning without drying out or irritating your skin. After bathing, use a moisturizer and a water-repellent barrier cream that protects your skin from urine.

Be patient. You may not see any improvement for six to eight weeks. Kegels, like any muscle-building plan, require practice, and doing them faithfully will pay off for you. Then again, don't overdo it. Overworking those muscles can cause pain.

Set a schedule to curb the urge

You can improve most cases of urinary incontinence by using self-help remedies. Kegel exercises are a good example. Another is bladder training, a technique designed to lengthen the time between bathroom visits.

Start out by going to the bathroom every one to two hours, whether you feel the need or not. As you gain control, gradually increase the time between trips until you are only urinating every three to four hours.

If you get an urge to urinate sooner than your scheduled time, stay where you are and wait until the urge passes. Then slowly make your way to the bathroom, even if you don't think you need to. Relaxation techniques, like breathing slowly and deeply, can help you control the urge.

> One survey found that 64 percent of people with incontinence don't do anything about it. And most adults wait an average of six years before discussing symptoms with their doctor.

Instead of a set schedule, some people can learn to put off urination after they first have the urge to go. Start by trying to hold your urine for five minutes. After you master five minutes, go for 10 and so on until you reach the goal of every three to four hours between bathroom stops.

As with Kegel exercises, bladder training is not an instant fix. It can take three to 12 weeks before you see any improvement.

5 ways to halt a leaky bladder

It might surprise you to find out that what you eat and drink, as well as your lifestyle, can have a considerable impact on incontinence. Why not make a few changes to help you control your leaky bladder.

Maintain a healthy weight. Carrying around excess weight weakens pelvic floor muscles. That's another good reason to stay at a healthy weight. If you're already overweight, taking off some pounds might solve your bladder control problem. In one study, overweight or moderately obese women decreased their incontinence accidents by 53 percent following a three-month weight loss program.

Women who have had a hysterectomy are 60 percent more likely to have urinary incontinence after they reach age 60.

Watch what you eat. Many foods can affect your ability to hold urine. Citrus fruits and juices, tomatoes, spicy foods, chocolate, sugars and honey, artificial sweeteners, and milk and milk products are known offenders. Carbonated, alcoholic, and caffeinated beverages — including tea and coffee — can also cause problems. Try eliminating one item a day over a 10-day period and see if it improves your symptoms.

Keep yourself "regular." Constipation contributes to incontinence, too. Eating fiber-rich fruits, vegetables, and whole grains — and drinking plenty of water — will keep constipation at bay. Exercising regularly also helps.

Stop smoking. Tobacco smoke affects your bladder and urethra, the tube that carries urine from your bladder to the outside of your body. In addition, smoker's cough places stress on your bladder, which can cause leaking. It's never too late to quit. Ask your doctor for help.

Check your medicine cabinet. Another cause of incontinence could be hiding in your medicine cabinet. High blood pressure pills, cold remedies, and other medications could cause problems. Recent studies have also found that estrogen, once thought to prevent incontinence, can increase your risk of developing it. If you already have a leaky bladder, estrogen can make it worse.

Talk to your doctor or pharmacist if you think medication you are taking could be causing bladder control problems. Just remember — never stop taking a drug your doctor prescribed without his approval.

What to expect from your doctor

Urinary incontinence is not a consequence of aging, and nearly everyone with a bladder control problem can be helped. Unfortunately, less than half of the people with incontinence tell their doctors, and two-thirds of doctors don't ask their patients about it. Many doctors are as embarrassed as their patients to talk about it, or they don't know how to treat it. If this is the case, ask your doctor to refer you to a urologist or urogynecologist. Both types of doctor specialize in treating bladder and urinary problems, but a urogynecologist only treats women.

Why you need to drink more water

Don't try to control your incontinence by drinking less water. Fewer fluids concentrate your urine, which irritates your bladder and urethra and leads to more leakage rather than less. Stronger urine also smells worse and calls more attention to you if you have an accident. Some experts say you need two to three quarts of fluids a day. Be sure to stop drinking two to four hours before bedtime, especially if you are prone to nighttime accidents.

The doctor will ask you for your medical history. Make sure you tell him about any past and present health problems and surgeries. Also, be prepared to give him the following information:

▶ when the problem first started

▶ how frequently you urinate

▶ the amount of fluids you take in every day

▶ how often you drink alcoholic or caffeinated beverages

▶ what you are doing when you have urine leakage

▶ names of medications you are taking

You can also expect a physical examination and several tests to determine the health of your urinary tract. If your doctor diagnoses your condition as urinary incontinence, he will probably suggest one of these treatments.

Behavioral techniques. Pelvic floor muscle exercises, or Kegels, and bladder training are usually the first line of treatment.

Medication. Your doctor may also prescribe medication to relax an overactive bladder or tighten the sphincter muscles that keep your bladder closed.

Surgery. If conservative treatments fail, your doctor might suggest one of nearly 200 surgical procedures. To choose the best one for you, he will consider the cause of your incontinence, including any physical abnormalities in your bladder or urethra. Surgery to treat incontinence is usually safe and effective. Just be sure to pick your surgeon wisely. In general, the more times a surgeon has performed the procedure, the safer for you.

Alternative treatments. Ask your doctor if one of these treatments could help you.

▶ an injection of certain materials into the urethra, which adds bulk for more resistance to urine flow

- a medical device, such as a pessary, urethral insert, or urine seal, inserted to prevent leaks

- mild electrical pulses to stimulate the nerves that control bladder function

Secrets for staying dry

Don't let incontinence interfere with your lifestyle. There are many products on the market that will keep you dry — without anybody knowing.

You'll find absorbent pads and underwear at discount stores, drugstores, supermarkets, and medical supply stores. Shop around to get the best price. Become familiar with different products so you'll choose the best one for your needs.

Disposable inserts. These are worn inside your underwear and protect against small leaks. They resemble sanitary napkins or mini-pads, but they are much more absorbent and have a waterproof backing. Feminine hygiene products don't absorb urine very well. You can also get cloth liners that are held in place by waterproof underpants and can be washed and reused.

Adult diapers. Disposable protective undergarments for larger amounts of urine come in a variety of styles, sizes, and absorbency levels. You can get pull-on briefs that you step into just like regular underpants.

Urge incontinence increases your risk of falling by 26 percent. That's because you're more likely to trip in your mad dash to the bathroom, especially at night.

Some are made from thinner, more absorbent materials and fit so it looks like you are wearing normal underwear. Be sure they fit snugly and have the right absorbency for your needs.

Reusable undergarments. Many styles of washable incontinence underwear look much the same as regular panties and briefs. They have waterproof panels and reusable liners. Newer styles have a unique design that wicks moisture away from the skin. They resemble normal underwear, but they are just as absorbent as adult disposable diapers.

Men's drip collectors. These are worn under briefs and are not noticeable with normal clothing. The pouch-like collector is made from absorbent material, has a waterproof backing, and fits over the penis. You can also buy washable briefs and boxer shorts with protective pouches that look and feel like normal underwear.

Find the product that fits your needs

Type of product	Average price	Advantages	Disadvantages
Disposable inserts	34¢ each	Use in regular underwear. You can carry spares in purse.	Best for only light to moderate leakage.
Adult diapers	73¢ each	Variety of styles, sizes, and absorbency. Many look and feel like regular underwear.	Some extra-absorbent styles may be noticeable under clothing.
Reusable undergarments	$20 each	Look and feel like regular underwear. Washable so they cost less in long run.	Higher initial cost. They must be laundered after use.
Men's drip collectors	33¢ each	Disposable pad designed specifically for men.	Lower absorbency.

Insomnia

Drug-free sleep solutions

You lie in bed and stare at the ceiling. You toss and turn. You even try counting sheep. But nothing works. When you suffer from insomnia, bedtime becomes a nightmare. Whether you have trouble falling asleep or staying asleep, you're simply not getting enough sleep.

Insomnia does more than ruin your night and leave you tired the next day — it is hazardous to your health. Sleep deprivation not only raises your risk of having a car accident, it may lead to serious health problems, including diabetes, migraines, and high blood pressure.

Insomnia may be a symptom of another condition, such as anxiety or depression, or a side effect of medication. Make sure you and your doctor rule out these possibilities before treating your insomnia. Read on to discover the safest and most effective remedies to send you to dreamland.

Sleeping pills not worth money or risk

Prescription sleep medicine is big business, and seniors are most likely to take them. New products hit the market regularly, accompanied by expensive advertising campaigns and supportive studies funded by drug companies. But are prescription drugs for insomnia worth the money? A recent Canadian study suggests not. These popular meds cause memory loss, fatigue, even falls and accidents, and the benefits are "unimpressive." If they are in your medicine chest, you may want to reconsider.

With new drugs come new risks of side effects. Most famously, people taking Ambien, the top-selling prescription sleep aid, reported episodes of binge eating in their sleep. Even more alarming, some also experienced episodes of driving while asleep.

Besides the unpleasant side effects, you can also become dependent on sleep aids. While the newer drugs claim not to be physically addictive like the older benzodiazepines, they still may be psychologically addictive. This means you may come to think you can't sleep without them.

Over-the-counter sleep aids may be even worse. They may not work as well as prescription drugs and are even more likely to leave you sluggish the next day. They also become less effective over time.

Remember, drugs should never be your first option when dealing with insomnia. If you do need to use them, use them with care as a short-term solution. See the chart on the following page.

Surprising effect of shorter sleep

Shorter sleep could mean a bigger waistline. Over a 16-year period, women who slept five hours or less per night gained an average of 2.3 pounds more than women who slept seven hours. They were also most likely to experience major weight gain — about 33 pounds. Those who slept six hours a night gained 1.5 pounds more than the seven-hour sleepers. Just one more reason to find a solution to your sleepless nights.

Beware of insomnia drug problems

Drug class	Generic (Brand)	Problems
antihistamines (nonprescription)	diphenhydramine (Nytol, Sleep-Eez, Sominex) doxylamine (Unison)	May leave you drowsy the next day. May not produce restful sleep.
antihistamine plus pain reliever (nonprescription)	diphenhydramine (Anacin P.M., Excedrin P.M., Tylenol P.M.)	Side effects include daytime sleepiness, dizziness, blurred vision, and dry mouth or throat.
benzodiazepines (prescription)	estazolam (ProSom) temazepam (Restoril) flurazepam (Dalmane) quazepam (Doral) triazolam (Halcion)	Side effects include headaches, dizziness, nausea, and temporary memory loss. Risk of dependency.
antidepressants (prescription)	trazodone (Desyrel) amitriptyline (Elavil) mirtazapine (Remeron)	Side effects include dizziness, low blood pressure, constipation, difficulty urinating, tremors, and mental impairment.
"Z" drugs (prescription)	zaleplon (Sonata) zolpidem (Ambien)	Reports of "sleep eating" or "sleep driving" with Ambien. Side effects include headaches, dizziness, and nausea.
other nonbenzodiazepines	eszopiclone (Lunesta) ramelteon (Rozerem)	Must take Lunesta right before bed. Side effects include unpleasant taste, headache, and dizziness.

Natural ways to get a great night's sleep

Better sleep leads to longer life. But, despite what those ads for prescription sleep aids promise, better sleep does not have to come in a pill. Check out these simple, drug-free tips.

▸ **Stick to a sleep schedule.** Go to bed and wake up at the same time each day, even on weekends.

▸ **Stop lying around.** If you're not asleep within 20 minutes, get up and do something else, like read a book or browse through a magazine, until you feel sleepy again.

▸ **Keep your bedroom dark, quiet, and cool.** Consider sleep masks, earplugs, or heavy window shades.

▸ **Avoid caffeine, nicotine, and alcohol.** Caffeine and nicotine can keep you wired and jittery. While a nightcap might seem like a good idea to help you relax before bed, alcohol actually leads to light, interrupted, unsatisfying sleep.

▸ **Boot pets from your bed.** You love the furry little creatures, but they can disrupt your sleep.

▸ **Exercise by day.** Daytime exercise helps you sleep better at night. But don't work out too close to bedtime or you might have trouble dozing off.

▸ **Relax and unwind.** Don't bring your day to a screeching halt. Ease into nighttime. A hot bath may help.

Don't let jet lag spoil your trip

If a temporary change in your sleep schedule, such as traveling to a different time zone, leads to insomnia, your insomnia may only be temporary as well. Often, your sleep schedule will naturally return to normal. In the meantime, it may help to have your meals, go to bed, and get up according to the new time right away. And get outside during the day. Sunlight will help your biological clock adjust faster.

▸ **Lighten up.** Avoid big, heavy meals before bed. You should also limit your beverages. Otherwise, you might have to get up in the night to use the bathroom.

▸ **Get rid of distractions,** like bright lights, a television, or a computer. Turn your alarm clock around so you won't keep staring at it.

▸ **Cater to your comfort.** Make sure you have a good mattress and pillow.

▸ **Put a cap on naps.** If you need a nap during the day, keep it under 30 minutes. Don't nap after 3 p.m.

▸ **Get some sunlight.** Spend at least 30 minutes a day in the sun. This helps control your biological clock and your body's production of the sleep hormone melatonin. If you have trouble falling asleep, an hour of morning sunlight may help.

If these lifestyle changes don't do the trick, try drug-free therapies. You can learn relaxation techniques, like slow, deep breathing. Or contact a sleep clinic and ask for information about sleep restriction and cognitive behavioral therapy — effective but costly treatments.

Turn on some music before you turn in. In a recent study, people between the ages of 60 and 83 improved their sleep when they listened to soothing music at bedtime.

Lull yourself to sleep with herbs

Sometimes the oldest remedies are the best remedies. The next time you have trouble falling asleep, try one of these five healing herbs that may work as well as drugs.

▸ **Valerian.** This is one of the most popular, effective, and versatile herbs for conquering insomnia. Drink it in a tea, swallow it in a capsule, or add five to 10 drops of the aromatic oil to a relaxing bath.

▶ **Chamomile.** Make a soothing cup of tea at bedtime to ease the stresses of the day. If you are allergic to pollen, however, choose a remedy other than this ragweed cousin.

▶ **Passionflower.** This flowering plant is particularly popular in England in preparations for calming the nerves. Brew a flavorful tea from the leaves and stems.

▶ **Hops.** Stuff some of these dried fruits into a small sachet bag or pillow and place it inside your pillowcase. Breathing the vapors from the alcohol in hops is probably what brings on the restful slumber.

▶ **Lavender.** To soak away your cares before bedtime, add a few drops of lavender oil to a warm foot bath. Or light a lavender-scented candle and enjoy the calming aroma.

Northwestern University researchers found that regular physical and social activity helped older people sleep better. Go for a walk, then talk with friends while playing cards or board games.

Keep in mind that just because herbs are natural does not mean they are safe. The Food and Drug Administration (FDA) does not regulate herbs, so you can never be sure exactly what you are getting. Herbs may interact with medication. Always tell your doctor about any herbs you are taking.

Rest easy with a simple supplement

You may not need potent drugs or mysterious herbs to get a good night's sleep. A dietary supplement may do the trick.

Melatonin, a hormone produced by the pineal gland, helps regulate your sleep-wake cycle. It kicks in at night, when it's dark, and promotes sleep. As you age, your body makes less of it, and a deficiency of melatonin may contribute to insomnia.

Fortunately, you can buy melatonin supplements — and millions of people do. However, experts disagree about the effectiveness of these pills.

One study found that melatonin supplements work best when your body is not producing melatonin on its own, such as in daylight hours. So it would help shift workers who sleep in the day or travelers with jet lag, but not most people trying to sleep at night.

Experts at the Massachusetts Institute of Technology say the amount of melatonin you take is key. And, in this case, less is more. They say small doses, such as 0.3 milligrams, work better than large doses, especially over time.

Keep in mind, the FDA does not regulate supplements, and the long-term effects of melatonin remain unknown. If you decide to try melatonin, take it up to 30 minutes before you plan to sleep.

> Women are twice as likely to suffer from insomnia as men. The risk of insomnia also increases with age.

Smart way to shush annoying snoring

Maybe you can't sleep because your spouse snores. Or maybe your own snoring startles you out of your slumber.

Here's an ingenious way to end the "buzz saw blues" without drugs or surgery. Simply sew a tennis ball into the back of your pajamas. This will prevent you from sleeping on your back, the position that makes you most likely to snore.

Other surefire ways to stifle snoring include losing weight, avoiding alcohol before bedtime, quitting smoking, elevating the upper part of your bed, and sleeping on your side.

Snoring is often a symptom of sleep apnea. Talk to your doctor about this serious condition that is widely undiagnosed.

Snack your way to a good night's sleep

A huge meal right before bed may not be the best recipe for a peaceful slumber, but the right snack can help you get some shuteye.

▸ **Cherries.** Just a handful of tart red cherries, or some tart red cherry juice, might do the trick. Cherries contain a significant amount of the sleep hormone melatonin.

▸ **Cheese.** One study found that eating cheese at bedtime helps you sleep and leads to pleasant dreams. Of course, that study was conducted by the British Cheese Board.

▸ **Chili peppers.** A Tasmanian study found that those who regularly ate chilies slept better than those who didn't.

Another good bet is the combination of the amino acid tryptophan and carbohydrates. Tryptophan promotes sleep, while the carbohydrates help deliver the tryptophan from your bloodstream to your brain. Snacks such as tuna on whole wheat or cereal with milk give you a double dose of sleepiness.

Make sure to get plenty of calcium, magnesium, and B vitamins in your diet, as well. They aid in the production of melatonin.

On the other hand, you should avoid certain foods close to bedtime. Spicy, sugary, or fatty foods can interfere with sleep.

Dollars&Sense
5 questions to ask about a new drug

Drug companies work hard to create new products to treat what ails you. But is newer always better? If you are thinking about trying a newly approved drug, first ask your doctor these questions.

Is it worth the extra cost? Television and magazine ads make the newest drugs seem almost too good to be true. But those ads — along with other costs of developing a new drug — mean a new brand-name drug costs more than older versions, and substantially more than their generic counterparts.

Is it better than old drugs? When a new drug receives Food and Drug Administration (FDA) approval, it's certified to be safe and more effective than a placebo. But the FDA does not compare new drugs to other treatments for the same condition. To see how it stacks up to well-established drugs, check the helpful charts at *www.aarp.org/health/comparedrugs/*.

How long has it been around? New drugs have limited testing on certain populations, so sometimes side effects or dangers come to light after more people use the drug. The arthritis drug Vioxx, for example, was pulled in 2004 after being on the market for five years. New studies showed that people who took the drug for 18 months or more doubled their risk of heart attack or stroke compared to those who took a placebo.

What does your doctor really think and why? Doctors, just like you, can be overly impressed with a new drug's promises. But sometimes a new drug may truly be better for your situation. Find out exactly why he is recommending it.

Is it covered by your health insurance? If the drug is not on your list of covered drugs, you'll need to pay for it yourself or file an appeal to ask your plan to pay for it.

Migraines

Reliable relief at your fingertips

Too many people with migraines don't realize they have them. The National Headache Foundation estimates more than half of migraine sufferers have been wrongly diagnosed with sinus and tension-type headaches. Maybe that's because most people think migraines always come with auras — flashing lights, dark spots, and other visual cues. But only one in five people see auras.

Diagnosing and treating migraines is critical. They can cause unnoticed mini-strokes, and women who have migraines with auras face twice the risk of heart disease, heart attack, and stroke as women without migraines.

Why suffer so much when new medicines and natural treatments can prevent attacks as well as ease symptoms? Stop settling for days filled with pain, and start living life on your own terms. You can do it safely without breaking the bank, and this chapter will show you how.

Maximize the power of migraine drugs

Taking migraine medications at specific times, in certain combinations, and in particular ways can boost their effectiveness, and a few clever tips can help cut the cost.

▶ Take triptans as soon as you feel a migraine coming on, while the pain is still mild. This makes them more effective, cuts the number of doses needed, and lowers the risk of headache recurrence.

▶ Discuss with your doctor taking an NSAID (nonsteroidal anti-inflammatory drug) with your triptan. In one study, taking the NSAIDs tolfenamic acid and naproxen sodium along with a triptan kept headaches from recurring better than the triptan alone.

▶ Talk to your doctor about splitting pills. Some high-dose triptans and other drugs can be safely split for great savings.

▶ Start looking for generic triptans. A generic version of sumatriptan (Imitrex) could become available as early as 2007.

▶ Consider combinations. Taking an NSAID, an ergot-derivative such as Cafergot, and the anti-nausea drug metoclopramide may be a cheaper alternative to triptans for some people.

▶ Ask about rescue medications if your regular medicine often fails to prevent attacks. A neuroleptic, sedative, corticosteroid, or DHE rescue drug can help avoid expensive visits to the emergency room.

▶ Use the nasal spray form of migraine medications if you get nauseous or vomit during attacks, or have trouble swallowing.

▶ Consider medications to prevent migraines (beta-blockers, anticonvulsants, antidepressants, serotonin antagonists) if you have more than two attacks a month, use pain relievers more than twice a week, or if pain relievers have stopped working for you.

Dodge hidden hazards of popular prescription

The class of drugs known as triptans makes life easier for millions of migraine sufferers, but like all medications, they can cause dangerous side effects.

Common drugs for migraine symptoms

Drug class	Specific drugs	Things you should know
over-the-counter pain relievers	aspirin/acetaminophen/ caffeine (Excedrin Migraine, Excedrin Extra Strength)	Inexpensive. Best for migraines without vomiting or bed rest. Relieved migraine better than ibuprofen in recent study. Avoid using more than twice weekly.
triptans	sumatriptan (Imitrex) rizatriptan (Maxalt) naratriptan, (Amerge) eletriptan (Relpax)	Take early during attack to boost effectiveness. Rizatriptan provides best value in terms of cost per pill times number of pills needed per attack.
ergot-derivatives	dihydroergotamine (DHE) (nasal — Migranal) ergotamine-caffeine (Cafergot)	Tablets and nasal sprays not as effective as sumatriptan for pain and nausea. Injected DHE does not work as quickly as injected triptan but lasts longer, which can stop headache from returning.
combination drugs	isometheptene mucate/ dichloralphenazone/ acetaminophen (Midrin, Duradrin)	Treat mild to moderate migraine about as well as sumatriptan when taken at first sign of attack.
antiemetics	metoclopramide neuroleptics (promethazine)	Combat nausea and vomiting. Taking metoclopramide with aspirin or other NSAID early in attack about as effective as triptans in people not severely disabled by migraine.
corticosteroids	prednisone (Deltasone) methylprednisolone (Medrol)	Rescue medication for prolonged migraine attack. Cuts risk of recurrence when taken alongside triptans. Use sparingly due to side effects.

Beware of heart problems. Triptans can narrow your heart's blood vessels. Do not take them if you have angina, peripheral vascular disease, uncontrolled high blood pressure, or have had a heart attack or stroke. Use caution if you smoke, are obese, or have diabetes, high cholesterol, or a family history of heart disease or stroke.

Shake rebound headaches. Certain migraine medications can cause chronic headaches if overused. Triptans, opiates, acetaminophen, aspirin, combination pain relievers, and drugs made with caffeine, barbiturates, ergotamine tartrate, and isometheptene have all been linked to chronic migraines. Dihydroergotamine (DHE) has not.

Dodge dangerous interactions. Tell your doctor if you take an antidepressant such as a selective serotonin reuptake inhibitor (SSRI) or selective serotonin/norepinephrine reuptake inhibitor (SNRI). Taking triptans alongside these drugs can cause a life-threatening condition called serotonin syndrome, especially when starting or increasing the triptan dose.

Split Imitrex at your own risk. GlaxoSmithKline, the maker of this drug, warns against splitting it. The pills are not scored, making them difficult to split evenly. They're also covered with a protective coating. Splitting damages this coating, causing the medication inside to begin breaking down. The first half may work fine, but the second half may be useless later.

3 new devices knock out pain

These nifty new gadgets could add to your arsenal of migraine relief. Keep your eyes peeled for these experimental devices to become available in the near future.

Start seeing red. Special red-tinted contact lenses may relieve light-sensitive migraines by blocking all but long wavelength-light from entering the eye. In a small study, people with light-sensitive migraines popped in the red contacts when an attack began. Five people felt complete relief in 10 seconds, while most others noticed a difference within five minutes. In 90 minutes, migraine pain had completely disappeared in all but five people.

Get a whiff of this. Researchers created a small device shaped like a pen that shoots carbon dioxide into one nostril and out the other, quieting the trigeminal nerve that carries migraine pain signals to your brain. More than one-third of people who tried the treatment in a recent study felt their migraines disappear within two hours.

Chocolate may not trigger headaches, after all. Research suggests people often crave sweets before a migraine strikes. The craving, not the chocolate, may signal a coming headache.

Zap away pain. Before a migraine sets in, you get an "electrical storm" in your brain. An experimental treatment called transcranial magnetic stimulation (TMS) uses a device that sends a strong, painless magnetic pulse into brain cells, short-circuiting the brain storm before it leads to a throbbing headache. Sixty-nine percent of people who tried it recently were pain free or only had mild migraine pain two hours later.

5 smart ways to fend off migraines

Certain things seem to trigger migraines, whether a poor night's sleep or a particular food. But you aren't at the mercy of these headaches. Establishing the right routines and eating habits can stop them from ever starting.

Set a sleep schedule. Changes in your sleep pattern, like sleeping in on weekends or going to bed later than usual, set the stage for migraines. Establish a regular sleep schedule and stick to it. Go to bed at the same time on weekends as on weekdays, and aim to get the same amount of sleep each night. See more tips in *Silence headaches with 8 sleep tricks* on the following page.

Eat right and regularly. Overweight and obese people are one-and-a-half times more likely to have chronic migraines. That could be due in part to poor eating habits. Evidence suggests a low-fat diet rich in complex carbohydrates, like whole-grain breads and cereals and legumes, cuts the frequency, duration, and severity of migraines. And don't skip meals — it lowers blood sugar, which can trigger an attack.

Track food triggers. Although no studies prove it yet, doctors and migraine sufferers swear certain foods set off headaches. Watch out for these common culprits.

▸ aged cheeses

▸ monosodium glutamate (MSG)

▸ processed meat, like hotdogs, made with nitrates and nitrites

▸ wine, dried fruits, and other foods containing sulfites

▸ beverages with tannins, such as coffee, tea, red wine, and apple juice

▸ beer and certain liquors

Keep a headache diary. Make an entry each time you have an attack, noting how long it lasts, the severity, and all food, beverages, and medication you took in the 24 hours before the attack, as well as what time you went to bed and woke up that day. Take your diary on doctor visits so he can look for a pattern behind the headaches.

Get moving. Exercise regularly to stay in shape and help relieve stress. Several studies show aerobic exercise, in particular, may help prevent migraines. Brisk walking and bike riding are good choices. Warm up first, since sudden, intense exercise can actually bring on a migraine.

Silence headaches with 8 sleep tricks

Daily migraines wreak havoc on your sleep, which causes more headaches. Making a few simple changes in your sleep habits can stop this vicious cycle, cutting down the number of migraines and their severity.

Sleep experts at the University of North Carolina asked 23 women suffering daily migraines to follow this advice each day.

▸ Do not take naps.

▸ Eat dinner at least four hours before going to bed.

▸ Limit the amount of fluids you drink for two hours before bedtime.

▸ Spend eight hours a night in bed.

▸ Go to bed at the same time every night.

▸ Do not watch television, read, or listen to music in bed.

▸ Use visualization exercises to help you relax and fall asleep faster. Thinking pleasant thoughts calms your mind.

▸ Avoid overusing headache medications.

After six weeks, these women had 29 percent fewer migraines, and their headaches were 40 percent less severe. After 12 weeks, more than half the women had only occasional migraines. The women who failed to follow three or more new sleep habits continued to suffer chronic migraines.

Smart alternatives bring sweet relief

Exciting new therapies are helping migraine sufferers cut back on expensive medications and live healthier, pain-free lives. Talk to your doctor to see if these options are right for you.

Acupuncture. Several strong studies have found acupuncture eases migraine pain and frequency. Experts think the needles may affect the way your brain processes pain. Other experts chalk it up to the placebo effect. Whatever the reason, it seems to work for some people. Discuss it with your doctor and look for a licensed acupuncturist.

Biofeedback. You can train your brain to stop headaches. Biofeedback and neurofeedback (EEG biofeedback) training teach you to control the physiological reactions, such as brainwave activity and muscle tension, that cause migraines, thereby short-circuiting the headaches early on. Look for a specialist certified in biofeedback or neurofeedback. Start by contacting the Biofeedback Certification Institute of America at 303-420-2902 or online at *www.bcia.org*.

Botox. Besides erasing wrinkles, Botox or *botulinum toxin* type A may treat migraines. In two recent studies, migraine sufferers who received Botox injections had fewer headaches and needed less medication to control them. People who had daily migraines and those who had had them for more than 30 years were least likely to benefit. Look for a headache specialist who has experience with Botox and expect to pay out of pocket, since insurance likely won't cover it.

Head off headaches naturally

Costly, conventional drugs aren't the only way to treat migraines. Many people find relief with natural herbs and nutrients. These four supplements show the most promise. As always, tell your doctor about any supplements you take.

Beat the ache with butterbur. This herb may cut migraine frequency in half, but not all supplements are made equal. Herbal experts only vouch for the safety and effectiveness of Petadolex, the most widely tested and used butterbur extract. Most people take it for three months, with excessive burping the most common side effect. Don't buy supplements containing whole butterbur, which is toxic.

Fend off headaches with feverfew. A species of chrysanthemum, feverfew has long been used to cut migraine frequency, and some research supports those claims. In clinical trials, powdered feverfew shows the most success. Only one brand of extract, called MIG-99 seems to work. Chewing the whole feverfew leaf may help, too, but can cause mouth ulcers. Taper the dose gradually if you stop taking feverfew to avoid withdrawal symptoms.

Manage migraines with magnesium. Scientists have linked some migraines to low brain levels of magnesium, and several studies show taking 360 milligrams (mg) to 600 mg of magnesium supplements a day can cut the frequency and severity of these headaches. People low in this mineral tend to benefit the most. People with kidney problems should not take magnesium. You may have to take supplements for three to four months before noticing a difference.

Banish pain with B2. Studies of vitamin B2 for migraines are limited, but early evidence shows it could help. In one study, nearly 60 percent of migraine sufferers taking 400 mg of B2 daily for three months cut their attacks in half. Common side effects include bright yellow urine, increased urination, and diarrhea in some people. Shop specifically for a B2 supplement rather than trying to get 400 mg from a multivitamin. This could put you at risk for an overdose of certain vitamins that can be toxic.

Osteoarthritis

Great ways to manage your pain and budget

You're not alone if you have osteoarthritis (OA). About 20 million Americans have this degenerative joint disease. It's the leading cause of disability in people over age 65, and it affects four out of every five people over age 75.

Since two popular pain-relieving drugs were taken off the market, many people have questioned the safety of their own prescription medications. Some OA sufferers are even turning to natural alternatives.

Keep reading to learn about safe and effective treatments, as well as treatments with dangerous side effects, and how to get the most for your money.

Get wise to the hidden hazards of pain relievers

While many prescription drugs help relieve OA symptoms, some drugs have dangerous side effects. Vioxx, a member of the Cox-2 inhibitor drug family, was pulled off pharmacy shelves for raising heart attack risk. Now it looks like Celebrex, another Cox-2 inhibitor, may have the same problem. In fact, Celebrex may even double your risk of a heart attack and also increase your risk of stroke.

Cox-2 inhibitors fall into the category of nonsteroidal anti-inflammatory drugs (NSAIDs). Many OA sufferers take NSAIDs for their arthritis pain. They're among the best all-around pain relievers in the world, and you don't need a prescription to get the over-the-counter variety — ibuprofen, aspirin, and naproxen.

> Opt for flat-heeled shoes next time you go shoe shopping. They may not be glamorous, but studies show wearing high heels can eventually cause knee OA or make it worse.

But NSAIDs have drawbacks, too. They can cause heartburn, ulcers, and gastrointestinal bleeding; increase your risk of heart failure and heart attack; and triple your risk of kidney failure. Older people with recent health issues are at the highest risk for dangerous kidney problems when they take this medicine.

Some evidence suggests using NSAIDs to relieve pain might make your OA worse. Drug companies don't want you to know that these common pain pills may speed up the breakdown of cartilage. Aspirin and ibuprofen seem to be especially guilty of this crime.

Does this mean you should stop taking NSAIDs? Not necessarily. It means you should talk with your doctor about whether they are right for you — especially if you have a history of high blood pressure or heart disease.

Smart way to protect your stomach

When you take heartburn medication with an NSAID, your risk of digestive problems goes down. Research shows that taking over-the-counter NSAIDs with a proton pump inhibitor, like Prilosec, carries a lower risk of stomach distress than taking the Cox-2 inhibitor Celebrex alone. Surprisingly, Celebrex was thought to cause fewer stomach problems. Plus, over-the-counter NSAIDs are cheaper than Celebrex, so the combo is easy on your stomach and your wallet. Remember — always talk with your doctor before changing medications.

Save money with generic NSAIDs

Drug	Common dose	Average price for generic (100 pills)	Average price for brand name (100 pills)
aspirin (Bayer)	325 mg	$1.99	$6.49
ibuprofen (Advil)	200 mg	$6.99	$8.79
naproxen (Aleve)	200 mg	$6.79	$9.49

Osteoarthritis sufferers use many of the same pain medications as people who suffer from back pain. Check out *The inside story on back pain drugs* in the *Back pain* chapter to learn more about your pain relief options.

Uncover common cause of joint pain

Could the medicine you're taking be the cause of your painful joints? Some medication side effects include joint pain. If you're taking statins for high cholesterol, you may have an increased risk of hip osteoarthritis. Here are 15 more drugs that can cause pain.

▶ adalimumab (Humira)

▶ anakinra (Kineret)

▶ etanercept (Enbrel)

▶ infliximab (Remicade)

▶ vitamin A (Aquasol A)

▶ cefaclor (Ceclor)

▶ cefadroxil (Duricef)

▶ cefditoren (Spectracef)

▶ cefixime (Suprax)

▶ cefpodoxime (Vantin)

▶ cefprozil (Cefzil)

▶ cefuroxime axetil (Ceftin)

▶ cephalexin (Keflex)

▶ cephradine (Velosef)

▶ loracarbef (Lorabid)

Talk with your doctor if you think a prescription drug is causing your joint pain. Never stop taking a prescribed drug without his approval.

Maximize benefits from insurance plan

One in three Americans now uses unconventional therapies to treat their health problems, and 5 percent have used acupuncture to relieve pain.

Because alternative treatments are in such demand, more health insurance companies are willing to cover therapies like acupuncture, massage, and herbal supplements. Last year, almost a third of major employers covered acupuncture in their health insurance plans. There's a good chance yours might, too.

Some arthritis sufferers have turned to bee venom for relief. They let bees sting them up to 100 times in one sitting. You can even mail-order live bees.

Take advantage of those benefits if you can. An eight-week study of people with knee OA found that acupuncture gave them twice as much pain relief as taking drugs alone, and there were no side effects. Although the benefits tapered off over time, if your insurance plan covers acupuncture, several months of relief might be worth it.

Soothe joints with sea supplements

Who knew shellfish and sharks could help relieve arthritis pain? Two popular supplements — glucosamine and chondroitin — may do just that, especially when taken together. Though they are both found naturally in your cartilage, the kind you get in supplements

Helpful advice for people who use a cane

Hold your cane on the opposite side of your pain. Research shows it takes stress off your hips and knees better than walking with your cane on the same side as the painful joint. In fact, not using a cane at all is preferable to using it on the same side.

comes from the ocean. Glucosamine is found in the shells of shellfish, and chondroitin is made from shark cartilage, as well as the cartilage of other animals. It's also made synthetically in a lab.

Some health professionals think glucosamine may even help restore damaged cartilage — something no other arthritis treatment can do. These supplements are best at treating moderate to severe arthritis pain. In fact, when taken together, they may even be as effective as the drug Celebrex and more effective than acetaminophen. Oddly enough, the combination doesn't work as well to relieve the pain and other symptoms of mild arthritis.

Not everyone is convinced glucosamine and chondroitin are worth the cost. Some researchers think the supplements are effective but only at doses higher than you can buy over the counter. And yet, they don't know if higher doses are safe. Stay tuned for the results of studies now in progress.

Because glucosamine is a sugar found in shellfish, if you have diabetes or a shellfish allergy check with your doctor before taking it.

Protect yourself from unsafe remedies

Let's face it. Not every arthritis treatment really works. But some sham treatments aren't just a waste of money — they can be dangerous. The Arthritis Foundation lists these alternative treatments as unsafe:

- arnica *(Arnica montana)*
- aconite *(Aconitum napellus)*
- kombucha tea
- chaparral
- autumn crocus *(Colchicum autumnale)*

- GBL *(gamma-butyrolactone)*
- GHB *(gamma-hydroxybutyrate)*
- 5-HTP *(5-hydroxytryptophan)*
- L-tryptophan
- adrenal, spleen, and thymus extracts

Some alternative treatments are harmless, but they aren't worth the money. SAMe (S-adenosylmethionine), for example, is an over-the-counter supplement that may or may not ease arthritis symptoms. Only one out of 10 studies show SAMe to be effective, and it can cause digestive problems, including diarrhea. What's more, you can pay up to $40 for just 30 pills. Spend your hard-earned dollars on something more reliable — but not on bracelets.

In a recent study, people with knee OA who received a ginger extract twice a day experienced less pain and required fewer painkillers than the people who received a placebo.

Magnetic bracelets have not been scientifically proven to treat arthritis pain, yet Americans spend about $500 million every year on this remedy. While some studies have shown benefits, many doctors think it's only a placebo effect. The same is true for copper bracelets.

Best way to take pressure off your knees

The single most important thing you can do to relieve the symptoms of knee OA is lose weight. For every pound of weight you shed, four pounds of pressure is taken off your knees each time you take a step. If you lost 10 pounds, the load on your knees would be

Exciting new cure for knee pain

Your aching knees may get new life, not through surgery, but through the miracle of Botox, according to a new study that showed the drug decreased severe knee pain 28 percent.

People who suffered from painful knee osteoarthritis experienced relief and improved function from Botox injections after just one month, researchers found. Those who received dummy injections showed no significant decrease in pain.

Although more research needs to be done, researchers are excited about Botox because it has the potential to replace knee surgery as an effective cure for osteoarthritis pain.

48,000 pounds lighter for every mile you walked. That's heavier than three African elephants. No wonder your knees hurt.

Regular exercise will not only help you lose weight, it will keep your joints flexible and strengthen your muscles. Research shows that regular aerobic or weight training exercises will also lessen your pain and improve your walking ability. Balance periods of activity with rest — and vary your routine. Try fitness walking, water aerobics, weight lifting, swimming, cross-country skiing, cycling, or dancing. Just remember to warm up and start slowly.

And here's another great benefit — exercising three or more times a week builds up collagen producers in your knees, making them less painful.

If you aren't sure which exercises are right for you, ask your doctor to refer you to a physical therapist who can develop an exercise program just for you.

Discover sweet relief from tasty treats

You can have a snack and baby your joints at the same time by eating two delicious fruits that relieve arthritis pain better than most drugs. These tasty fruits go above and beyond the call of duty to combat arthritis.

Team up with cherries. This delicious, vitamin-packed fruit is proven to relieve arthritis pain better than aspirin, ibuprofen, and other drugs without stomach upset or other side effects.

Anthocyanins, the pigments that make cherries red, fight painful inflammation by protecting your body from damaging free radicals. In a study at Michigan State University, tart red cherry juice was 10 times more effective in relieving pain and inflammation than aspirin. And cherries won't cause any of the harmful side effects you can get from painkillers like NSAIDs.

> Leeches may not be all bad. German researchers have found that leech saliva may have painkilling properties, and putting the little buggers on achy joints can relieve pain.

If you want to give cherries a try, experts recommend drinking two tablespoons of cherry juice concentrate mixed with one cup of water each day. That's equal to the pain-fighting power of 50 to 60 cherries.

Discover the power of pomegranates. This exotic fruit has received a lot of attention lately for its heart-healthy benefits. What you may not know is how it helps foil arthritis.

Researchers at Case Western Reserve University School of Medicine recently discovered that pomegranate extract protects your joints from enzymes that destroy cartilage. Its antioxidant and anti-inflammatory power, combined with its ability to prevent cartilage deterioration, could make this a safe, effective treatment for OA sufferers.

Although the study was done using pomegranate extract, you might want to eat more pomegranates. This delicious fruit is full of vitamin C, the vitamin that works as well as medicine for relieving your arthritis pain. Your body needs vitamin C to make collagen, a protein that helps build new cartilage and bone. People with OA who don't get enough vitamin C — less than 150 milligrams (mg) a day — will lose cartilage three times faster than people who do. Sweet red peppers, strawberries, and citrus fruits are also high in vitamin C.

Make life easier with these clever products

You don't always need a pill to beat arthritis pain. You can find a variety of products made especially for OA sufferers. Whether it's a heat wrap to stop pain where it starts or a kitchen device that gives your hands a break, you're certain to find something that can make life easier for you.

Turn on the heat for fast relief. Go straight to the source of your pain and place a heat wrap on your achy joint. These devices can ease arthritis pain better than some over-the-counter drugs. Reusable wraps usually contain gel or beads that you warm in your microwave.

Capsaicin, the active ingredient in hot peppers, is an effective arthritis pain reliever. Capsaicin cream, made from dried cayenne peppers, is absorbed through your skin and works by deadening local nerves.

Some disposable wraps use capsaicin, the active component of hot peppers, or menthol to make the painful area feel warm without actually heating your skin. The sensation of warmth lasts about 30 to 60 minutes. ThermaCare disposable wraps use iron that lets off heat when it's exposed to air. These wraps come two in a box for about $7. The warmth from each wrap lasts about eight hours.

Disposables are more convenient, but they can get expensive if you use them every day — more than $1,000 a year. Luckily, you don't have to wear one all the time since the effects last long after you remove the wrap.

Make your home arthritis friendly. Pain isn't the only symptom of osteoarthritis. You have to deal with loss of joint function, too. It's easy to take care of that problem with a few helpful devices around your house. Have trouble opening jars? An automatic jar opener will have that lid off in no time. Can't reach shelves in your closet? Easily grab objects more than 2 feet away with a reach extender. Key turners, book holders, and doorknob levers all turn potentially painful tasks into pain-free ones.

> Mozart and Bach can soothe your achy joints. A study found that listening to classical music eased chronic OA pain by distracting sufferers from their condition.

You can find the latest information about arthritis friendly products and packaging at the Arthritis Foundation's Web site. Go to *www.arthritis.org/resources/sponsors* and click on "Ease of Use Commendation" to find out more about everything from golf club grips to hot tubs.

Dollars&Sense
4 ways to cut prescription drug use

Americans spend billions of dollars on prescription drugs each year. But do you really need all the drugs you take? You may be able to sidestep side effects and save money with these strategies.

Evaluate your situation. Don't assume you need commonly prescribed drugs. Here are some you may want to think twice about.

▸ **Antibiotics.** Just because you have an infection doesn't mean you need antibiotics. Studies show most ear infections and uncomplicated sinus infections clear up without antibiotics.

▸ **Statins.** These drugs, such as Lipitor and Zocor, work well to bring down high cholesterol, but their side effects may include muscle problems, liver damage, and memory loss. The lower the dose you can use, the better. Some research shows changing your diet may work nearly as well as drugs to lower cholesterol.

▸ **Aspirin.** Many people at risk for heart disease take a preventive daily aspirin. But people with a history of certain stomach problems are more likely to develop an ulcer from taking aspirin. This risk may outweigh the benefits for your heart.

Change your lifestyle. To help yourself live longer and avoid heart disease, try exercising and watching your diet instead of popping a pill. These simple moves toward a healthy lifestyle repeatedly prove most effective.

Check OTC options. Sometimes a prescription drug is a stronger version of a cheaper over-the-counter drug. For example, nonprescription Aleve is a less-expensive form of prescription Naprosyn. Ask your doctor to help figure out the correct dose.

Consider your changing situation. As you age, your drug needs change. Make sure you review your medications annually with your doctor. He should help you weigh each one's benefits and risks based on your age, health, and long-term expectations.

Osteoporosis

Fight for stronger bones

Fifty-five percent of Americans over age 50 have osteoporosis, or they are in danger of getting it, reports the National Osteoporosis Foundation (NOF). What's more, you may have no symptoms until this sneaky disease causes a fracture in your wrist, hip, or spine.

Osteoporosis leaches away solid bone until it looks more like Swiss cheese or a lattice fence. This can lead to fractures, as well as loss of height, back pain, or a broken hip.

Although women get osteoporosis more often than men, men who break a hip have higher odds of dying within a year. Both women and men who fracture a hip are more likely to lose their independence. Start fighting back right now to prevent bone damage and its serious consequences.

Protect yourself from shocking side effects

Some medications may increase your risk for brittle bones, falls, fractures, and other health problems. For example, Worstpills.org reports that steroid medicines can raise your risk of brittle bones, and the anti-anxiety drug Xanax can make you more prone to falls. Ask your doctor or pharmacist to check your medications for any drug that might weaken your bones or make you drowsy or dizzy. Alternatives without these side effects may be available.

Controversy is raging over a suspected side effect of alendronate (Fosamax), risedronate (Actonel), ibandronate (Boniva), and other bisphosphonate drugs, which strengthen bones. Osteonecrosis of the jaw, a rare rotting of the jawbone, develops in as many as 10 percent of cancer patients who take high doses of bisphosphonates intravenously. But a smaller number of cases have been reported in people taking lower-dose bisphosphonates for osteoporosis, usually for several years. More research is needed because doctors aren't sure how common this disease is, and they lack the evidence to issue guidelines about osteonecrosis risk.

> Taking naproxen sodium (Alleve) with Fosamax could raise your risk of ulcers. Doctors suspect frequent use of other NSAIDS, like aspirin and ibuprofen, with bisphosphonates might raise your risk, too.

Meanwhile, dentists and oral surgeons are debating whether people taking bisphosphonates should avoid invasive dental procedures, like tooth extraction, or if stopping the drug for several months before the procedure would help. Talk to your doctor, dentist, and oral surgeon about osteonecrosis, especially if you've experienced complications after an invasive dental procedure.

Long-term use of bisphosphonates hinders bone turnover, which is essential for healthy bones. Some doctors proposed that people stop taking bisphosphonate after five years. However, you should never stop taking any medicine without your doctor's approval. Talk with him about whether you should continue taking biophosphonates.

If your doctor recommends a bisphosphonate for osteopenia, a precursor to osteoporosis, ask him about your risk of fracture and find out if you can try nondrug alternatives first.

Bone up on osteoporosis drug concerns

Drug class	Generic (Brand)	Consumer concerns
Bisphosphonates	alendronate (Fosamax) risedronate (Actonel) ibandronate (Boniva)	Take the pill with a full glass of water at least 30 minutes before the day's first meal. Stay upright at least 30 minutes after taking the pill. If you have difficulty swallowing, chest pain, or heartburn, see your doctor right away. Once-a-week doses of these medicines are available, and Boniva comes in a once-a-month pill.
Selective estrogen receptor modulator (SERM)	raloxifene (Evista)	May cause hot flashes or other menopause symptoms. May raise your risk of blood clots and fatal stroke. Talk with your doctor about stopping this drug before surgery, prolonged bed rest, or a long flight.
Human parathyroid hormone	teriparatide (Forteo)	Only drug that stimulates bone growth. Unlike most treatments, benefits may continue after the drug is stopped. Side effects include dizziness, nausea, and leg cramps. Animal studies suggest a possible risk of bone tumors. Only available as an injection.
Hormonal bone resorption inhibitor	calcitonin (Miacalcin, Fortical)	Used to treat, not prevent, osteoporosis. Available as an injection or nasal spray. Some people may develop an allergy to this drug over time. Side effects include flushing, diarrhea, nausea, and vomiting (injection) and nasal irritation (nasal spray).
Hormone replacement therapy (HRT)	estrogen/ progesterone (Premarin, Estrace)	HRT is no longer recommended as a first choice for treating osteoporosis.

Get the lowdown on regular screening

Health professionals recommend osteoporosis screening for any man or woman who has had a fracture or any woman age 65 or older. They also recommend that postmenopausal women under age 65 be tested if they have one or more of these risk factors.

▶ having a small frame

▶ being a smoker

▶ having a family history of fractures

▶ using steroids for longer than three months

Medicare will cover the cost of a painless DEXA or DXA bone density scan once every two years if you are an estrogen-deficient woman declared at risk for osteoporosis by her doctor — or for any of these reasons.

▶ An X-ray shows you have problems with your vertebrae, or bones of the spine, with possible osteoporosis, low bone mass, or vertebral fractures.

▶ You have taken daily steroids equal to at least 7.5 milligrams (mg) of prednisone for longer than three months.

▶ You have primary hyperparathyroidism, a thyroid disease.

Medicare may also cover more frequent screenings if your doctor recommends them. As of 2006, you pay only 20 percent of the Medicare approved amount for the screening after your yearly Part B deductible.

Bone density scans done at shopping centers, or ultrasounds offered at health fairs, may not accurately predict your risk for fractures. A third scan called Quantitative Computed

The makers of the shoe-hugging product, Yaktrax, claim it will help prevent falls in wintry conditions. Ask about it at Ace Hardware, REI, or Dick's Sporting Goods.

Tomography (QCT) exposes you to radiation and may not give you accurate results either.

Eat your way to tougher bones

Nab these nutritional tips to help keep your bones strong and healthy.

▸ Eating 12 dried plums a day could contribute to healthier bones in just a few months, according to a study at Oklahoma State University.

▸ Research has linked vitamin B12 deficiency to bone loss and fractures in older women. Get extra B12 from foods like fish, poultry, milk, and fortified breakfast cereals.

▸ High amounts of vitamin A from retinol, found in foods of animal origin, may boost your hip fracture risk. Get up to 40 percent of your vitamin A from beta carotene instead. Carrots, sweet potatoes, and apricots are good sources. Check your multivitamin bottle to see where your vitamin A comes from.

▸ The DASH diet for high blood pressure could help protect against osteoporosis, too. To get started on this mineral-rich diet, eat veggies, fruits, and whole grains daily. Limit salt to retain calcium. Avoid saturated fat but include calcium-rich nonfat or low-fat dairy products. Get some of your protein from oily fish, like salmon, which is high in vitamin D. For more information, visit *www.nhlbi.nih.gov*.

> To get vitamin D from light canned tuna, buy the kind packed in oil. Canned light tuna in water is D-free.

Fend off fractures with vitamin K

Why take Fosamax when these delicious vegetables slash your risk of weak bones and hip fractures! Kale, turnip greens, broccoli, and spinach are all rich in vitamin K — a key ingredient for building and strengthening bones. Even better, research shows that just getting more of this vitamin helped cut women's risk of hip fracture. But don't freeze K-rich veggies if you want their full value. Freezing destroys vitamin K.

And that's not all. Researchers have discovered a higher risk of hip fractures in men who take warfarin, a commonly used blood thinner, for more than a year. Scientists suspect warfarin affects the strength of your bones because it interferes with vitamin K.

Recent research suggests that supplements of another form of vitamin K might show more bone-fortifying promise than regular vitamin K. So keep an eye out for news about vitamin K2, and talk with your doctor to learn more. Meanwhile, you can get small amounts of K2 from chicken and cheddar cheese.

Defend bones with calcium

Get enough calcium regularly, and you'll be more likely to keep your bones strong and prevent a fracture. It's easy to get calcium from food. Start with low-fat dairy products. Add calcium-fortified versions of foods like orange juice, oatmeal, cereal, waffles, and energy bars. Top off by sneaking nonfat dry milk into recipes, and eat foods like kale, sardines, turnip greens, and salmon.

Just be sure you absorb the calcium in the foods you eat. Caffeine might keep many people from absorbing calcium and may also play a role in bone loss and hip fractures. Play it safe and limit or avoid caffeinated beverages like tea, soda, and coffee. But there's even more.

You'll absorb more of your Actonel, Fosamax, or Boniva if you take it with plain water only and don't eat or drink anything for two hours afterward.

A chemical called oxalate, found in spinach, rhubarb, nuts, chocolate, tea, wheat bran, and strawberries, can also block calcium absorption. And dried beans contain phytate, a less-powerful calcium blocker. If you like these foods, just make sure you eat them an hour before or two hours after eating calcium-rich foods or taking calcium supplements.

Here's another smart idea. You can disarm phytates by soaking the beans for several hours, draining well, and cooking them in fresh water.

All that calcium won't do your bones any good if you aren't getting enough vitamin D. Your body needs vitamin D to absorb calcium. Salmon, fortified milk, and eggs are good sources.

Get more value from calcium supplements

Tests show that some supplements won't dissolve enough to deliver the calcium you paid for. What's more, some tablets contain lead — including several coral calcium brands. To dodge both problems, look for a supplement with the United States Pharmacopeia (USP) symbol on it. This means the supplement is free of dangerous amounts of lead and other toxic metals, and it will break down so your body can use it.

Worried you're not absorbing the calcium from your supplement? Drop one in a glass of white vinegar for 30 minutes. If it breaks down, the supplement will be absorbed well.

Choose the right form. Read supplement labels to find out which form of calcium a supplement contains. Coral calcium may not be your best value. The Federal Trade Commission has charged the people marketing this product with making unsubstantiated claims. Consider these forms of calcium instead and decide which one is right for you.

Calcium carbonate	Calcium citrate
40 percent of pill is calcium	24 percent of pill is calcium
Side effects may include constipation and bloating	Best choice for people who take acid blocker medicines or have low stomach acid or other digestive problems
Must take with food	Can take without food
Less expensive	More expensive
Interferes with iron absorption	Doesn't interfere with iron absorption like most calcium supplements
Difficult for your gut to absorb	Better absorbed but the pills are larger, and you have to take more of them

Take the right dose. Ask your doctor how much calcium you need. Most older adults require 1,200 mg each day. You need less calcium from supplements if you get more of this mineral from food. Read labels to estimate how much calcium you get daily from dairy products and calcium-fortified foods. Subtract that from the amount you need.

If you also take Tums antacids regularly, count how many tablets you use daily. According to the makers of Tums, one "regular strength" tablet gives you 200 mg of calcium, while "maximum strength" provides 400 mg.

Next, figure out how much calcium your body can harvest from a particular supplement. The NOF suggests you find the "percent daily value" on the label and tack on a zero. For example, a tablet with 60 percent daily value supplies 600 mg of calcium.

But don't forget that your body can't absorb more than 500 mg of calcium at a time. For a better value and better bones, consider small dose tablets that will allow you to get a few hundred milligrams of calcium every few hours.

Increase absorption. You may get little or no calcium if you take a calcium supplement with steroids. Ask your doctor or pharmacist if drugs you are taking can keep you from absorbing calcium.

> Research shows that a once-a-month version of Boniva is just as effective and well-tolerated as the daily version.

Vitamin D helps your body absorb calcium. It also strengthens your legs and muscles, which could prevent falls. Ask your doctor about vitamin D deficiency and find out if you need supplements. Before you buy a vitamin D supplement, check to see if your existing supplements contain vitamin D. Too much vitamin D could be dangerous.

Save money. If you take calcium supplements to treat osteoporosis or your doctor has recommended calcium supplements, you may be able to pay for the pills with pre-tax money from your flexible spending account. Call your plan administrator to find out.

Or consider buying discounted supplements from Freeda Vitamins, Inc. Call 800–777–3737 for a free catalog or visit *www.freedavitamins.com*. You can also try *www.drugstore.com* or *www.allstarhealth.com*.

Fun ways to fight bone loss

Exercise is a powerful weapon to strengthen your bones and reduce your risk of falls. Although you need 90 minutes of moderate exercise a week, you don't have to do it all at once.

Do some weight-bearing exercises — the ones you do standing up, such as gardening, brisk walking, or dancing. Weight training with light weights also helps keep your bones strong. If you'd like to chop your risk of falling and build balance, tai chi may help. Beware of high-impact aerobics, like step aerobics, because these exercises could increase your risk of fractures.

> You'll get more calcium from calcium-fortified orange juice if you shake the container before drinking.

Avoid falls and keep your independence

Falls are responsible for 90 percent of hip fractures that can lead to a nursing home or other long-term care, but simple changes around your house can help prevent falls.

▸ Put night lights near stairways and in bedrooms, bathrooms, and hallways.

▸ Use a rubber bathmat in showers or tubs. Add grab bars to walls near your tub, shower, and toilet. Check prices on grab bars at Independent Living Aids. Call 800–537–2118 or write to 200 Robbins Lane, Jericho, NY 11753 to request a free catalog.

▸ Give carpets and area rugs a skid-proof backing or tack them to the floor.

▸ Add ceiling lights to lamp-lit rooms. Keep rooms and stairs well lit.

▸ Keep kitchen cabinet items within easy reach.

▸ Clear loose cords, clutter, and low furniture from traveled areas that might make you trip.

Wise daily habits and smart medical decisions can help prevent falls, too.

▶ Wear low-heeled shoes with good support even at home. Consider thinner, hard-soled shoes. Athletic shoes may offer less stability.

▶ Avoid walking in flip-flops, socks, stockings, or slippers.

▶ Limit alcoholic drinks to no more than two a day.

▶ Sit on the side of your bed for several minutes before you stand. Standing up quickly can make you dizzy.

▶ Keep a flashlight by your bed.

▶ Have regular eye and hearing checkups. See the *Cataracts* chapter for inexpensive eye exam options.

▶ Use a cane or walker for added stability. Check prices at Independent Living Aids.

▶ Try hip pads. The new thinner hip protectors are worn under clothing, but they still help protect hipbones during falls.

Bear hormone offers hope for strong bones

Hibernating black bears could hold the secret to keeping your bones strong. A researcher from Michigan Technological University discovered that bears maintain strong bones despite long periods of inactivity. Although bears lose some bone during hibernation, they can grow new bone cells quickly. Parathyroid hormone, or PTH, could be the key. This hormone, known to promote bone growth, increases during hibernation. Not surprisingly, black bear PTH is different than human PTH. Understanding how it works might help researchers develop better ways to prevent or treat osteoporosis.

Psoriasis

Don't break the bank handling this heartbreak

The red, scaly, itchy skin patches that show up in psoriasis affect more than 6 million Americans — about 2.5 percent of the population. It's no wonder such famous people as singer Art Garfunkel; writer John Updike; and actor Jerry Mathers, "The Beaver," are among the sufferers. Statesman Benjamin Franklin, in fact, wrote of his trials with "the Scurff" over much of his trunk, arms, and legs, which a doctor's remedies failed to cure.

If you suffer from "the heartbreak of psoriasis," as the old television commercial called it, you may feel misunderstood and isolated. But you are not alone. More powerful drugs have been developed to send this heartbreak on its way. Along with traditional drugs, light treatments, and creams, these potent remedies can help you spend less time battling the flakes and more time forgetting you have psoriasis.

New drugs offer hope for healing

If you've suffered with psoriasis for any length of time, you know traditional treatments can have serious side effects. Drugs like methotrexate or cyclosporine can damage your liver or kidneys, cause high blood pressure, and increase your risk for infections. Because of these risks, doctors usually have their patients alternate with other treatments.

For less-severe psoriasis, you may have tried a variety of steroid creams, which can be effective, or other so-called "miracle cures" available over the counter. These products typically offer bigger promises than results. The steroid creams work for fewer than 40 percent of people and can cause dryness, irritation, and thinning of the skin. Even worse, they tend to stop working after a while. As for any lotions or creams that promise to "cure" your psoriasis, buyer beware. Psoriasis is still considered a lifelong condition with no known cure.

> Scientists see a link between being overweight and suffering with psoriasis. Very low-calorie or vegetarian diets — even fasting — seem to reduce the body's inflammatory response so psoriasis flare-ups stay away.

Some topical treatments can reduce symptoms. Coal tar ointments or shampoos can help clear up patches on the skin, called plaques, for people with mild to moderate psoriasis. Calcipotriene (Dovonex), a cream containing a synthetic form of vitamin D3, has been used in Europe and is becoming more popular stateside. It works well alone or in combination with other treatments, has few side effects, and is available in easy-to-apply foam.

If you have severe psoriasis covering more than 10 percent of your body, there's hope for relief. New drugs, called "biologics," work by targeting certain cells of the immune system. These drugs — alefacept (Amevive), efalizumab (Raptiva), and etanercept (Enbrel) — are injected once or twice a week. Studies suggest they prevent flare-ups and reduce symptoms for many people not helped by other treatments.

Unfortunately, biologics are expensive, and they don't work for everyone. In addition, long-term side effects are still unclear. Ask your doctor if one of these drugs might be right for you.

Remicade: 2 treatments for the price of 1

Up to 30 percent of psoriasis victims also develop psoriatic arthritis, a potentially crippling form of arthritis. The biologic drug Remicade (infliximab), used to treat the condition, now has FDA approval as a remedy for chronic, severe psoriasis. The ability of one drug to treat both conditions is a bonus for psoriasis sufferers.

Remicade works by blocking a chemical in the immune system called tumor necrosis factor-alpha (TNF-alpha) that promotes inflammation. People with psoriasis have too much of this chemical in their skin, and the drug helps bring the levels back to normal, leading to an improvement in symptoms.

On the downside, the drug may worsen heart failure and contribute to liver damage, so talk to your doctor about whether it's the right choice for you.

Improve your quality of life for free

The discomfort and pain of psoriasis, along with people's comments on your skin's appearance, can make psoriasis an emotional challenge. In fact, people with psoriasis are more likely than others to smoke and be overweight, maybe because they hide at home rather than lead active lives. Depression, embarrassment, and feelings of isolation can make it hard to meet new people.

Here's an idea you might want to try — join a support group for people with psoriasis. These small, informal groups often meet monthly and are open to people with psoriasis and their guests, like a spouse or caretaker. You can talk about the chal-

Let the cure fit the symptoms

Symptom severity	Common treatment	Method of use	Cost per month
Mild — affects less than 2% of body	coal tar steroid cream calcipotriene (Dovonex)	ointment or shampoo cream cream	$14 $37 $143
Moderate — affects 2 to 10% of body	PUVA UVB light	oral and UVA light treatment UVB light treatment	$1,200 – $1,500 $300 – $1,200 (doctor's office treatments, three a week)
Severe — affects more than 10% of body	methotrexate cyclosporine retinoids (acitretin) alefacept (Amevive)	oral oral oral injection by nurse	$91 $603 $407 $2156

lenges of living with this condition, get ideas on treatments that work, and learn about the newest advances in drugs. Most importantly, you'll get to share with other people who understand what it's like to live with psoriasis. Finding a caring listener can help you cope with everyday life. You can find a support group near you through the National Psoriasis Foundation's Web site at *www.psoriasis.org.*

Lighten up the cost of phototherapy

Ultraviolet (UV) light therapy, or phototherapy, fends off psoriasis outbreaks by interfering with skin cells that grow too quickly. If your doctor wants you to try UV treatment for your psoriasis, you might be baffled by the varying costs and therapy options.

Studies show that psoralen-UVA (PUVA) therapy is the most effective phototherapy, but it causes reddening of the skin and is linked with skin cancer. PUVA therapy involves using the drug psoralen, in the form of a cream or capsule, to make your skin more sensitive to light. You're then exposed to UVA light, one component of sunlight. PUVA therapy must be done in a doctor's office.

> Sunlight and seawater can help clear psoriasis, so many people hit the beach for relief. The Dead Sea, with its extra-salty water and low-altitude filtered sunlight, is an ideal spot.

The safest form of phototherapy is exposure to UVB light, the other element of sunlight. You can receive UVB light treatment in a doctor's office, usually a few times each week. In one study, narrow-band UVB therapy cleared up psoriasis plaques on 86 percent of the people who tried it. UVB treatment has fewer side effects than drug therapy or psoralen-UVA therapy, and it costs about $25 to $100 per treatment.

If UVB treatment works for you, consider investing in a home light box. You'll save money in the long run and enjoy more convenient treatments. Models range from small hand-held units to larger panels and even booths. Naturally, the prices vary along with the size of the machine, from $600 for the smaller styles up to $3,000 for the larger units.

Don't be alarmed at the cost. If your doctor recommends this treatment, most health insurance companies will pay some or all of the cost. Otherwise, look for used or discontinued models at online outlets, like eBay at *www.ebay.com*. But don't start shopping without calling your doctor. Phototherapy equipment for home use is available only with a doctor's prescription.

Get wise to psoriasis myths

Psoriasis is one of the oldest known skin conditions. Although it has been around for generations, there's still confusion and misunderstanding about the disease.

▶ **Psoriasis is an old person's problem.** Most people develop this skin disorder before they reach 40 years old.

▶ **You'll always suffer from flaky plaques.** New treatments can do wonders to clear up the condition for extended periods of time in most people.

▶ **Scrubbing scales from flaky patches will make them disappear.** This irritation can make the plaques worse. Follow your doctor's advice.

▶ **Like father, like son.** Although psoriasis tends to run in families, having a parent with the condition is no guarantee you'll get it.

Attack psoriasis from the inside out

Psoriasis is more than skin deep. Like many skin conditions, it's related to your body's inner health and can be affected by what you eat. If you have severe psoriasis, seek your doctor's advice on the best treatment. But these supplements might help.

▶ **Fish oil.** Many supplements claim to fight psoriasis, but fish oil might really work. In several clinical trials, fish oil supplements improved symptoms of psoriasis, including scales, redness, and itching. Because fish oil is taken in large doses to get the desired effect, talk with your doctor before you try this treatment. As a bonus, fish oil, which is rich in omega-3 fatty acids, can help protect you from heart attack and stroke.

▶ **Turmeric.** This spice, the main ingredient in curry powder, is an ancient remedy for wounds and infections. Now, researchers are testing a chemical in turmeric — curcumin — to see how it can help other conditions, including cancer, arthritis, and psoriasis. According to clinical trials, turmeric can reduce the severity of psoriasis. It can be taken in capsule form as a dietary supplement or added to food.

Drinking coffee may reduce your symptoms if you take methotrexate or sulfasalazine for psoriasis. Researchers think coffee helps these drugs reduce inflammation.

Sweet relief from your pantry

For mild psoriasis, try making this economical, home-brewed mixture of honey, olive oil, and beeswax to treat scaly plaques. In a small study, this remedy helped clear up symptoms in 60 percent of the people who used it. Although in the study steroid cream was added to the mixture, when the amount of steroid cream was cut way back, it still worked.

Psoriasis balm

1/4-cup unprocessed honey

1/4-cup olive oil

1/4-cup beeswax

Melt beeswax in a double boiler over low heat, stirring frequently. Remove pan from heat and slowly stir in honey and olive oil. After it cools to a comfortable temperature, rub the warm mixture on affected areas of your skin. If you plan to store any leftover balm, mix in vitamin E from one gel capsule to help preserve it longer. Store in an airtight container.

Dollars&Sense
Top 7 Rx questions to ask your doctor

When you visit your doctor, get the information you need to protect yourself from mistakes your well-meaning doctor or pharmacist could make — mistakes that could cost you your life. Ask him these seven questions about every prescription.

Bring a friend or relative with you if you are worried about understanding or remembering what he tells you. Write down your questions beforehand, and jot down the answers he gives.

▶ What are the generic and brand names of this medicine?

▶ What exactly is it for, and does it replace anything I already take?

▶ How many times a day do I take it? For how long? Do I need to take it with water or food, or at a specific time?

▶ Should I avoid any foods, drinks, or activities while taking it?

▶ What side effects might occur, and can I do anything to minimize them?

▶ Will I need to come in for tests or monitoring while on this medicine? How often?

▶ Will it interact with the other drugs, herbs, vitamins, and supplements I take? Does it contain the same ingredients as any over-the-counter pills? Are they safe to take together?

Once a year, bring all your medications to the doctor's office for a "medicine check-up" — including all prescriptions, over-the-counter drugs, supplements, vitamins, and herbal remedies you use regularly. Ask him to go over the dosage instructions, warnings, and possible interactions with you, and ask if there are any you can stop taking.

If you have trouble remembering your medication schedule, talk to your doctor about prescribing once-a-day versions of your medicines. You can even have him write out your schedule.

Raynaud's syndrome
Smart, inexpensive ways to short-circuit the pain

Raynaud's syndrome affects between 5 and 17 percent of the population — mostly women. It can strike out of the blue or stem from an underlying condition, like scleroderma, atherosclerosis, lupus, or rheumatoid arthritis. The attacks can be triggered by stress, holding a cold item, reaching into the fridge, or even air temperatures below 60 degrees Fahrenheit.

Raynaud's skews the way your blood vessels react to cold. Normally, cold makes blood vessels near your skin's surface narrow slightly to retain heat. In people with Raynaud's, blood vessels narrow dramatically. The resulting attack reduces blood flow to fingers, toes, and sometimes the nose, lips, or ear lobes.

As your skin turns white and then blue, you may feel pain, tingling, and numbness. In rare cases, lost blood flow may even cause tissues to die. Near the end of the attack, your skin turns red as blood rushes back in. Fortunately, driving back attacks may be easier than you think.

Stop an attack before it starts

Prevention is your best weapon in fighting Raynaud's. Follow these tips to lessen your chances of suffering painful fingers and toes.

▸ Spend more time indoors during cold weather.

Antibiotics help some sufferers

A recent study uncovered a connection between Raynaud's and *H. pylori*, the bacterium that can cause ulcers. After taking a week of antibiotics, 17 percent of those cured of *H. pylori* infection saw their Raynaud's symptoms disappear. Among those who still had Raynaud's, 72 percent experienced fewer and milder attacks.

▸ Wear layers of loose clothing to combat chilly temperatures. Include gloves or mittens, insulated boots, hat, scarf, earmuffs, thick socks, and a coat.

▸ Don gloves, mittens, or oven mitts before handling refrigerated or frozen foods at home or in the supermarket.

▸ Wear mittens and socks to bed on cold nights.

▸ Turn the thermostat up when using air conditioning or dress warmly, including a sweater or jacket, while in an air conditioned place.

▸ Drink hot liquids or eat hot foods before facing cool temperatures.

▸ Warm up your car before driving in cold weather.

▸ Talk with your doctor if you are taking beta blockers; headache drugs containing ergotamine, like Imitrex; estrogen; medicines with pseudoephedrine or other over-the-counter cold remedies, allergy medicines, or weight loss pills. These drugs can affect blood flow.

▸ Limit the use of vibrating tools and repetitive hand actions, like typing or piano playing.

If you are experiencing an attack, you can help ease the pain with these tricks and tips.

▸ Go indoors or move to a warmer spot.

▸ Soak your hands and feet in warm water or run warm water over them. Try rubbing your hands together or rubbing other affected areas to warm them. Thaw hands or feet with a heating pad.

▸ Swing your arms in circles or shake your arms and feet. Wiggle or massage fingers and toes.

Savvy shopping secrets for cold weather

Stock up on cold weather clothes at after-Christmas sales or end-of-season closeouts in February or March. And don't forget to check sporting goods stores, ski supply stores, and even military surplus shops for bargains on battery-powered warming socks, winter clothing, and more. Consider battery-heated gloves, for example. Here are a few mail-order prices without sales tax. If you catch a closeout sale at your local sporting goods store, you might even beat the Carol Wright Gifts price.

Mail order source	Price (battery-heated gloves)
Dick's Sporting Goods	$35.78
The Sports Authority	$35.78
Carol Wright Gifts	$20.99

Meanwhile, remember these other shopping tips for clothing and accessories to keep you warm.

▸ Bypass cotton socks and choose wool, synthetic, or cotton-blend instead. These keep your feet drier and toastier.

▸ Look for chemical warming packets or pouches. Tuck the small ones into pockets, mittens, or footwear for long periods in the cold.

▸ Use insulated drinking glasses and insulated glass or bottle holders.

Get wise to risky drug interactions

Ask your doctor about monitoring your blood pressure and pulse rate if you're prescribed any of these drugs. In addition, if you are going to have surgery, tell the surgeon you are taking one of the following medications.

Drug class	Generic (Brand)	Interactions
Calcium channel blockers	nifedipine (Adalat, Procardia) isradipine (DynaCirc) felodipine (Plendil)	Do not take with grapefruit juice or grapefruit. Tell your doctor if you're over age 65 or have heart problems, low blood pressure, or liver disease. These drugs may interact with melatonin, ginkgo, alcohol, ginseng, antibiotics, warfarin, high blood pressure drugs, NSAIDs, and more.
Angiotensin II receptor blocker	losartan (Cozaar)	Avoid salt substitutes. Tell your doctor if you're on a low-salt diet or if you've had kidney disease, liver disease, or heart problems. This drug may interact with ibuprofen, blood pressure drugs, and more.
Sympathetic nervous system blockers	prazosin (Minipress)	Tell your doctor if you have kidney disease or angina. These drugs may interact with over-the-counter weight loss pills; sildenafil (Viagra); high blood pressure drugs; cold, allergy, or sinus medicines; and more.

4 alternative treatments worth a look

Herbs and other nonstandard medical treatments may work for some people, but talk to your doctor first to avoid problems with side effects and drug interactions.

Fish oil. Two studies suggest that fish oil supplements show promise in helping improve circulation, but more research is needed before experts reach a definite conclusion.

Evening primrose oil. A small study found that evening primrose oil (EPO) supplements did not improve blood flow or temperature in study participant's fingers, but the supplements did reduce the number of attacks and weaken their severity.

Ginkgo. Two small studies suggest you might restore healthy blood flow to your painful hands and feet without drugs, vitamins, or exercise. The study participants, who took 120 milligrams (mg) of ginkgo every day for 10 weeks, showed improvements in blood flow and frequency of attacks. Just make sure you don't take ginkgo if you are taking blood-thinning medicines, such as aspirin or warfarin.

Biofeedback. Biofeedback uses devices to frequently measure body functions, like blood flow, to help you learn how to gain more control over that function. With practice, you may learn how to use your brain to help warm your fingers and toes. This seems to work for some people, but research has yet to prove its effectiveness. If you'd like to try biofeedback, ask your doctor where you can get training.

Don't worry if part of your nifedipine tablet turns up in your stool. The tablet's outer casing is designed to stay intact so it can control the gradual release of the medicine.

Pay less for supplements

If you decide to try supplements, mail order catalogs and Web sites may help you find a good deal. Call The Vitamin Shoppe toll-free at 800-223-1216 to order a catalog or visit them at *www.vitaminshoppe.com.* You can also get a free catalog from Swanson Health Products by calling 800-824-4491, or shop online at *www.swansonvitamins.com.*

3 ways to stifle stress

Stress can make your blood vessels narrow just like cold temperatures can. Try these tips to calm your mind and your body.

▶ Contact your local hospital and other community organizations and ask if they offer classes in stress management.

▶ Talk to your doctor about starting an exercise program. If he approves, try walking, gardening, dancing, sports, or fitness classes. Exercising regularly fights stress and gets your blood flowing.

▶ Read and watch more funny stuff. Laughter fights stress and increases blood flow by widening your blood vessels.

Restless legs syndrome
Wise ways to calm fidgety legs

Bedtime means darkness, quiet, and stillness — unless you have restless legs syndrome. Then you feel tingling, burning, creeping, crawling, or prickling sensations in your legs. Moving them relieves the symptoms, but it doesn't help you get any sleep.

Not surprisingly, restless legs syndrome often results in insomnia. This lack of sleep leads to impaired concentration and performance during the daytime. It can also lead to anxiety and depression.

Genetic factors, chemical imbalances in the brain, certain medical conditions, and some drugs may cause restless legs syndrome. This frustrating condition can also strike when you're sitting for long periods. It affects more women than men and is more common in older people. Although there is no cure for restless legs syndrome, there are things you can do to help you cope.

New drug approved to treat RLS

You may finally be able to rest easy if you have restless legs syndrome (RLS). A new drug called ropinirole (Requip), the first drug specifically approved for restless legs syndrome, recently hit the market.

Like some other drugs used to treat RLS, ropinirole belongs to a class of drugs called dopamine agonists that boost your levels of the brain chemical dopamine. Experts think low levels of dopamine may cause RLS. Originally prescribed to treat Parkinson's disease, ropinirole has been shown to improve RLS symptoms in several trials.

Other dopamine agonists include pergolide (Procalamine), cabergoline (Dostinex) and pramipexole (Mirapex), the most potent drug used for RLS. Common side effects of these drugs include nausea, drowsiness, and dizziness.

But you may not need the latest, greatest drug to control RLS. Before resorting to prescription drugs, try treating your symptoms with over-the-counter pain relievers, like acetaminophen, or NSAIDs (nonsteroidal anti-inflammatory drugs), like ibuprofen or naproxen. Just be aware that long-term use of NSAIDs can lead to ulcers, gastrointestinal bleeding, and even heart problems.

About 80 percent of people with restless legs syndrome also suffer from periodic limb movement disorder, a condition that involves the repetitive jerking and twitching of legs during sleep.

Another common drug treatment is the dopamine precursor levodopa (L-dopa), which has the advantage of working quickly. It's often combined with carbidopa in brands like Sinemet and Atamet. Be aware that long-term use of dopamine precursors or dopamine agonists can intensify RLS symptoms. These drugs can also lose their effectiveness over time.

If dopamine drugs don't work for you, your doctor may prescribe sedatives, opiates, or anticonvulsants. While these drugs may help you sleep or feel less pain, they also have serious side effects, including risk of addiction. Try them only as a last resort.

When you have restless legs syndrome, you also need to be careful about which drugs you take for other conditions. Several drugs can make your RLS symptoms worse. These include antidepressants, antipsychotic drugs, anti-nausea drugs, beta blockers, diuretics, asthma drugs, and even over-the-counter antihistamines and cold medicines.

Prescription for success

Not all victims of RLS need drug treatment. If you do, the following chart details some approaches — according to *Family Practice News* — your doctor may take to treat the condition.

For treatment purposes, restless legs syndrome is divided into three categories — intermittent, daily, and refractory. Refractory RLS means you have been treated for daily RLS with a dopamine agonist but that treatment is no longer effective or tolerable.

Intermittent RLS	Daily RLS	Refractory RLS
one half or one whole tablet of carbidopa/levodopa (25/100 formulation)	dopamine agonists — pramipexole (Mirapex) (.125 to .5 mg) or ropinirole (Requip) (.25 to 2 mg)	switch to gabapentin or a different dopamine agonist
dopamine agonists ropinirole (Requip) or pramipexole (Mirapex)	anti-seizure drug — gabapentin (Neurontin) (1300-1800 mg)	add gabapentin, a benzodiazepine, or an opioid
propoxyphene (65-200 mg), codeine (30-60 mg), tramadol (50-100 mg), or benzodiazepines	codeine, propoxyphene, or tramadol	switch to oxycodone (5-15 mg), hydrocodone (5-15 mg), methadone (5-10 mg), or tramadol (50-100 mg)

Simple tips soothe restless legs

When you have restless legs syndrome, you may feel helpless, but you're not. There are many ways to manage this frustrating condition — even without drugs. Try these tips to make your restless nights more peaceful.

▶ **Stick to a sleep schedule.** Go to bed and wake up at the same time every day. It's important to follow good sleep habits. Check out the *Insomnia* chapter for more details.

▶ **Sleep in.** If your schedule allows it, go to bed later in the evening and sleep later in the morning. Some people find that pushing back their sleep schedule reduces RLS symptoms.

▶ **Warm up or cool down.** A hot bath before bed may help. Cold compresses can also provide relief.

▶ **Get moving.** Mild to moderate exercise can help, but don't overdo it. Also, try stretching before bed.

▶ **Butt out.** Don't smoke cigarettes.

▶ **Make adjustments.** Find ways to accommodate your fidgety legs. For instance, sit on a high stool so you can dangle your legs. Or work standing up if you can.

▶ **Calm down.** Stress can contribute to restless legs. Try relaxation techniques or get a massage. Acupuncture has also been used to treat RLS.

▶ **Sock it to 'em.** Wear long socks to bed.

▶ **Keep busy.** Do activities like crossword puzzles or needlework when seated to keep your mind off your legs.

Shake off jittery legs with iron

Restless legs syndrome may be triggered by an iron deficiency. Your doctor can do blood tests to determine if your iron levels are too low. If they are, you can take steps to correct the problem.

First, make sure your diet contains plenty of iron. Eat iron-rich foods like clams, oysters, liver, and red meat. You can also get iron from eggs, dairy products, dried beans and peas, dark-green leafy vegetables, dried fruits, nuts, seeds, and iron-fortified cereals, bread, and pasta.

Vitamin C helps your body absorb iron, so eat foods rich in vitamin C, like broccoli, cabbage, citrus fruits, melon, tomatoes, and strawberries.

You can also boost your iron intake by cooking your food in cast iron skillets. Boiling, steaming, or stir-frying food in any type of pot or pan may also enhance its iron content.

If dietary measures don't work, your doctor can prescribe iron supplements to get your iron levels up to normal. Take supplemental iron between meals and watch out for common side effects like constipation and diarrhea. Too much iron can lead to more serious gastrointestinal problems.

> Between 3 and 15 percent of all people experience restless legs syndrome. But among people over age 65, the estimated percentage jumps to between 10 and 35 percent.

Eat right to sleep tight

Iron isn't the only nutrient that plays a role in restless legs syndrome. Deficiencies in other nutrients can contribute to the development of the condition, and some foods can trigger flare-ups. With the right choice of foods and supplements, you can take a bite out of RLS. Here's how.

Cut out caffeine and alcohol. They can make symptoms worse and hamper your ability to get a good night's sleep. Stay away from coffee, tea, cola, and chocolate — especially late in the day.

Elevate your E. Vitamin E supplements have been reported to help with restless legs syndrome. Aim for 800 to 1200 international units (IU) a day. You can also get vitamin E from vegetable oils, dark leafy greens, nuts, seeds, and wheat germ.

Make room for minerals. Calcium, potassium, and magnesium supplements may help. Food sources of these important minerals include dairy products, small bony fish, and legumes for calcium; fresh fruits, vegetables, fish, and legumes for potassium; and nuts, legumes, whole grains, dark leafy greens, and seafood for magnesium.

Several conditions have been linked to restless legs syndrome. They may trigger RLS or share a common cause. These include osteoarthritis, varicose veins, obesity, diabetes, high blood pressure, rheumatoid arthritis, sleep apnea, and snoring.

Fill up on folate. A deficiency in folate may contribute to RLS. Make sure you get enough of this B vitamin, which is found in dark leafy greens, legumes, seeds, and enriched breads and cereals. Folic acid supplements will also do the trick.

Rheumatoid arthritis
Ideas to improve your quality of life

Your immune system protects you from harmful bacteria and viruses. When you have an autoimmune disease, like rheumatoid arthritis (RA), something triggers your body to attack itself.

In RA, the membrane that lines your joints is the main target. The attack causes inflamed and painful joints, but it can wreak havoc on your whole body. Flu-like symptoms, like fatigue, low fever, and loss of appetite, are also part of the package.

Treating rheumatoid arthritis early can prevent damage. See a doctor as soon as you notice symptoms. It's possible you can take back your life from this debilitating disease.

Screenings protect you from drug dangers

Even miracle drugs have a downside. While Remicade and Humira can make all the difference in the world to someone with severe RA, these drugs can also carry deadly risks.

Mayo Clinic researchers found that a high percentage of people who took Remicade and Humira developed serious infections, like tuberculosis, while others got skin, lung, or breast cancer. Taking the drugs actually tripled the patients' chances of getting cancer, and the higher the dose, the worse their odds.

Humira and Remicade fall into the category of TNF inhibitors. They make life easier for RA sufferers by blocking tumor necrosis factor-alpha (TNF-alpha), a chemical that attacks your joints. For some people, TNF inhibitors are the only treatment that helps.

Because the drugs are so effective at relieving symptoms, they've become very popular. Sales of Humira and Remicade have reached billions of dollars in the past several years. That means more and more people are being exposed to these dangerous side effects.

But health professionals say don't give up on these medications just yet, especially if they relieve your RA symptoms. Simply be mindful of the risks, so you and your doctor can decide if TNF inhibitors are right for you.

Get tested for tuberculosis and other infections before you start taking Humira or Remicade. And if you've had cancer before, get screened for it on a regular basis. As long as you're vigilant, you can still get relief from these "miracle drugs."

2 new drugs get to the root of the problem

You've tried everything, and your rheumatoid arthritis is still going strong. Orencia and Rituxan, two new medications that hit the market recently, could be worth looking into. These drugs halt or slow the deterioration of joints and bones.

These newcomers are biologic DMARDs (disease-modifying anti-rheumatic drugs). Remicade and Humira also fall into the category of biologic DMARDs. Before biologics came along, RA sufferers had to take corticosteroids, which relieved symptoms, but caused long-term side effects, like high blood pressure, osteoporosis, and diabetes. There were other options, but their effects were only temporary.

Until recently, the only other choice was to take the cancer drug methotrexate, another DMARD, and combine it with a TNF inhibitor, like Humira or Remicade. These drugs treat inflammation, but they can't get to the root of the problem — your immune system. Plus, you have to inject yourself once or twice a week with TNF inhibitors, and they can cost up to $28,000 a year.

Today, your doctor can pull out the big guns and combine either Orencia or Rituxan with methotrexate. These new drugs stop the damage before it's done by launching a defensive campaign against your T cells and B cells — soldiers in your immune system that attack your joints. Orencia defends against T cells, while Rituxan takes on the B cells.

> The upside to rheumatoid arthritis is you're 50 percent less likely to have seasonal allergies. But if you have both, the allergies may keep your RA from being as severe.

Unfortunately, no medication is perfect. Both Orencia and Rituxan can cause infections. And taking Orencia means you need an infusion every four weeks. That can cost up to $17,500 a year if you don't have insurance. You may only need two infusions of Rituxan to bring on remission, but those two infusions will cost about $18,000. Talk with your doctor and weigh the benefits, risks, and costs of these two new drugs.

Well-known cholesterol drugs chase away RA

The drug you take to lower your cholesterol might keep your joints healthy. In a recent study, researchers discovered that statin drugs,

Doctors aren't sure what causes RA. They think some people have an inherited trait that combines with an unknown factor, possibly something in the environment, triggering the disease.

usually prescribed to lower high cholesterol, might play a role in treating rheumatoid arthritis.

One possible cause of RA is malfunctioning synovial cells, cells that make up the protective sac around your joints. The sac is usually thin and delicate, but sometimes the synovial cells multiply too fast and the sac gets wrinkly and thick, leading to rheumatoid arthritis. The only way to stop synovial cells is to "help" them die so they don't build up around your joints.

That's where statins come in. Fluvastatin, in particular, keeps the synovial cells from getting the protein they need to survive. No more protein, no more synovial cells, and no more inflammation. Statins aren't a sure-fire cure, but researchers think the drugs could eventually be the best therapy available.

Statins may also protect you from RA in a more obvious way — by lowering your cholesterol. According to a recent study, the lower your lipid (cholesterol and other blood fats) levels, the lower your odds of developing rheumatoid arthritis.

RA sufferers run a higher risk of heart disease than most people. Doctors once thought inflammation was to blame, but this study found that people with rheumatoid arthritis were more likely to have high cholesterol before they developed RA. Their total cholesterol level was higher, and their levels of HDL or "good" cholesterol were lower.

It's possible having unhealthy lipid levels makes you more susceptible to inflammatory diseases, like RA. Since statins help combat high cholesterol, researchers think they could prevent rheumatoid arthritis at the same time.

5 great reasons to exercise every day

Exercise might not sound like a great idea when you have arthritis, but the truth is regular exercise will help, not hurt, your achy joints. Here's what exercising regularly can do for you:

▶ reduce pain

▶ improve joint function

▶ strengthen your bones

▶ build up your muscles

▶ help you feel good about yourself

Plan to get 20 to 30 minutes of aerobic exercise each day, as long as your doctor approves. If you can't manage it every day, just do what you can. A little is better than nothing. Avoid high-impact activities, like running and heavy weight lifting that stress your joints. Try these low-impact exercises instead.

Ride a bike. Cycling is a great way to work out without pounding your joints. A recumbent bike or a stationary exercise bike is your best option because it won't strain your knees as much. Stationary bikes are easier on RA sufferers with balance problems because they won't fall over.

If you already have a bicycle, you can turn it into a stationary bike with a cycling trainer, a piece of equipment you attach to the rear axle. The wheel will spin without going anywhere so you can cycle in front of your TV if you want. You can take it off when the weather is nice if you'd rather cycle outside.

Arthritis is the number one cause of disability in America. And you don't have to be a certain age. Three out of five arthritis sufferers are under age 65.

You'll find the Bell Motivator Cycling Trainer for about $100 at these stores — Sports Authority, Dick's Sporting Goods, and Dunham's Sports.

Jump in the pool. Take a water aerobics class in a heated pool. Not only will the exercise strengthen your muscles, the water's warmth and buoyancy will help ease stiffness in your joints and reduce pain. In a new study, RA sufferers who took two water aerobic classes a week for 12 weeks improved their flexibility and endurance.

Women are two to three times more likely to get RA than men. But they are less likely to report symptoms to their doctors, so they don't get the aggressive treatment they need.

The Arthritis Foundation offers an Aquatic Program in pools throughout the United States. To find a program in your area, call the Arthritis Foundation at 800-568-4045.

When you exercise, recognize the difference between normal pain and arthritis pain. If your muscles hurt for a day or two after exercising, they are probably sore from working out. If your joints are swollen and feel warm when you touch them, your arthritis is flaring up. You might want to take a break or choose a lower-impact exercise. Talk with your doctor to come up with a fitness plan that works for you.

Eat your way to healthier joints

Your entire body is connected. This can be a good thing or a bad thing. Take rheumatoid arthritis. If your immune system goes haywire, your whole body feels the effects. The good thing is taking care of yourself and eating the right foods will help you feel better.

Mix in a little curry. Banish arthritis, not with powerful anti-inflammatory drugs, but with turmeric — the soothing spice you taste in curry. Ancient Ayurvedic medicine and traditional Chinese healers have used turmeric for thousands of years to treat inflammation. Now modern medicine has found evidence to support that practice.

Turmeric prevented joint inflammation in animals with RA in a recent study, especially when they took it before the inflammation started. The secret ingredient is curcumin, a compound in turmeric that fights inflammation right down to your cells' molecules. Look for this spice at your grocery store and use it to perk up stir-fry or your favorite vegetables.

Make friends with flaxseed. Everyone agrees omega-3 fatty acids are good for you. And flaxseed has more than any other plant. This essential fatty acid can reduce inflammation, relieve joint pain, and reduce morning stiffness. Eating flaxseed to get omega-3 fatty acids is a cheap and easy way to take control of RA.

Take one to two tablespoons of ground flaxseed or one to two teaspoons of flaxseed oil to get these benefits. Ground flaxseed is easier to digest than whole seeds, and it goes well with other food. You can sprinkle it on cereal, mix it with yogurt, or bake it into muffins. Flaxseed oil works, too. Put it in cold foods, like salad dressings and smoothies.

Add color to your diet. When it comes to fruits and vegetables, brighter is better. Brighter colors mean more antioxidants, like carotenoids, that help fight inflammation and prevent rheumatoid arthritis.

Researchers found that oranges, bell peppers, pumpkins, tangerines, and papayas were full of the carotenoid beta cryptoxanthin, an antioxidant that lowers your risk of developing RA. People who ate the most of these fruits and vegetables were half as likely to suffer from rheumatoid arthritis. Just one glass of freshly squeezed orange juice a day will reduce your risk.

Arm yourself with antioxidants. What do vitamin C, vitamin E, beta carotene, and the mineral selenium all have in common? They may prevent rheumatoid arthritis. Studies have shown that not having enough of these powerful antioxidants in your blood can lead to RA. In one study, people with the lowest level of Vitamin C in their diets were three times more likely to develop rheumatoid arthritis. And the ones who skimp on vitamin E, beta carotene, and selenium are eight times more likely to develop RA.

Not sure where to look for selenium? You can find it in seafood, meat, and whole grains. Brazil nuts are also a great source. You can get all the selenium you need for the day by eating just two nuts — but don't eat them by the handful. Too much selenium can be toxic.

Popular beverage cuts your risk in half

A cup of tea could protect you from the ravaging effects of rheumatoid arthritis. But don't count on coffee to do the same. Women who drank four or more cups of decaf coffee every day doubled their chances of developing RA, according to the results of the Iowa Women's Health Study. Researchers think a by-product related to the processing of decaf coffee could be to blame.

Tea is rich in antioxidants. It also helps to reduce swelling. The women who drank more than three cups of tea a day reduced their risk of developing RA by 60 percent.

Brew some green tea, too. Research from the Medical College of Georgia shows that green tea protects you from autoimmune diseases, like rheumatoid arthritis, because of the way it affects your immune system. Green tea lowers your levels of autoantigens, chemicals that trigger an immune response. Fewer autoantigens means your body is less likely to attack itself.

The leaves of green and black teas come from the same plant, *Camellia sinensis*. The difference is in how they're prepared. Green tea leaves are steamed right after they've been picked, which helps preserve the antioxidants. For black tea, the leaves are allowed to ferment. To make a great cup of tea, steep black tea and green tea for about three minutes in water that's hot but not boiling. Boiling water destroys some of the antioxidants.

Pamper yourself with touch therapy

Massage therapy is perfect for RA sufferers because it gets your blood circulating and eases pain, swelling, and muscle spasms. It also reduces stress, shakes depression, strengthens your immune system, and helps you sleep better.

Massage is no passing fad when it comes to healing. Your levels of endorphins and serotonin, compounds produced in your brain, shoot up during a massage to give you natural painkilling action. Your first massage doesn't have to be full of surprises. Here are a few things to expect.

▸ The massage therapist will ask you some questions to find out what kind of massage would be beneficial for you and to rule out any potential health risks.

▸ You will have a chance, in private, to take off your clothes and remove any jewelry. Only take off what you're comfortable with. She will give you a towel or sheet to cover yourself and keep you warm. The therapist will only uncover the areas being massaged.

▸ You'll lie on a padded massage table in a peaceful room. The therapist may play relaxing music. She might use lotion or massage oil during the massage to smooth out her movements. Tell her if you have any allergies to ingredients in oils or lotions.

▸ The massage will last between 30 and 90 minutes, but most sessions take an hour. The therapist will leave the room when she is done to let you get dressed.

An hour-long massage can cost anywhere from $65 to $80, but many insurance companies will cover some of the cost if you have arthritis. Look for a massage therapist at your local gym or YMCA.

Dollars&Sense
Dodge dangerous drug interactions

Interactions between drugs, herbs, vitamins, foods, and over-the-counter (OTC) remedies can cause unpleasant side effects and even death. You can help your doctor and pharmacist catch dangerous interactions before they occur with a few simple steps.

Carry a list. Take a list to each doctor appointment naming all the prescription and over-the-counter (OTC) drugs, vitamins, and herbs you use, including creams and ointments. Note how much you take, how often, the condition each treats, and who prescribed it. You can get ready-made forms off the Internet. Go to *www.themedform.com* to print out full-page and wallet-size medication forms. Another program, Vial of Life at *www.vialoflife.com* provides decals and medical forms to place on your refrigerator door to help emergency responders find out what drugs you take and learn your medical history.

Stick to one pharmacy. Try to fill all your prescriptions at one pharmacy, so the pharmacist can check for interactions. Each time you pick up a prescription, show the pharmacist your list of herbs, supplements, OTC remedies, and prescription drugs you take regularly. She may spot dangers the doctor missed.

Know food no-nos. Ask your doctor or pharmacist if you need to avoid any foods while taking your medication. Grapefruit, for instance, can interfere with 60 percent of oral drugs, boosting their strength to toxic levels. Avoid grapefruit and its juice while taking oral medicines and for 48 hours before starting a new drug, unless your doctor says it's safe.

Document side effects. Pay attention to how you feel after starting a new medicine. Write down any changes you notice, both emotional and physical, and share them with your doctor during the next visit. He may offer advice on how to lessen side effects or prescribe a different drug.

Avoid dangerous combinations

Food, herb, or OTC drug	Commonly overlooked interactions
alcohol	ibuprofen (Advil), naproxen (Aleve), acetaminophen (Tylenol), antihistamines (Benadryl), dextromethorphan (cough/cold remedies), tricyclic antidepressants, anti-diabetics, benzodiazepines (Valium), nitroglycerin, morphine, codeine, propranolol (Inderal), bronchodilators (albuterol), metronidazole (Flagyl), ketoconazole (Nizoral)
grapefruit juice, limes, pumellos, Seville oranges	anti-inflammatories (aspirin, ibuprofen), statins (especially lovastatin and simvastatin), calcium-channel blockers, estrogen, histamine (H1) antagonists, sedatives, erectile dysfunction drugs, amiodarone, immunosuppressives, cyclosporine, carbamazepine, saquinavir
St. John's wort	selective serotonin reuptake inhibitors (SSRIs), monoamine oxidase (MAO) inhibitors, digoxin, warfarin (Coumadin), sedatives, loperamide (Imodium A-D), imatinib, cyclosporine
ginkgo biloba	blood thinners, MAO inhibitors, digoxin, anti-diabetics
aspirin	alcohol, other nonsteroidal anti-inflammatory drugs (ibuprofen), insulin, garlic, ginger, ginkgo biloba
ibuprofen or indomethacin	blood thinners, steroids, aspirin, alcohol, some high blood pressure medicines
nasal decongestants	antidepressants
antihistamines	alcohol; cold medications; kava kava; sedatives; tranquilizers; sleep aids (Sominex); certain drugs for anxiety, depression, and high blood pressure

Rosacea

Attack common skin problem at first blush

Red in the face? Got more pimples than you did as a teenager? You may have rosacea, a skin condition affecting 14 million Americans that usually appears between ages 30 and 50.

Rosacea is most common among light-skinned women with ancestors from England, Scotland, Ireland, and Sweden — so common it's been called the "curse of the Celts." The red cheeks and bumpy skin of former President Bill Clinton, along with the enlarged nose of British statesman Winston Churchill, are due to rosacea.

If rosacea makes you feel more self-conscious than stately, your doctor can prescribe creams or pills to flush out the redness. You can also avoid common triggers, like heat, cold, and certain foods considered red flags for a rosacea flare-up.

New use for an old drug

Here's good news for people suffering with the emotional and physical pain of rosacea. The Food and Drug Administration (FDA) recently approved a new drug to treat this common inflammatory skin disease.

Called Oracea, it contains doxycycline, an antibiotic used to treat pneumonia and other bacterial infections. In this new version, however, the doxycycline is in such a low dose it does not kill bacteria. Instead, it fights inflammation to reduce redness and pimples. Unlike some antibiotics, Oracea doesn't make your skin more sensitive to sunlight.

An added benefit of Oracea is that it's a controlled-release capsule you only take once a day. This makes it a great choice for people who have found other rosacea drugs too bothersome. Even if you've used other pills in the past to treat rosacea, you may want to ask your doctor about this new drug.

Several other prescription drugs are used to treat rosacea. Lotions, creams, or gels containing either azelaic acid or the antibiotic metronidazole help banish pimples and redness. Antibiotics in pill form, including tetracycline, minocycline, or erythromycin, can kill the bacteria that may be causing pimples.

Although these antibiotics work well, they can become less effective over time. Antibiotics can also cause yeast infections in women. According to the experts, Oracea can be used long term without these side effects.

Household cleaners, especially aerosol or pump sprays, can make rosacea flare up, according to the National Rosacea Society. Use soap and water instead, or wear a mask when you're cleaning.

Terrific way to expose common food triggers

People prone to rosacea quickly discover that certain foods can bring on a flare-up. Alcoholic beverages can cause flushing in anyone, while spicy foods can make you sweat or flush. Hot beverages heat up your body temperature, which also causes flushing. Here are some other common dietary triggers:

- yogurt
- cheese
- sour cream
- liver
- eggplant, avocados, and spinach
- soy sauce
- vinegar
- citrus fruits
- chocolate and vanilla

To figure out what foods trigger a bout of rosacea for you, keep a journal of what you eat and how those foods affect your skin. The National Rosacea Society offers a free diary booklet that can help you identify all of your personal triggers — not just food. To get a copy, call the society's toll-free number, 888-NO-BLUSH (888-662-5874) or print the booklet from their Web site, *www.rosacea.org*.

6 ways to beat the heat when exercising

Strenuous exercise is good for your heart, but it's not so good for rosacea. A recent survey by the National Rosacea Society found that more than 83 percent of people with rosacea remembered having a symptom flare-up after a hard workout.

Everyone can get flushed from overheating during exercise, but it's worse for people with rosacea. To keep up your exercise routine without triggering a flare-up, try these simple tips.

A recent study found that people who used a lotion containing antioxidant-rich red tea extract saw a 70-percent improvement in their rosacea symptoms compared with people using lotion without it.

Exercise in a cool place. During the summer, exercise outside in the early morning or evening when it's cooler. If you must exercise during the heat of the day, find an indoor gym or swimming pool to help you keep your cool.

Get the red out with light therapy

Erythema or red patches on the nose, cheeks, forehead, and chin cause the most distress to many people with rosacea. Antibiotics and creams work well on other symptoms, but sometimes this redness, which is caused by extra blood flow through the tiny capillaries, remains.

Dermatologists can treat this redness using several forms of light therapy — lasers, photodynamic therapy, and intense pulsed light (IPL). IPL, which has been available for about 10 years, is now commonly used. The treatments are done every three to four weeks, with the best results showing after four to six treatments. Combination therapy, joining light therapy with medicated skin creams and antibiotics, can help in severe cases.

Avoid the sun. Sun exposure can worsen rosacea symptoms, so walk, run, or bike in the shade. If you must be in the sun, wear a sunscreen with an SPF of 15 or higher. Avoid alcohol-based sunscreens, which can be irritating.

Go for shorter bursts. Rather than exercising for a full hour, divide your workouts into shorter sessions of 15 minutes. You'll get all of the benefits without overheating.

Lower the intensity. Instead of working at full capacity, go for less-strenuous forms of exercise. Your body will be conditioned, but your body temperature will stay in check.

Keep your cool with a damp towel. Wet a small towel with cool water and wear it around your neck while you exercise. You can also find special towels that will keep you cool for several hours. Look for Frogg Toggs Chilly Pad Sports Towel or Cramer Stay Cool Sports Towel at your favorite sporting goods store or online.

Suck on ice chips or a cool drink. Cool your body from the inside out by keeping a bottle of cool water handy while you exercise. If you overdo it and feel flushed and overheated, cool down quickly by sucking on ice chips.

Smooth on minerals for natural beauty

Rosacea isn't a serious physical illness, but if you are a victim, it can take a heavy toll on your emotional health. In a recent survey, almost 70 percent of people with rosacea said the condition had damaged their self-confidence and self-esteem. It's not uncommon for people to miss work or shun social situations to avoid being seen.

To deal with unwanted redness, many people use cosmetics and other skin-care products. Unfortunately, these products often have ingredients that can make rosacea worse.

Not surprisingly, several manufacturers have designed makeup made of minerals for people with sensitive skin, including those with rosacea. These new cosmetics are composed of finely ground minerals, like zinc oxide, titanium dioxide, and iron dioxide, with inorganic pigments added for color. Zinc oxide, the same calming agent in diaper-rash cream, may help with skin irritation.

Mineral makeup even offers a bit of sun protection, which is especially important if you have rosacea. The best thing about mineral makeup, however, is that it contains none of the usual makeup ingredients that can cause a rosacea flare-up — no fragrances, talc, preservatives, chemicals, or dyes. It won't clog pores or irritate your skin. That's why many dermatologists recommend mineral makeup for people with rosacea.

> Lotions and creams containing oatmeal may provide relief for rosacea sufferers by stopping itching and fighting inflammation.

What you should know about rosacea

Symptoms of rosacea	Doctor's treatments	Self-help remedies
flushing, redness, visible blood vessels, scaliness, facial swelling (erythematotelangiectatic rosacea)	metronidazole (MetroGel, MetroCream) azelaic acid (Finacea) laser therapy or intense pulsed light therapy	avoid excessive heat, cold, strenuous exercise, and trigger foods use mineral makeup or concealer
redness and pimples that look like acne (papulopustular rosacea)	doxycycline (Oracea), tetracycline, minocycline, erythromycin	wash face with warm water and gentle soap use a light, oil-free moisturizer
thickened skin, bumps, enlarged nose (phymatous rosacea)	dermabrasion, electrosurgery	treat rosacea at an early stage to avoid facial disfigurement
watery or bloodshot eyes, sometimes with burning or itching, sties on eyelids (ocular rosacea)	erythromycin ointment cyclosporine ointment (Restasis)	warm, wet compress several times a day, wash eyelids with baby shampoo solution seek treatment to avoid vision loss

This remarkable makeup provides great coverage for redness. Some types go on a bit heavy, so take time to practice to get them to look natural. You can choose from foundation, blush, powder, eye shadow, and lipstick. Mineral makeup might cost a bit more than regular makeup, but a few economical brands are available. Try Neutrogena Mineral Sheers, Bare Escentuals BareMinerals, or Jane Iredale Mineral Cosmetics.

Symptoms you should not ignore

Rosacea is not just a skin disease. It can also affect your eyes, causing redness, watering, burning, itchiness, dryness, sensitivity to light, blurred vision, and sties on your eyelids. You may be unable to wear contact lenses, and your vision may seem to get worse. More than half the people with skin rosacea also have these eye problems, called ocular rosacea.

You may think having bloodshot, watery eyes is only an annoyance, but ocular rosacea can damage your eyesight if you don't get treatment. Over time, it can lead to scarring of the cornea, the transparent tissue covering the front of your eye.

To treat ocular rosacea, your doctor might prescribe doxycycline or tetracycline, antibiotics used to treat skin problems. An ointment of erythromycin for the eyes and eyelids can also help take care of any infections. Cyclosporine ointment for eyes is a new way to treat the condition.

If you have ocular rosacea, ask your doctor if there's anything you can do at home. He might suggest using a watered-down solution of baby shampoo to wash your eyelids every day. If you have a stye — an infection of a gland on the eyelid — don't try to drain it. That will only spread the infection. Instead, hold a warm, wet compress, like a clean washcloth, to the stye for a few minutes several times a day until it heals.

Shingles

Get tough on a mysterious virus

A shingles outbreak, whether brief and mild or severe and lingering, always causes pain. The herpes virus known as varicella-zoster virus, which triggers chickenpox in children, is also responsible for shingles. If you had chickenpox, the virus hides in nerve cells and can reappear years later. In fact, if you live to be 85 years old, you'll have a 50-percent chance of getting shingles.

Like chickenpox, shingles causes an itchy rash, as well as pain. True to its name, which means "belt" or "girdle" in Latin, a shingles rash forms a band on one side of the body and lasts for about seven to 10 days.

Pain can continue for weeks or months after the rash has healed. When the pain lasts longer than a month, it's called postherpetic neuralgia. But new drugs can fight the symptoms, and a new vaccine can keep you free of shingles.

New vaccine to the rescue

You're at risk for developing shingles if you had chickenpox as a child. That includes about 95 percent of Americans older than age 60. But there's good news.

In 2006, the Food and Drug Administration approved Zostavax, a vaccine to prevent shingles. Zostavax is a more powerful form of the chickenpox vaccine, which children have been getting since 1995. It

Shingles cases are increasing, possibly because most children in the United States are getting the chickenpox vaccine. That means less protective exposure to the virus for adults.

can cut in half your risk of getting shingles. Even if you develop shingles after you get the vaccine, you'll have less discomfort from the rash and a lower chance of suffering the severe, lingering pain of postherpetic neuralgia. This complication can make shingles sufferers miserable for weeks or months after the rash has cleared up.

The shingles vaccine is approved for people 60 years and older. They are at the highest risk of developing the disease. If you have a weakened immune system from cancer treatments, organ transplants, or other causes, you may not be a good candidate for the vaccine. Side effects of Zostavax can include redness, pain, itching, and swelling at the injection site.

The vaccine is expensive — $150, but health insurance should pay at least part of the cost. Zostavax is included under Medicare's Part D prescription program.

Take action to outsmart shingles

It's not too late to fight back, even after you come down with shingles. Anti-viral drugs, which work by keeping the virus from reproducing, can help. They do the most good if you start taking them within 72 hours of your first symptoms. These drugs can make the shingles attack milder, help you heal faster, and possibly ward off the discomfort of postherpetic neuralgia.

In a recent study, people began taking two anti-viral drugs soon after shingles symptoms began. They took the drugs acyclovir (Zovirax) for two weeks, then valacyclovir (Valtrex) for one month. By the end of the treatment, more than half the people who completed the study had significantly less pain. Unfortunately, the study was small, and no comparison group was used to find other possible reasons for the reduced pain. Still, the results are promising.

Because younger people who develop shingles usually get well quickly with few complications, these anti-viral drugs are not usually recommended for them. Instead, they are most important for people with shingles who:

▸ are elderly.

▸ have a shingles rash near their eyes.

▸ have very severe pain.

▸ have a weakened immune system.

▸ develop a shingles rash over a large area of skin.

Other anti-viral drugs that might help early on with shingles symptoms include famciclovir and foscarnet. See your doctor as soon as you have symptoms so you can take advantage of anti-viral drugs.

Help yourself to pain relief

You'll need to see your doctor if you think you have shingles. Once the diagnosis is confirmed, follow your doctor's orders and take some extra steps to ease the pain. To treat an acute attack of shingles — and all the pain and itching that come with it — try these self-help ideas.

Soak away the pain. Soothing baths help reduce itching for children with chickenpox, and they can help shingles sufferers, too. Pour one

If you have shingles, you can't give it to someone else. However, exposure to the fluid from shingles blisters can cause chickenpox in people who have never had it.

or two cups of colloidal (finely ground) oatmeal into a tub of warm water and soak for about 20 minutes. You can also try one-half to one cup of baking soda or a cup of cornstarch.

Grab an old standby. You probably have aspirin or ibuprofen in your medicine cabinet. These or other NSAIDs (nonsteroidal anti-inflammatory drugs) can help with the discomfort of a severe shingles outbreak.

If you have postherpetic neuralgia (PHN) after your shingles rash has healed, you'll need to try other ways to get rid of the pain.

Rub on relief. To battle PHN, you can try a variety of topical treatments. Health professionals say lidocaine patches work well, although they are a bit pricy at more than $6 each. Topical salicylates, like Aspercreme, or creams with menthol, such as maximum-strength Flexall 454, may also help, and they are less expensive.

Get help from peppers. Capsaicin, the ingredient that makes hot peppers hot, is available in an over-the-counter cream. Over time, applying the hot pepper cream to your skin actually makes the area less sensitive to pain and heat. Capsaicin cream seems to be a good remedy for PHN pain, but don't use it until the blisters have healed completely.

The price of topical pain relief

Brand	Active ingredient	Form	Price
Lidoderm	lidocaine	patch	$6.22/patch
Aspercreme	trolamine salicylate	patch	$1.57/patch
Aspercreme	trolamine salicylate	cream	$1.89/ounce
Flexall 454	menthol	cream (maximum strength)	$3.98/ounce
Zostrix	capsaicin	cream	$9.43/ounce

Quiet the virus with peaceful exercises

Want to silence shingles? Practice the steps of Tai Chi Chih, or "meditation with movement." This traditional Chinese style of exercise, adapted from a form of martial arts, was developed to help keep older people fit. It uses a series of slow movements and balance poses.

In a recent study, researchers in California found that seniors who participated in Tai Chi Chih classes three times a week for 45 minutes boosted their immunity to the virus that causes shingles. In the study, participants followed an instructor through a series of 20 Tai Chi Chih movements.

After 15 weeks of classes, the exercisers were given a blood test. It showed certain immunity factors, which protect against shingles, had increased by 50 percent. People in a control group, who did not take the classes, had no change in these immunity factors. Along with keeping shingles at bay, the Tai Chi Chih classes also helped the exercisers with their everyday movements, such as climbing stairs and walking.

Ward off shingles with fruits and veggies

A new study shows eating a diet rich in fruits and vegetables — or taking a special blend of vitamins and minerals — helped stave off shingles by boosting the immune system.

The nutrients studied were vitamin A, vitamin B6, vitamin C, vitamin E, folic acid, iron, and zinc. Researchers believe these vitamins and minerals, by working together, can strengthen your immunity. When people took just one of the seven nutrients, no improvement was observed. In the study, the people who didn't get enough of these nutrients were five times more likely to get shingles.

The study also showed that people who ate less than one serving of fruit a week had three times the chance of developing shingles than people who ate three or more servings a day.

Dollars&Sense
4 steps to prescription safety

Even doctors and pharmacists make mistakes, and it's up to you to catch them. Keep prescription mistakes from killing you by following a few precautions.

Shop the same pharmacy. Have all your prescriptions filled at the same pharmacy. Each one tracks the medications you have filled there and checks for potential interactions — a safety check which could save your life.

Get to know your medications. Read the leaflets that come with your prescriptions. They contain important information about side effects, warnings, and drug interactions. If you have trouble understanding the leaflet, ask the pharmacist to go over it with you.

Do a double-check. Before you leave the pharmacy, open the bag and carefully read the label on each medication. Look for your name and check that the drug names, strengths, and dosage instructions match what your doctor told you. Ask the pharmacist to print your medicine labels in large type if you have trouble reading them.

Learn the lingo. You can decode your prescriptions with these common Rx abbreviations and their meanings.

Rx abbreviation	What it means	Rx abbreviation	What it means
a.c.	before meals	p.r.n.	as necessary
ad lib	as much as wanted	q.	every
b.i.d.	twice a day	q.4 h.	every four hours
h.	hour	q.d.	every day
h.s.	at bedtime	q.i.d.	four times a day
p.	after	q.o.d.	every other day
p.c.	after meals	Stat.	immediately
p.o.	by mouth	t.i.d.	three times a day

Sinusitis

Simple steps to unblock serious distress

Cold, allergy, or sinusitis? Many people have trouble telling the difference. They all produce similar symptoms — like a stuffy nose — but sinusitis is an inflammation that can develop into a serious infection. More than 37 million Americans share this misery and shell out $5.8 billion every year on sinus-related health care.

Acute sinusitis usually starts with a cold. If you treat it right, it may go away when the cold ends. Or it may develop into a painful infection and last a couple of weeks more, even after a trip to the doctor. With chronic sinusitis, sinus problems keep coming back or hang on for months at a time.

Whatever the extent of your sinusitis, you can get rid of some — if not all — of the suffering with a few simple practices. Most don't even cost much money. It's all about keeping your airways open, taking action that truly helps, and avoiding medicines that don't do any good.

Cheap and easy home solutions

Some of the best solutions to clogged sinuses are sitting right under your nose. And they don't require spending money at the drugstore for "miracle" sinus pills that may not give you relief.

Your sinuses are air-filled pockets located above and behind your eyes and nose. They have a lining that produces mucus to trap and carry away bacteria and irritants. When the sinuses swell, the mucus can't drain properly and it builds up, creating the perfect breeding ground for infection. That leads to more inflammation and swelling as well as painful pressure.

The trick is to drain those sinuses and get rid of the pressure and the mucus before it becomes infected. See how many of these time-tested home remedies will work for you.

Drink lots of water. Six or more glasses of water is the best way to lubricate your mucous membranes and keep them moist, so you can resist infection and your sinuses can drain easier. Experts say keeping hydrated may be the only treatment needed for mild sinusitis with no signs of infection.

Get the right rest. Not enough sleep can make your sinus problems more painful and longer lasting. Too much sleep can have the same effect. Help your sinuses drain at night by sleeping with your head slightly elevated. If one side is stuffier than the other, sleep with that side tilted down.

Breathe some steam. Fill the sink with hot water, put a towel over your head and the sink, and breathe in the warm vapors to get moisture into your sinuses. You can also hold a warm wet towel over your face, take a long steamy shower, or just breathe the steam from a cup of hot water or tea.

Try not to blow your nose when you have a cold. It forces mucus into your sinuses along with bacteria and viruses that can lead to sinusitis.

Wash out your nose. Rinsing nasal passages with salt water relieves congestion and other sinus problems. Researchers believe the salt helps break down mucus, but the main benefit is from the rinsing itself. Make your own wash with a quarter teaspoon table salt in 8

Xylitol: a sweet way to stop bacteria

A sweetener that prevents tooth decay may also help slow down sinusitis. Xylitol, a natural sugar alcohol, is used in toothpaste, chewing gum, and mints, and is proven to reduce cavities. It does not kill dental plaque bacteria, but it keeps them from growing. The same type of bacteria also causes ear infections and sinusitis, so doctors came up with a xylitol nasal spray that cut ear infections in children by a third or more. It is now a promising treatment for sinusitis, too, and more research is under way.

ounces of warm water. Use a bulb syringe to squirt this solution into one nostril and let it run out the other. Repeat with the other side, and after 30 seconds or so, gently blow out the remaining solution.

Spice up your food. Spicy foods and seasonings cut through sinus blockages. Eat more hot peppers, horseradish, and garlic. Use hot seasoning in soups and other dishes, and keep a bottle of hot sauce on the table.

Go for a brisk walk. Mild to vigorous exercise opens up nasal passages and clears breathing for many people. Others find it makes clogged sinuses worse. You need exercise anyway, so give it a try and see if it helps.

Smart tips for choosing OTCs

You can look to the drugstore for sinus relief, but choose over-the-counter remedies cautiously. It is easy to waste money on drugs that don't help, actually make your sinusitis worse, or have risky side effects.

It's important to know what causes your sinusitis so you can tailor treatment to your exact symptoms. Your doctor can help you figure that out. Then, stick to single-ingredient products instead of the drug combinations advertised as cold and sinus remedies so you won't load up on ingredients you don't need.

Nebulized antibiotic therapy — inhaling a mist of antibiotics — appears to work better for sinusitis than taking a pill, say researchers at Stanford University.

Use caution with decongestants. Decongestants may help your symptoms temporarily. They shrink your nasal passages, which promotes drainage. Unfortunately, they also thicken your mucus, making it more difficult to clear out your sinuses.

Inhaled decongestants have a dangerous rebound and dependency effect if you use them longer than three to five days. Oral decongestants can raise blood pressure and cause difficulty urinating. The Food and Drug Administration (FDA) has concluded that decongestants do not help with sinusitis and has ordered drug companies to take that information off their labels.

Steer clear of antihistamines. The only time they help sinusitis is when it's caused by allergies. Antihistamines dry out your sinuses and make your mucus more concentrated, which adds to inflammation and infection. And the older drugs that cause drowsiness intensify sinusitis fatigue.

Thin mucus with expectorants. These drugs generally cause mucus to be coughed up from the lungs and are sometimes recommended for sinusitis. They contain mucolytics — ingredients that thin mucous secretions — and help promote draining and reduce tissue swelling. Drink plenty of water to loosen mucus even further. Expectorants also may cause drowsiness or nausea.

Use standard pain relievers. If you suffer from mild fever and pain from sinus pressure, take your usual pain relievers like aspirin, acetaminophen, and ibuprofen. Remember that you will save money by buying the generic versions rather than brand names.

5 reasons to see the doctor

Sinusitis that turns into a sinus infection needs a doctor's attention. It's often hard to know when the viruses that cause colds and flu have given way to a bacterial infection you can stop with antibiotics. Signs you have progressed from a viral to a bacterial infection include:

▶ nasal congestion with a thick discharge that is yellowish to yellow-green or gray.

▶ facial or tooth pain, especially when you bend over.

▶ cold or flu symptoms that last 10 or more days.

How to tell if it's sinusitis

	Sinusitis	Colds	Allergy
Common symptoms	nasal congestion, sore throat or coughing, facial pain or pressure		
Discharge	dark, thick, green, gray, or yellow mucus from nose or back of throat	runny nose with thin, clear-to-yellow mucus	runny nose with clear, watery mucus
Duration	acute, 1 to 3 weeks; chronic, 8 weeks or more	3 to 7 days	seasonal, lasts only when allergens are present
Other symptoms	fatigue, post-nasal drip	fatigue, sneezing	itchy eyes or nose

- symptoms that worsen after five to seven days or return after initial improvement.

- high fever and sudden or severe illness.

Your doctor can decide if you need antibiotics, allergy medicine, or something else. If he thinks it is bacterial, he will probably give you an antibiotic that stops the most common bugs since the exact strain is difficult to determine. If you don't start improving in five or six days, you may need a different drug.

You should take your medication at least 10 to 14 days and maybe as long as three weeks, even though you think you feel fine. Follow your doctor's instructions to the letter. If you stop the medicine too soon, you may not wipe out all the remaining bacteria. They will then continue to multiply and possibly become resistant to the antibiotic.

Secret to solving chronic sinusitis

Chronic sinusitis is a sinus problem that won't go away. It may be one continuous condition that lasts for months, or it may go away and then come back again. Even though it's likely to be less severe, it's something you just can't shake.

The secret to solving your problem is to pinpoint exactly what is causing it. If your sinus misery won't quit, it's time to see a specialist — an otolaryngologist or an allergist — to help you do just that. A specialist has more experience with the condition and can perform more sophisticated tests than your family doctor.

The first step is to rule out underlying conditions like allergies, asthma, immune problems, gastraoesophageal reflux disorder (GERD), and structural blockages. If it appears your condition resulted from previous sinus damage, the specialist will look for a specific type of bacterial infection and treat it with more potent antibiotics. If

Fungus — the key to sinusitis?

You may be growing fungi in your sinuses. As unpleasant as that sounds, it may also be the key to curing your sinusitis. Some doctors believe all chronic sinusitis is an immune response to fungus rather than an infectious disease. They think your immune system may damage your sinus membranes when it overreacts to certain fungi, much the same way it causes allergic reactions.

Their theory is supported by research at the University of Buffalo and the Mayo Clinic that found fungi in the mucus of chronic sinusitis surgery patients. The good news is that treatment with a fungicide proved successful, so a new sinusitis cure may be on the horizon.

the problem is allergies, he will deal with them instead of continuing treatments that don't affect the root cause of your sinusitis.

Along with antibiotics, your doctor may prescribe corticosteroids to reduce inflammation. Steroids are also helpful in treating allergy and asthma. Both nasal and oral steroids have their downsides, so be sure and discuss side effects if your doctor recommends them.

One unusual thing your specialist may check for is the presence of fungi in your mucus. Recent breakthrough research shows some people with chronic sinusitis may have intense immune and inflammatory responses to fungi. (*See box above.*) Scientists are considering both anti-fungal and anti-inflammatory drugs to treat fungal sinusitis.

New hope for sinus sufferers

A lifetime of sinus problems can end up costing you a fortune between doctor's visits and medications. If nothing has worked, surgery may be your best option. Sinus surgery is almost always successful and is now done as a minimally invasive procedure that usually requires only a local anesthetic. But you should only consider it when medical treatment falls short.

You might have surgery to:

▸ clean out infected sinus membranes.

▸ enlarge sinus openings and promote drainage.

▸ remove polyps or repair other obstructions.

▸ eliminate stubborn fungal infections.

The most common surgery today is called functional endoscopic sinus surgery (FESS), and it uses fiberoptics and instruments inserted through a flexible tube in a small opening. Serious complications are rare, and 85 to 90 percent of the people who have FESS surgery report good to excellent relief. But it may take several months for mucous membranes to heal, and you may experience a dull ache around your nose and sinuses. Severe sinusitis cases may still require conventional scalpel surgery to remove infected areas.

Replenish "good" bacteria wiped out by broad-spectrum antibiotics with acidophilus or lactobacillus found in live-culture yogurt.

A few doctors are trying balloon sinuplasty to clear nasal passages. It's similar to the technique surgeons use to open clogged heart valves, called angioplasty. They insert a catheter-mounted balloon into the sinus cavity, and as the balloon inflates, it expands the sinus opening and restores its ability to drain normally.

The procedure is still new, so long-term results of its effectiveness aren't yet available. But it may offer new hope to those who suffer with chronic sinus problems.

Top tips for healthy sinuses

Preventive measures can do as much to keep your sinuses healthy as steps you take to cure sinusitis.

Make wise food choices. The right diet helps heal and protect your mucous membranes and strengthen your immune system. Choose foods with lots of vitamins and minerals, particularly the ones below.

▶ **Vitamin C.** Fend off colds, allergies, and sinus infections with colorful fruits and vegetables like apricots, cantaloupe, strawberries, red and green peppers, kale, and broccoli.

▶ **Vitamin A.** Keep mucous membranes healthy with carrots, sweet potatoes, mangoes, and winter squash. They're full of beta carotene, which your body converts to vitamin A.

▶ **Zinc.** Strengthen your immunity with the zinc in beef liver, dark turkey meat, and black beans. It also helps change beta carotene to vitamin A.

Breathe the best air. Avoid cigarette smoke and other pollutants. If allergies fire up your sinus inflammation, take extra care to identify and avoid your particular allergens. Use a humidifier to put moisture back into the air, especially during dry winter months if you heat your home with a forced-air furnace. It makes it easier to breathe and keeps your sinuses from drying out.

Avoid pressure situations. Air travel can be difficult for sinusitis sufferers because of changes in pressure as the plane takes off and lands. Try decongestant nose drops or inhalers before a flight to avoid this problem.

Diving into a swimming pool isn't good for sinuses because it forces water up through your nasal passages. Chlorine in the pool irritates your nose and sinus lining. Drinking alcohol can also lead to sinus problems because it causes swelling in nasal and sinus membranes.

Sleep apnea

Say goodnight to bedtime breathing problems

British writer Anthony Burgess wrote, "Laugh and the world laughs with you; snore and you sleep alone." If you or your spouse snores, you know the truth in this saying. Loud snoring can be bothersome to those within earshot. It can also be a sign of sleep apnea, a dangerous condition affecting 12 million people in America.

People with sleep apnea stop breathing during the night, from about 10 seconds to as long as a minute at a time. They awaken briefly to start breathing again, usually not realizing they have woken up. These incidents can happen hundreds of times each night.

Comic strips and television shows make fun of people who snore loudly, but sleep apnea is no joke. Recent research links sleep apnea to many serious health problems, including depression, strokes, heart attacks, high blood pressure, diabetes, and weight gain. It also makes you tired and cranky during the day, and it can lead to deadly traffic accidents.

Foolproof way to pin down your problem

Your doctor might send you for a sleep study, or polysomnograph, at a sleep center if he thinks you have sleep apnea. A sleep study can be expensive, easily costing $2,000 to $4,000. Some insurance companies require a referral from your primary doctor. Some cover the cost of a study only if it's done in a sleep center accredited by the American Academy of Sleep Medicine.

If you've heard of home sleep-monitoring equipment, you may wonder if this cheaper option is just as good as a full study in a center. Some home devices test for insomnia, while others look for sleep apnea. But a recent study found that the home units don't do a good job of detecting breathing problems during sleep. In spite of the high cost, a sleep study is the best way to find out if your snoring is really a sign of a dangerous breathing condition.

> Don't take sleeping pills or tranquilizers if you have sleep apnea. These sleep aids can relax soft throat tissue, causing it to sag and making sleep apnea worse.

What happens in a sleep study? Basically, you sleep overnight in a sleep center while your breathing, brain waves, muscle movement, and heart activity are monitored. You'll be hooked up to machines so sleep technicians can keep tabs on how you're doing and record your sleep. Follow these suggestions to make your sleep study as comfortable and productive as possible.

Pack your bags. Take your pajamas, toothbrush, clothes for the morning — the same things you need when you stay overnight in a hotel. A sleep center has individual sleeping rooms similar to hotel or hospital rooms, including facilities to shower in the morning. If you like a certain pillow or blanket, take it with you.

Watch what you drink. Avoid caffeine and alcohol before your sleep study, since they can change your sleep patterns and alter the test results.

Prepare to get connected. Many sleep centers ask that you avoid using lots of hair gel, spray, or other products before a sleep study for easier attachment of electrodes and tapes to your head and scalp. Remove fingernail polish and artificial nails from at least two fingers. You'll wear a device called an oximeter on your finger to check your blood oxygen level through the nail. Also, avoid makeup, which can keep electrodes from sticking to the skin on your face.

Get there early. You'll be asked to arrive a couple hours before bedtime, since it takes about 45 minutes to connect leads, belts, and monitors, then more time for you to get relaxed for sleep.

Relax and enjoy the ride. Basically, the rest is up to you. Sleep as you normally do at home while the technicians and machines keep track of your sleep activities. Some people fear they won't be able to sleep connected to wires, but most people are so tired they have no trouble falling asleep.

Drivers who fall asleep at the wheel cause as many accidents as drunk drivers, according to the National Highway Transportation Safety Association. About 1,550 deaths occur each year because of sleepy drivers.

For a list of accredited sleep disorders centers and laboratories for sleep-related breathing disorders in your area, check the American Academy of Sleep Medicine's Web site at *www.sleepcenters.org.*

Clever gadgets help you cope

How you treat your sleep apnea depends on the type of sleep apnea you have. Obstructive sleep apnea, caused when your tongue and throat muscles relax and block your airway, is the most common type. Central sleep apnea, when the brain doesn't send the right signal for breathing during sleep, is more common among people older than age 65. Complex sleep apnea is a combination of both types.

There's hope for people struggling to get a good night's sleep. Several gadgets can treat obstructive sleep apnea, helping you breathe and sleep better.

Mouth guards. For mild sleep apnea, doctors recommend you first try using a special dental appliance, similar to a sports mouth guard. These guards work by moving the jaw and tongue forward to allow for better breathing and less snoring. Your dentist should fit the guard to your mouth. Then, you should have a sleep study to be sure it's doing its job. Guards approved to treat sleep apnea are usually covered by health insurance.

Pillows. Specially made pillows that stretch the neck to improve air flow while you sleep work well for some people. Other pillows, such as the Sona Pillow, are designed to encourage you to sleep on your side. The Sona Pillow is approved by the Food and Drug Administration to treat snoring and mild sleep apnea. For more information about the Sona Pillow call 866-935-9166 toll free or visit *www.sonapillow.com* on the Internet.

Continuous positive airway pressure (CPAP). CPAP devices work by sending a constant stream of air through a mask over the nose and/or mouth to keep the airways open. This treatment works for about 80 to 90 percent of people, and it has the

Sleep apnea linked to impotence

Men with sleep apnea are more likely to have impotence, also called erectile dysfunction (ED), or trouble getting or maintaining an erection. A recent study found that one commonly used treatment for impotence may only make things worse. In the study, men with severe sleep apnea took one dose of the drug Viagra, used to treat ED.

Researchers noted that the men had more incidents of interrupted breathing and lower oxygen levels in their blood as they slept — signs of worsened sleep apnea. The study was small, so more information is needed to know the full effects of Viagra on sleep apnea.

added benefit of lowering your blood pressure. But some people have trouble getting used to wearing a mask while sleeping, and it can cause side effects, like nasal congestion and dryness. In fact, one-third of those who try CPAP give it up. To increase your odds of success, see the following story *11 tips to make CPAP work for you*. CPAP machines can be rented or purchased, and they are usually covered by health insurance.

Bilevel positive airway pressure (BiPAP). Similar to CPAP, this system works by changing the amount of air pressure as you breathe in and out. BiPAP is most helpful if you have a lung disease along with sleep apnea or if your carbon dioxide levels are too high. Health insurance doesn't always cover this treatment, and the machines can be more expensive than CPAP units.

11 tips to make CPAP work for you

Using a continuous positive airway pressure (CPAP) device is the best way to treat obstructive sleep apnea, but it can be difficult to use. Give it your best shot, and try these hints from the American Academy of Sleep Medicine.

▶ **Start slowly.** Wear your CPAP for short periods during the day, perhaps while you relax or watch television.

▶ **Ramp up.** Use the setting that allows the machine to increase air pressure slowly.

▶ **Be consistent.** Use the CPAP every night and during naps. It works best if you sleep with it regularly. You'll get used to it sooner, too.

▶ **Muffle the noise.** Place the unit under your bed to dampen the sound if it keeps you awake. Newer CPAP models are nearly silent.

▶ **Adjust for fit.** The mask, headgear, tubing, and straps can be adjusted for the most comfort.

▶ **Ease congestion.** For mild nasal congestion, try a saline nasal spray. If you have serious congestion, ask your doctor if you should take a decongestant.

▶ **Dampen the air.** If you have trouble with breathing dry air, find a humidifier that fits your CPAP unit.

▶ **Try nasal pillows.** They add cushioning to the CPAP mask, making it more comfortable.

▶ **Keep it clean.** Once a week, clean the mask, tubing, and headgear.

▶ **Change the filter.** Check and replace the filters in the CPAP unit and humidifier regularly.

▶ **Ask for help.** Your doctor and machine supplier can make sure you have the correct machine, mask, and air pressure settings. Don't give up on CPAP without asking for help.

Latest news on surgical treatments

Surgery can treat sleep apnea, but it's not for everyone. Depending on how your mouth and throat are built and what is causing your sleep apnea, you may not be a good candidate. For many people, the problem can be solved through less-drastic measures, like losing weight or trying a CPAP machine.

Health insurance may not cover some surgical options, and they can be expensive. But for people with specific mouth or throat abnormalities, one of these procedures might be a good choice.

UPPP. Short for uvulopalatopharyngoplasty, UPPP is surgery to remove excess soft tissue at the back of the throat. If you still have tonsils or adenoids, they are also taken out. UPPP can expand your airway, allowing for better breathing at night, but it works only about 65 percent of the time. It's one of the most painful treatments, and recovery takes weeks. Common side effects include infection, voice changes, swallowing problems, changes in sense of smell, and excess mucus in the throat. Even worse, if you try UPPP and it doesn't work, using a CPAP machine can be less effective.

LAUP. This is a simpler version of UPPP that can be done in a doctor's office. Technically called laser-assisted uvulopalatoplasty, LAUP uses a laser to cut away the uvula, or tissue that hangs down at the back of the throat. It may take more than one session, and it's only good if the uvula is causing your trouble. This surgery also has low success rates, and it can cause throat dryness, narrowing, and scarring.

Radiofrequency ablation. Radio waves aimed at the base of the tongue heat, stiffen, and shrink small sections of tissue. It can be done in a doctor's office, requires about 10 treatments, and works best for mild sleep apnea.

Get help from the experts

Kathleen, a 58-year-old research librarian, snored loudly and didn't sleep well for a year before her husband urged her to get help. Her doctor referred her for an overnight sleep study to determine if she had sleep apnea. Kathleen expected the worst when she agreed.

"My preconceived idea was that I would be sleeping on a cot in a lab," she recalls. "It was not at all like that." Instead, the sleep room was similar to a nice hospital room, with an adjoining bathroom, television, and simple furniture. And although she felt she didn't sleep well, she was successfully diagnosed with sleep apnea and fitted with a CPAP device to help her breathing. Now she's happy to be able to fall asleep quickly and get a good night's rest using the machine.

Pillar implants. This new, reversible option shows promise, and it's less expensive and less painful than other surgical procedures. Braids of polyester are injected into the soft palate on the roof of the mouth, making it more rigid and less likely to collapse during sleep. Scar tissue forms around the braids to make them even stiffer.

Jaw or tongue restructuring. Surgeons can advance your jaw, move your tongue forward, or fix a deviated septum. These major surgeries might make your face look different, but they can help solve your breathing problem.

Tracheostomy. A last-chance option, tracheostomy is done only if your life is in danger from severe sleep apnea. In this surgery, the surgeon makes a quarter-size breathing hole in the front of the throat. It's extreme, but it's nearly 100 percent successful.

Playing the didgeridoo — that long, wooden, horn-like instrument from Australia — may reduce snoring and daytime sleepiness from sleep apnea. Researchers think regular practice strengthens muscles of the upper airway.

6 simple steps to more restful sleep

Not all people with sleep apnea snore, and not everyone who snores has sleep apnea. A National Sleep Foundation survey found that 32 percent of people ages 55 to 84 say they snore at least a few nights a week. If you or your spouse snores on most nights, it's likely someone is longing for some peace and quiet.

People who may have sleep apnea should see a doctor for a diagnosis and treatment advice. You wouldn't want to merely quiet the snoring if it's a sign of a more serious health condition. But if snoring is your only problem, follow these steps to cut down on snoring and create a more peaceful bedroom.

Lose excess weight. Here's another reason to pay more attention to your diet and exercise habits. Snoring is much more common among people who are overweight, probably because extra fat deposits in the throat make the airway narrower.

Stop smoking. If you avoid the nasal congestion that can come from smoking, you can probably also avoid the snoring it causes.

Avoid alcohol near bedtime. Alcohol narrows your breathing passages by relaxing the muscles in your airway, which leads to snoring. Although drinking alcohol may help you fall asleep faster, you'll wake up more during the night and have trouble falling back to sleep.

Sleep on your side. Sleeping on your back can cause your mouth to fall open and your throat to collapse, making snoring louder. If you have trouble staying on your side during the night, try sewing a pocket into the back of your pajamas and inserting a tennis ball. That'll send you back to your side.

Raise the head of your bed. One study found that sleeping in a more upright position could ease snoring. Raise yourself by propping up your back or head with pillows. You can also raise your bed by putting blocks of wood under your headboard.

Open your nasal passages. Some people only snore when they have a stuffy nose from colds or allergies. If that's you, try using the nasal strips many football players wear to breathe better. Studies show the strips reduce snoring in people with stuffy noses. Breathe Right is a well-known brand, but less-expensive, generic versions are also available.

What about the many other over-the-counter nasal sprays, drops, and remedies that promise to cure snoring? Research says these products claim to do a lot more good than they really do for most people. Don't waste your money.

Dollars&Sense
Medicine safety at home

Simple, clear instructions, with no confusing doctor-speak, on ways to take, store, and use medicines properly, can keep you safe from deadly drug interactions and accidental overdoses. Start with these tips for taking prescription drugs safely.

Focus on your task. Pay attention to what you are doing each time you take a pill, and you will be less likely to make mistakes.

▸ Keep medicines in their original bottles, unless placing them in pill boxes. Never store different drugs together in the same bottle.

▸ Take each medicine exactly as prescribed. Taking medicine too frequently in an effort to "speed up" the effects is a big mistake and can cause dangerous overdoses, even with seemingly harmless drugs like acetaminophen (Tylenol).

▸ Check with your pharmacist about the proper way to handle your meds. Not all pills can safely be crushed, dissolved, or split.

▸ Mark the lids and labels of your medicines with different colored stickers or nail polishes to help tell them apart.

▸ Read the label every time you take a medicine to make sure you are taking the right one, the right way.

▸ Turn on the light when you take medicines at night to be sure you get the right ones. Read the label under bright light. Your eyes need about three times more light to read at age 60 than they did at age 30.

▸ Don't take anyone else's drugs. They can mask important symptoms from your doctor and interact dangerously with other medications.

▸ Continue taking a medicine for as long as your doctor tells you to, even if you start feeling better. Always talk to your doctor before you stop taking a drug.

Store them properly. Store medications in a cool, dry, dark place like a kitchen cabinet or bedroom shelf. Don't keep them in the bathroom, where heat and moisture can damage them, and don't store them in the refrigerator unless your doctor, pharmacist, or the drug's label says to do so.

Toss out the old. Clean out your medicine cabinet every six months and toss expired over-the-counter (OTC) and prescription drugs. Old medications are not only unsafe, but they probably won't work. Don't flush them down the toilet, however. Drugs leach into the water supply, contaminating streams, fish, and eventually people. Instead, ask your pharmacy or doctor's office to dispose of them.

Never forget another dose. Remembering to take all your medicines is no small challenge, especially if you have complicated dosing schedules. Try this advice to stay on track.

▸ Plan ahead by organizing pills in a pillbox.

▸ Tape notes strategically around the house on the bathroom mirror, by the coffee pot, on the bedside clock, and elsewhere to remind you to take your meds.

▸ Establish a buddy system with a friend who also takes pills daily. Take turns calling each other when it's time for the next dose.

▸ Use a small chalkboard or dry erase board to stay on track. Put a check mark and the time next to each drug name when you take it. Erase them all the next day and start over.

Get an annual Rx check-up. Once a year, bring all your medications to the doctor's office for a "medicine check-up" — including all prescriptions, OTC drugs, supplements, vitamins, and herbal remedies you use regularly. Have him go over the dosage instructions, warnings, and possible interactions with you, and ask if you can stop taking any of them.

Fill him in on OTCs. Let your doctor know if you use OTC remedies regularly. Most are not meant for long-term use, and your doctor may be able to prescribe a more effective medication.

Stroke

Best ways to thwart a brain attack

Every 45 seconds someone in the United States has a stroke. Stroke, also called brain attack, ranks third behind heart disease and cancer as a cause of death.

Ischemic stroke, the most common type, occurs when a blood clot blocks blood vessels to the brain, or in the brain, cutting off the brain's supply of oxygen. In a hemorrhagic stroke, a blood vessel bursts, leading to bleeding in or around the brain. Both types of stroke can have devastating results. Besides killing you, stroke can also affect your motor skills, speech, memory, behavior, senses, and thought processes depending on which parts of your brain are damaged.

Who does stroke target? Older people, blacks, men, and those with a family history of stroke are at higher risk. Other risk factors include high blood pressure, high cholesterol, heart disease, diabetes, smoking, and obesity. Luckily, you can protect yourself from a brain attack. Discover what steps you can take to prevent, recognize, and recover from a stroke.

Save a life with swift action

Every second counts when it comes to a stroke. The longer oxygen remains cut off from your brain, the more damage occurs.

You definitely grow older on your birthday. But, according to a recent study, you are also 27 percent more likely to have a stroke, TIA, or heart attack. The added stress could be to blame.

Often, acting quickly can be the difference between life and death. That's why it's so important to know the symptoms of a stroke and how to respond to a brain attack.

Recognize the signs. Symptoms of a stroke include sudden weakness or numbness of the face, arm, or leg, especially on one side of the body; confusion; trouble speaking or understanding; difficulty seeing; dizziness, loss of balance or coordination; and a sudden, severe headache.

Even if the symptoms pass quickly without any lasting effects, don't ignore them. They could be warning signs of a transient ischemic attack, or TIA. These "mini-strokes" often come before a full-blown stroke, and they should be taken seriously.

Give a pop quiz. When you suspect someone is having a stroke, ask the person these three simple questions:

▶ Can you smile?

▶ Can you raise both arms above your head?

▶ Can you speak a complete sentence?

If the person has trouble with any of these tasks, take immediate action.

Call for help. If you think you — or someone else — may be having a stroke, call 911 right away. You can also drive the person to the hospital. But never let someone having a stroke drive himself — and never attempt to drive yourself if you are the one experiencing the stroke.

Once at the hospital, you'll get quick treatment. If you arrive within three hours of the start of an ischemic stroke, you may receive the emergency drug alteplase (Activase). Also called a tissue plasminogen activator (t-PA), this clot-busting drug can stop an ischemic stroke in progress. In the case of a hemorrhagic stroke, surgery may be necessary.

Identify stroke type for best treatment

When you arrive at the hospital, diagnostic tests, such as a CT scan, help determine whether your stroke is ischemic or hemorrhagic. Once doctors know the type of stroke, they take different approaches. Here are some steps they may take.

Ischemic stroke	Hemorrhagic stroke
Control blood pressure and body temperature. Blood pressure should not be too high or too low. Fever can worsen damage to the brain.	Lower blood pressure slowly to minimize bleeding from ruptured artery.
Administer the clot-busting drug alteplase, or t-PA, if it's within three hours of the stroke's onset.	Use the sugar mannitol and diuretics to reduce fluid retention and swelling of the brain.
Use the anticoagulants heparin or warfarin — or aspirin to prevent and control blood clots.	Use calcium channel blockers, like nimodipine (Nimotop), to reduce damage from spasms of blood vessels in the brain.
Perform a carotid endarterectomy to remove plaque from carotid artery. A carotid angioplasty, with or without stents, may also be performed to re-open a blocked carotid artery.	Perform surgery to clip aneurysm and stop bleeding. Emergency surgery to drain accumulated fluid may also be needed.

2 ways to prevent a second stroke

Once you've had a stroke, you increase your risk of having another one. That's where blood thinners come in. Antiplatelet drugs, like aspirin, and anticoagulants, like warfarin, help prevent blood clots from forming. Your doctor may suggest these drugs if you are at high risk for stroke, if you've had a transient ischemic attack (TIA), or to prevent a second stroke.

Antiplatelets. Aspirin and other antiplatelet drugs, including clopidogrel (Plavix) and ticlopidine (Ticlid), keep the platelets in your blood from clumping together. Aspirin, the most common antiplatelet drug, can lower your risk of a second stroke by 25 percent.

Anticoagulants. These drugs thin your blood and prevent it from clotting. The most common anticoagulant is warfarin

Reclaim your life with rehab

Recovering from a stroke takes hard work. You may have to learn to walk, talk, or function all over again. Two recent studies provide hope for stroke survivors.

At the University of Alabama – Birmingham, researchers found that constraint therapy helps improve movement even years after a stroke. This strategy involves restraining your good arm so you are forced to use your weakened arm for everyday tasks.

In another study, researchers in Taiwan showed that thermal stimulation also spurs recovery in paralyzed arms and hands. This technique involves alternating hot and cold packs, wrapped in towels, on your hand and wrist. Not all rehab is physical. Depression often strikes stroke survivors, and it should be treated.

(Coumadin), which is often prescribed to people with multiple risk factors for stroke.

However, blood-thinning drugs come with risks. Because they prevent your blood from clotting, they may increase your risk of bleeding. While they protect against ischemic stroke, they slightly increase your risk for hemorrhagic stroke.

> During a stroke, it's as if your brain ages in dog years — 8.7 hours every second, 3.1 weeks every minute, 3.6 years every hour, and a whopping 36 years for an untreated stroke.

When taking these common prescription drugs, you should never consume too much vitamin K. This vitamin, found in broccoli, spinach, cabbage, kale, and brussels sprouts, makes warfarin less effective, which increases your risk of blood clots. This is critical news you probably haven't heard from your doctor or pharmacist. Several drugs and supplements can also interfere with warfarin, so make sure to tell your doctor about any medication you are taking.

Similarly, the FDA recently issued a warning about the danger of taking ibuprofen with aspirin. Mixing these two painkillers can lessen the antiplatelet effect of aspirin.

Simple strategies for stroke prevention

Experts estimate that more than half of all strokes could be prevented. Here are some terrific tactics to sidestep stroke.

▸ **Control high blood pressure.** High blood pressure, the No. 1 risk factor for stroke, contributes to 70 percent of all strokes. Keep your blood pressure within a healthy range. For helpful tips on how to do that, check out the *High blood pressure* chapter.

▶ **Quit smoking.** Smokers have a 50-percent greater risk of stroke than nonsmokers. Cigarettes boost your risk of both ischemic and hemorrhagic stroke. You should also do your best to avoid secondhand smoke.

▶ **Lose weight.** Obesity, especially abdominal obesity, dramatically boosts your risk of stroke. Cut back on calories and become more active to shed those extra pounds.

▶ **Exercise regularly.** Being a couch potato can triple your risk of stroke compared to people who are physically active. Exercise helps you overcome stroke risk factors like obesity and high blood pressure. Aim for at least 30 minutes of activity a day.

▶ **Avoid alcohol.** Drinking moderately may reduce your risk of ischemic stroke, but it boosts your risk of hemorrhagic stroke. Heavy drinking causes several health problems, like raising your blood pressure and producing irregular heartbeats, that can increase your stroke risk. Limit yourself to no more than two drinks a day.

'Plane' truth about blood clots

Your next flight may leave you with more than just jet lag. Flying increases your risk of deep vein thrombosis, or painful blood clots in your legs. That may have something to do with the low cabin pressure during flights or just sitting still for so long. Deep vein thrombosis is a common complication following a stroke because of the stroke victim's limited mobility.

No matter what the reason for the risk, you can take steps to lessen it. On long flights, get up and stretch your legs often. Drink plenty of water to stay hydrated, and avoid alcoholic beverages and sleeping pills. Compression stockings may also help. You can find them for as little as $16, but a good pair will cost about $60.

▶ **Improve your cholesterol.** Boosting your HDL, or good, cholesterol can reduce your risk of stroke. So can lowering your total and LDL, or bad, cholesterol. Eat a healthy diet, exercise, and take cholesterol-lowering medication, if necessary, to achieve your goals.

Negative emotions, such as anger, fear, irritability, or nervousness, may also contribute to stroke. Find ways to stay calm or avoid stressful situations. Air pollution may also boost your risk of ischemic stroke, so moving from the city to the country might do you some good.

It's not just the Beach Boys who feel good vibrations. Vibrating insoles may improve your balance after a stroke, according to Boston University researchers. More studies of this technology are planned.

Foil stroke with healthy foods

What you put in your belly can help safeguard your brain. To ward off stroke, make sure your menu includes plenty of the following foods.

Fruits and veggies. Several studies have found that eating more fruits and vegetables reduces your risk of stroke. In fact, a recent British study determined that eating three to five servings of fruits and vegetables each day lowers your stroke risk by 11 percent. If you eat more than five servings, you've slashed your stroke risk by 26 percent. Here's why — fruits and veggies are loaded with potassium, folate, fiber, and antioxidants like vitamin C, beta carotene, and flavonoids.

Orange juice. Why take Bayer when you can eliminate blood clots with a juicy, natural "formula" that won't upset your stomach? Rich in vitamin C, which has been shown to reduce the risk of stroke, oranges also contain more than 60 flavonoids. Many of these antioxidants have the power to stop blood clots from forming.

Other fruit juices, like grape or cranberry, can also help. One glass a day should do the trick.

Spinach. Popeye's favorite veggie, a great source of the B vitamin folate, has protected against stroke in both human and animal studies. Other good sources of folate include legumes, peas, asparagus, and enriched breads, cereals, and pastas.

Fish. Fatty fish contain omega-3 fatty acids, which help with stroke risks like high blood pressure, high cholesterol, and inflammation. But how you prepare your fish makes a difference. A recent Harvard study found that eating tuna or other baked or broiled fish lowers your risk of stroke, but munching on fried fish and fish sandwiches actually increases your risk.

Whole grains. The fiber in whole grains fights both high blood pressure and high cholesterol, making it an ideal weapon against stroke. Cereal fiber, the kind in oats, wheat, rye, and barley, provides the most protection.

Dairy foods. A recent study found that calcium may lessen the severity of a stroke and improve your chances of recovery. Besides low-fat dairy products, good sources of calcium include legumes, green vegetables like broccoli and kale, and canned fish with bones, like sardines.

Your diet should also include plenty of potassium and magnesium, two more minerals that help regulate blood pressure and guard against stroke. Bananas, dried fruits, molasses, cereals, nuts, and raw vegetables provide potassium, while you can find magnesium in seafood, dry beans, whole grains, and nuts.

Urinary tract infections

Head off problems before they start

Bad bacteria sometimes multiply in the urethra, kidneys, or bladder, resulting in a urinary tract infection (UTI). Women are 30 times more likely to get one than men. Diabetes, kidney stones, and an enlarged prostate also up the risk, as does wearing a catheter.

While some people experience classic UTI symptoms — a frequent urge to urinate, burning, and cloudy or reddish urine — seniors may not. Instead, they may experience nausea, vomiting, abdominal pain, confusion, coughing, or shortness of breath.

Seeing a doctor for diagnosis is important. Although most urinary tract infections are mild and easily treated, they can lead to kidney stones, kidney scarring, and, in postmenopausal women, incontinence.

You'll probably need a course of antibiotics to kick a UTI, but the easiest remedy is to prevent infection in the first place. Start with these natural home remedies to help urinary problems, all without drugs or surgery.

'Berry' the burn of UTIs

Long before antibiotics, cranberries reigned as a popular remedy for urinary tract infections (UTIs). Science proves they still do.

Drinking cranberry juice daily can prevent UTIs and curb the need for expensive antibiotics and doctor visits.

The red pigments, or proanthocyanidins, in cranberries and blueberries seem to keep UTI-causing bacteria from clinging to the walls of your urinary tract. Without a good grip, bacteria such as *E. coli* can't dig in and cause infection. Cranberry juice, in particular, seems to keep regular bacteria as well as antibiotic-resistant super bugs from getting a foothold in the urinary tract.

But these berries work best as preventive measures, not treatments for existing infections. Some evidence suggests sexually active adult women could see a 50-percent drop in recurring UTIs with cranberry juice or supplements. However, no solid evidence shows the fruit can cure existing infections.

Experts suggest anywhere from 8 ounces of 100-percent pure, unsweetened cranberry juice daily, to 8 to 16 ounces of cranberry juice cocktail a day. If you prefer supplements, try taking one 300- to 400-milligram cranberry tablet twice daily. It may take four to eight weeks to see results.

People prone to oxalate kidney stones should talk to their doctor before starting cranberry therapy, as long-term use could raise the risk of these stones. Also, discuss it with your doctor if you take the blood thinner warfarin (Coumadin), as the berries could boost its effect.

Say good-bye to urinary problems

Simply adding a few common foods to your diet could spell the end of urinary tract infections. What could be easier? Experts believe some foods help keep bacteria from invading the urinary tract.

Cool the burn with creamy treat. Most UTIs are caused by bad bacteria from stool contaminating the urethra. In premenopausal women, the vagina is home to *lactobacilli*, a family of good bacteria that includes acidophilus. *Lactobacilli* create an unfriendly environment for bad bugs such as *E. coli*, the main cause of uncomplicated UTIs. *Lactobacilli* levels naturally drop after menopause, perhaps one reason older women are prone to UTIs. Adding back the good bugs through diet could help reverse that trend.

A Finnish study involving more than 200 premenopausal women found those who ate fermented dairy products like yogurt and cheese at least three times a week were almost 80 percent less likely to develop a UTI as women who ate them less than once a week. Fresh dairy such as milk had no protective effect. Other studies show taking probiotics supplements helps restore the natural balance of bacteria in the urinary and genital areas.

Over-the-counter remedies such as AZO Standard can temporarily ease UTI symptoms like burning and itching, but they will not cure the underlying infection.

Move over, cranberries. This same Finnish study delivered more good news. Along with cranberries, eating fresh strawberries, raspberries, cloudberries, lingonberries (a European relative of cranberries), or drinking juices made from these berries all lowered women's risk for UTIs. Researchers say you can thank flavonols, natural compounds plants make to ward off their own microbial infections. Fruits such as apples, plums, and cherries are packed with flavonols, but in general berries boast the highest amounts.

Find big relief with tiny seeds. Grapefruit seeds seem to have antibacterial powers that could be used to treat urinary tract infections. Four case studies from Nigeria found eating five to six grapefruit seeds every eight hours for two weeks cleared up urinary tract infections without the need for antibiotics. In one man's case, the seeds even seem to have worked against antibiotic-resistant bacteria. Research has confirmed that grapefruit seed extract has the same antimicrobial properties. Get your doctor's advice on this remedy before trying it. Remember, UTIs can become serious if not treated properly.

The bottom line on UTI treatments

Antibiotic	Pros and cons
trimethoprim-sulfamethoxa-zole (TMP-SMX) (Bactrim, Cotrim, Septra)	First choice treatment for most UTIs. Should not be used by people allergic to sulfa drugs or if infection occurred after dental work.
ciprofloxacin (Cipro), ofloxacin (Floxacin), other quinolones	Usually second-choice treatment. Expensive. Seems to work better than TMP-SMX in the elderly. Commonly used in complicated or catheter-related UTIs, in infections that don't respond to TMP-SMX, and in people allergic to TMP-SMX.
nitrofurantoin (Furadantin, Macrodantin)	Relatively inexpensive and a good alternative to TMP-SMX or quinolones. Tends to cause upset stomach. Interacts with many other drugs. Not for use in people with kidney disease.
tetracyclines (doxycycline, tetracycline, minocycline)	Used in long-term treatment of UTIs caused by Mycoplasma or Chlamydia. Can cause skin reactions to sunlight, burning in throat, and tooth discoloration.
amoxicillin	Until recently, was the standard treatment for UTIs. Is now ineffective against *E. coli* UTIs in up to 25 percent of cases.
fosfomycin (Monurol)	Comes as an orange, soluble powder. Not as effective as other antibiotics, but fewer bacteria are resistant to it.
amoxicillin-clavulanate	Not useful in treating *E. coli*.

Clean up your act for a healthy tract

How you handle matters "down there" has a lot to do with whether or not you get urinary tract infections. Practicing a few hygiene tips could help slash your incidence of UTIs.

▶ Wipe front to back after using the restroom. Wash urinary and genital areas with soapy water or wet wipes after each bowel movement.

▶ Urinate both before and after sex to empty the bladder and flush bacteria from the urethra.

▶ Wear underwear and stockings with cotton crotches, and change them at least once a day. Avoid wearing tight pants.

▶ Avoid using bath oils, feminine hygiene sprays, powders, or any other perfumed products near the genital area, especially if you have skin allergies.

▶ Use sanitary napkins rather than tampons, and change them after each urination. Some experts think tampons encourage the development of UTIs.

▶ Take showers instead of baths. Soaking in a tub helps bacteria enter the urethra.

▶ Drink plenty of fluids, such as water and cranberry juice, each day. Many experts believe emptying the bladder often keeps it from getting irritated, cutting the risk of infection.

> About half of women with UTI-like symptoms actually have a different condition such as vaginitis, interstitial cystitis, or irritation of the urethra.

New catheters cut UTI risk

Catheters cause about four out of five of the UTIs people get in hospitals. The longer you wear a catheter, the higher your risk of infection. Having diarrhea while wearing a catheter pushes that risk even higher.

Researchers are testing new devices in an effort to cut down infections. One for men, a condom-style catheter, fits over the penis rather than inserting into the urethra, like indwelling catheters. In a new study of men without dementia, those who wore condom-style catheters experienced less pain and discomfort, while men with indwelling catheters were nearly five times as likely to develop bacteria in their urine, UTIs, or to die.

Experts are also testing catheters coated with antibiotics, silver nitrate, and other compounds to lower infection rates. One, LoFric, shows some promise, but none are foolproof.

Whether you need a catheter for a few days or few months, you can take steps to protect yourself from bacterial infection.

▶ Remember to drink plenty of fluids, and aim for three glasses of cranberry juice daily.

▶ Wash your hands before touching the catheter or the area around it.

▶ Clean the catheter and the surrounding area gently with soap and water daily and after each bowel movement.

▶ Keep the catheter tube free of kinks and knots.

▶ Stabilize the drainage bag against your leg using tape or bandages. Be careful not to wrap them so tight you cut off blood flow in the leg.

▶ Keep the drainage bag off the floor.

Dollars&Sense
Spot the truth behind health claims

New treatments spring up every day promising to cure whatever ails you. Scam artists tend to target people with chronic or incurable conditions like arthritis, obesity, memory loss, Alzheimer's disease, cancer, or diabetes. Don't get taken for a ride.

Proven treatments undergo years of study before experts start recommending them. Look at the evidence backing a remedy, and consider these questions.

▸ Who funded the research? Did the company selling the product pay for the studies or did a nonbiased group like the National Institutes of Health?

▸ Was the study done with people, animals, or test tubes? Results from animal and lab experiments don't mean a treatment will work in people.

▸ If the trial involved people, did it meet the "gold standard?" That is, was it randomized, double-blinded, and placebo-controlled?

▸ How many people took part in the study, and for how long? In general, the more people tested and the longer a study lasts, the more meaningful the results.

One place to find easy-to-read, unbiased information about herbs, nutrition, and alternative supplements is the Office of Dietary Supplements, a department of the National Institutes of Health. Visit the Web site *http://dietary-supplements.info.nih.gov,* and click on "Health Information."

The Food and Drug Administration (FDA) issues warnings and recalls via a toll-free information line at 888-463-6332 and on its Web site at *www.cfsan.fda.gov.* The FDA and the Federal Trade Commission take legal action against companies making false health claims. You can see who has been caught by visiting the Web sites *www.ftc.gov* or *www.fda.gov/oc/enforcement.html.*

Weight gain

Proven solutions for a serious problem

More than a billion people in the world are either obese or overweight, and the numbers are expanding rapidly. Excess weight boosts your risk of serious diseases like type 2 diabetes, heart disease, stroke, and some forms of cancer. Obesity costs Americans more than $117 billion every year in medical costs and lost productivity.

Weight gain is not a mystery. When you put more fuel — or food — into your body than you burn, the excess energy is stored as fat. To manage your weight, you must balance intake with output.

The search is always on for a quick and easy solution — a miracle diet, magic pill, or super exercise machine. But in the end, the only proven solution is a combination of sensible eating habits and regular exercise.

Get the skinny on diet pills

Americans spend $2 billion a year on diet pills of one kind or another. Do they work? Sometimes — but only when you adopt some lifestyle changes, like cutting calories and exercising more. What they won't do is magically melt pounds away while you sit on your couch and eat whatever you want.

Your doctor may prescribe one of several drugs to either curb your appetite or prevent your body from absorbing some of the fat you eat if you are obese. Most of these weight loss drugs are only approved for short-term use, and they all have unpleasant side effects. Some are mild, like headaches or stomach cramps, but others are serious, like high blood pressure.

And here's something else to consider — most weight loss drugs lose their effectiveness over time, and some can become addictive or trigger depression. These drugs don't work the same for everyone, so the exact dosage and results vary. Weight loss drugs can be put into three general categories:

Appetite suppressants. These include the many herbs, drugs, and supplements sold to either curb your appetite or make you feel full. Phentermine — the "phen" part of the discontinued diet drug Fen-phen — is the most-common prescription appetite suppressant. Brand names, including Adipex, Ionamin, and Fastin, can cost two or more times as much as generic phentermine. Fen-phen was banned several years ago because fenfluramine, the "fen" ingredient, was linked to heart valve problems. Phentermine is not associated with heart problems.

Other prescription appetite suppressants include sibutramine (Meridia) and diethylpropion (Tenuate). Rimonabant (Acomplia) is an appetite suppressant sold in Europe that is expected to receive U.S. Food and Drug Administration approval in 2007.

Fat absorption inhibitors. These drugs reduce your body's absorption of some of the fat you eat. They come with unpleasant side effects, like gas and diarrhea, and also interfere with absorption of the fat-soluble vitamins A, D, and E, and other important nutrients. The only FDA-approved fat absorption inhibitor is orlistat (Xenical).

Metabolism boosters. This approach to weight loss, known as thermogenic therapy, suggests that certain natural compounds, like chromium, coenzyme Q10, and pyruvate, encourage your liver to increase energy in your cells and stimulate metabolism. These compounds are part of a host of unregulated diet remedies, which also includes appetite suppressants not approved by the FDA. They all have numerous side effects — many of them serious.

Experts say the best — and safest — way to lose weight and keep it off is to eat less and exercise more. Over-the-counter pills and so-called natural remedies are expensive, and they can cause dangerous side effects. Plus, their reactions with other drugs are unknown.

Promising new weight-loss remedy

An Australian pharmaceutical company is testing a chemical called AOD9604 — a synthetic fragment of human growth hormone that reduces body fat in mice. Weight-loss experts say people who are obese have lower levels of this substance, which stimulates fat metabolism. Researchers hope a daily dose of AOD9604 will bring their fat-burning ability back to normal — without side effects. Results of the study, which includes 480 people, are expected some time in 2007.

Win the fat war

It's easy to find a diet plan that will knock off several pounds fairly quickly, but the trick is keeping off those pounds for good. In a recent study, researchers concluded it doesn't make much difference which diet plan you use as long as you stick with it.

The study results showed weight loss was about the same for the Atkins, Ornish, Weight Watchers, and the Zone diet plans. Unfortunately, only 50 to 65 percent of the participants stayed with their diets for the full year of the study. Here's a look at some of the most popular diet plans.

▶ **Restricted calories.** The more you cut calories, the faster you'll lose weight. But watch out for cutting back too much. Extreme diets of less than 1,100 calories can have serious health consequences, and you're more likely to binge or overeat when you go off the diet.

▶ **High protein, low carbohydrate.** These diets are proving to be effective for short-term weight loss, but experts are concerned about their long-term effects on your health. The Atkins diet emphasizes high-protein and low-carbohydrate intake, while the South Beach and the Zone diets allow certain types of carbs.

▶ **Low fat, high-fiber.** This approach is to replace fat with complex carbohydrates, like fruits, vegetables, and whole grains. You count grams of fat instead of calories. But when you eliminate fat, you may miss out on some important nutrients. Commercial "low-fat" products are also likely to be loaded with sugar and other ingredients with no nutritional value.

The simplest and least expensive weight loss plan is to cut back on calories and exercise for at least 30 minutes a day, five times a week. Cutting fat, protein, or carbohydrates may make a diet fashionable or easy to follow, but it only works when you burn more calories than you take in. Depending on your age, gender, and activity level, you need 12 to 15 calories a day per pound of your desired weight.

Avoid overeating at a restaurant by ordering a to-go box with your meal. Place half the meal in the box before you eat. You'll take in fewer calories and enjoy two meals for the price of one.

The best way for you to lose weight — and keep it off — is to find a plan you'll stick with. It should give you proper nutrition, yet allow you to control your calories. You could also rely more on making healthy food choices rather than following a strict diet. No matter what plan you choose, make sure you find time to exercise.

Where to find help to reach your goal

Weight Watchers, the Zone, and other commercial programs offer weight loss tips and support groups to help you make lifestyle changes. Some programs, like Jenny Craig and Nutrisystem, also sell prepackaged meals. These programs can be expensive, but they could help you reach your weight loss goal. Take Off Pounds Sensibly (TOPS) is a nonprofit group and the least expensive of the programs.

	Fees	Plan structure	Food	Support
Jenny Craig	$6 a week and up, plus cost of food	diet control with Jenny Craig prepackaged food	buy from Jenny Craig for $11-$15 a day	one-on-one counseling, either in person or by phone
Nutrisystem	cost of food only	diet control with Nutrisystem prepackaged food	buy from Nutrisystem for $289 a month	counseling, classes, newsletter, all at home or online
Take Off Pounds Sensibly (TOPS)	$24 a year plus nominal chapter fees	encouragement to stick with food and exercise plans from member's own doctor	buy and prepare your own	weekly chapter meetings, newsletter
The Zone	$52 every 13 weeks	meal planner, recipes, shopping lists	buy and prepare your own	daily tips, online nutritionists
Weight Watchers	$39.95 a month	instruction on eating plans for weight loss	buy and prepare your own	weekly meetings, lower fee for online plan

7 no-nonsense ways to shed extra pounds

The average American over age 55 has added nearly 40 pounds of fat during adulthood. Much of the blame for this ugly fact goes to poor eating habits. Without making a few lifestyle changes, you'll always have a hard time maintaining a healthy weight. Here are some tips to help you.

Practice portion control. Researchers at Cornell University discovered something interesting while hosting an ice cream social. When people serve themselves, they tend to put more food on their plates if the plates and serving utensils are large. Think small and cut back on the size of your helpings by using smaller plates, bowls, and serving utensils. And when you're eating out, don't fall for the fast food "supersize" craze.

Pound the pillow. Women who sleep only five or six hours a night gain more weight than those who get seven hours of sleep a night, according to the Nurses' Health Study. Another study found that two key hormones that regulate appetite get out of whack when you don't get enough sleep. Leptin, which tells your body you've eaten enough, decreases, and ghrelin, which stimulates your appetite, increases.

Turn off the TV. Your risk for obesity increases 23 percent for every two hours a day you spend in front of your TV. Americans now burn 111 less calories a day than in years past, and that adds up to 11 pounds a year. When you're sitting around watching TV, not only does your metabolism slow, you might be tempted by clever advertisers to reach for high-sugar, high-fat snacks — and empty calories.

> Many so-called "healthy foods" are actually loaded with sugar and fat. Read the nutritional labels when you replace junk food with yogurt, granola, and low-fat snacks.

Volunteer your services. Retirees who joined a program to help mentor and tutor children in local elementary schools more than doubled their physical activity, a Johns Hopkins University survey shows. Not only did the volunteers get off the couch and away from the TV, they had more energy for daily activities like household chores and gardening.

Find strength in numbers. You can lose more weight by joining an organized weight loss group than trying to go it alone, says a study funded by the U.S. Department of Agriculture. Women dieting on their own have higher stress levels, and that leads to less success overall. A group also gives you support and nutritional information you won't get by yourself.

Don't use food as a crutch. When you eat to cope with anger, depression, or stress, you're loading up on food that makes you fat. Find something else to help you deal with your emotions — go for a walk, take a relaxing bath, or play a game.

Simple secret makes losing weight easier

Eating breakfast helps you lose weight — and keep it off. Nearly four out of five people in the National Weight Control Registry, a survey of almost 3,000 people who have lost at least 30 pounds and kept it off for a year or more, eat breakfast every day.

The right kind of breakfast keeps you from getting hungry and loading up on calories later in the day. Choose whole grain cereals and fruit, but steer clear of sugary cereals. Sugar, a simple carbohydrate, raises your blood sugar quickly — then it falls, and you're hungry again. Both whole grains and eggs, another breakfast favorite, will help you feel full longer.

Forget about skipping meals. Eating three meals a day and a healthful snack or two keeps your blood sugar stable and your hunger pangs under control. In addition, missing a meal can encourage you to overeat at the next meal. Overeating stretches your stomach, which continues to signal hunger until it gets back to normal size.

Foolproof way to burn fat and build muscle

Exercise is a double-barreled weapon in the fight against weight gain. It not only helps you burn more calories, it builds muscle, which burns calories faster than fat tissue. On top of that — people who exercise are more likely to stick to a weight loss plan.

Here's more good news. Taking a brisk walk might help you shed more pounds than a fast run, according to a small study in Greece. In the three-month study, 14 women who exercised at a moderate pace lost more weight than the women who exercised more vigorously. The researchers suggest striving for a combination of moderate and vigorous exercise — with your doctor's approval — for the most benefits. When you exercise strenuously, you rev up your metabolism, and you'll continue to burn more calories long after you stop exercising.

If you are thinking about buying an exercise machine, consider this — the best choice for burning calories is a treadmill. Wear your walking shoes when you shop for a treadmill so you can try it out in the store. Make sure the controls and handrails are located comfortably and the belt fits your stride. You can probably get along fine with a less durable — and less expensive — treadmill if you are only using it for walking. Hop on for 10 minutes at a time about four times a day for the best results.

Resistance, or strength, training is a great way to replace fat with muscle. You can do these exercises at home with equipment ranging from simple household items to sophisticated gear from a sporting goods store. You can also join a health club or fitness center for a wider range of equipment and trainers to help you decide the exact exercises you need.

People age 55 and older account for about 25 percent of all gym and health club memberships, and many programs are designed for middle-age and older adults. One program, available to people who have reached age 65, is the SilverSneakers Fitness Program. Benefits include a free membership at a participating fitness center, as well as exercise classes geared for seniors. Leading Medicare health plans and Medicare Supplement carriers offer the program at no extra cost. For more information, call 888-423-4632 toll free or visit *www.silversneakers.com* on the Internet.

When to seek surgery

Surgery isn't the answer for people who want an easy way to lose 10 or 20 pounds. Only people who are 100 pounds or more overweight or people 85 to 100 pounds overweight who have obesity-related medical problems, like type 2 diabetes, should consider this surgery — and only if other weight loss treatments have failed.

Weight reduction, or bariatric, surgery has increased from 36,700 cases in 2000 to 171,000 in 2005. An increase in the number of obese people, improved surgical techniques, and a number of high-profile success stories are responsible for the rise. It seems to work — most people lose about two-thirds of their excess weight within two years, as well as improving their health. The following are two types of weight loss surgery.

Laparoscopic gastric banding. In this procedure, an adjustable silicone band is placed around the upper part of your stomach. This makes your stomach smaller so you can't eat as much, and you feel full faster. This procedure has several benefits, like less time in surgery, a shorter hospital stay, and fewer complications after surgery. The band can also be removed. On the downside, there is very little information about its long-term effectiveness. Gastric banding costs about $18,000.

Gastric bypass. With bypass surgery, a pouch about the size of an egg is created in your upper stomach, and the small intestine is attached to it. You feel fuller faster, and food bypasses most of the stomach and upper intestine. That means fewer calories are absorbed, which leads to weight loss. This operation costs about $25,000 to $30,000 — if there are no complications. Although this surgery has a better record for both losing weight and keeping it off, it's a more difficult procedure with a higher risk of complications, like nutritional deficiencies.

Medicare has recently eased its criteria for paying for these surgeries and other insurers are expected to follow suit. Check your health insurance plan to see if weight loss surgery is covered.

Enviga, an expensive soft drink that contains green tea extracts, calcium, and caffeine, claims to burn 60 to 100 extra calories if you drink three cans in 24 hours. Unfortunately, the study was based on healthy, normal weight people ages 18 to 35.

Natural alternatives to common drugs

Herb	May replace*	What it does	May interact with
aloe	Metamucil	Relieves constipation	hypoglycemic drugs, insulin
black cohosh	hormone-replacement therapy (HRT) drugs	Eases menopausal symptoms	birth control pills, tamoxifen
garlic	aspirin, ibuprofen	Reduces pain and inflammation of rheumatoid arthritis	sequinavir, warfarin and other anticoagulants, antiplatelet drugs, NSAIDs, thyroid drugs, fish oil
	cholesterol-lowering drugs	Lowers cholesterol, stops blood from clumping, and slows the stiffening of arteries	
ginger	Dramamine	Relieves motion sickness, including dizziness, nausea, and vomiting	antacids, anticoagulants, NSAIDs, insulin
peppermint	Milk of Magnesia	Relieves indigestion, upset stomach, and gas	felodipine (Plendil), simvastatin (Zocor)
	Nyquil	Relieves nighttime cold symptoms and cough	chamomile, red clover, St. John's wort, and other herbs
	Pamprin	Acts as a muscle relaxant to relieve cramps	

Natural alternatives to common drugs

Herb	May replace*	What it does	May interact with
peppermint oil	Tylenol Vicks VapoRub Ben-Gay	Relieves headaches Reduces congestion Relieves muscle pain	felodipine (Plendil), simvastatin (Zocor) chamomile, red clover, St. John's wort, and other herbs
red clover	Proscar (finasteride)	May relieve prostate enlargement in benign prostatic hyperplasia (BPH)	anticoagulants, HRT, birth control pills, NSAIDs
saw palmetto	Proscar (finasteride)	Increases urine flow while decreasing urination frequency. May reduce prostate size in BPH	testosterone (Androderm), HRT, anticoagulants, NSAIDs
St. John's wort	antidepressants	May relieve mild depression	antidepressants, cyclosporine, protease inhibitors, birth control pills, warfarin, anesthetics, statins
valerian	Ambien, Valium	Helps relieve anxiety and tension while providing a good night's sleep	antidepressants, alcohol

Do not stop taking any prescription drugs without talking to your doctor first.

Index

Q

R

S